FOR A PHILOSOPHY
OF
FREEDOM
AND STRIFE

SUNY Series in Contemporary Continental Philosophy
Dennis J. Schmidt, editor

FOR A PHILOSOPHY
OF
FREEDOM
AND STRIFE

Politics, Aesthetics, Metaphysics

Günter Figal

Translated, with notes, by Wayne Klein

State University of New York Press

Original title of the German language edition: Günter Figal: *Für eine Philosophie von Freiheit und Streit. Politik, Ästhetik, Metaphysik*, published by J. B. Metzler Verlagsbuchhandlung und C. E. Poeschel Verlag Stuttgart © 1994. Chapters 4, 9, and 13 were not included in the German language edition.

Published by
State University of New York Press, Albany

For information, address State University of New York Press,
State University Plaza, Albany, N.Y., 12246

Production by Marilyn P. Semerad
Marketing by Dana E. Yanulavich

Library of Congress Cataloging-in-Publication Data

Figal, Günter, 1949–
    [Für eine Philosophie von Freiheit und Streit. English]
    For a philosophy of freedom and strife : politics, aesthetics,
metaphysics / Günter Figal : translated by Wayne Klein.
        p.   cm. — (SUNY series in contemporary continental
philosophy)
    Includes bibliographical references and index.
    ISBN 0–7914–3697–7 (hc : alk. paper). — ISBN 0–7914–3698–5 (pb :
alk. paper)
    1. Metaphysics. 2. Political science—Philosophy. 3. Aesthetics.
4. Liberty. 5. Struggle. 6. Philosophy, German—19th century.
7. Philosophy, German—20th century.   I. Title. II. Series.
B3240.F493F8713   1998
193—DC21   97–19141
                                            CIP

10 9 8 7 6 5 4 3 2 1

Contents

Preface

Few think badly of freedom, and one ought not think badly of strife if freedom and strife are bound up with one another. The essays collected here aim to show that this is the case by considering and representing the relationship between freedom and strife in its various manifestations. The essays do not by any means exhaust their subject but are meant as examples, repeated reflections, which in their complementarity and thematic variation attempt to say the same thing.

If it were possible to say directly and satisfactorily what this is, it would not be necessary to present it by means of examples. The more general thoughts are, the more they appear to say nothing when considered in isolation. They only first become interesting when one continually comes up against them and becomes convinced that there is very little or nothing at all that can be understood without them. This is the case, I believe, with freedom and strife.

The foregoing makes it clear that freedom and strife are not here meant as restricted phenomena. Freedom is not synonymous with the ability of persons to make decisions, and strife does not denote all possible types of conflict, from differences of opinion to armed life and death struggle. Rather freedom is the openness, the play-space,[1] which every activity requires to be carried out at all; and strife, to speak with Heraclitus, is the father of all things,[2] the necessary coherence of each and every essential thing with its opposite.[3]

The interpretations of freedom in the sense outlined above are based on the conviction that every activity, every comportment, can be understood correctly only when one understands them within their play-space. The interpretations of strife in the sense outlined above express something similar insofar as they, too, oppose the isolation of that which is taken to exist independently.

With regard to freedom, everything which belongs to a play-space is, on the one hand, individual, particular, and contingent; it could be otherwise, but it is now as it is, like a successful move in a game at this moment and at this place is unique and attracts our attention precisely because it is not made of necessity. On the other hand, that which belongs to a play-space is only meaningful within it; a move in a game is what it is only in the context of the rules which make it possible and allow it to be made. The interest in the play-spaces of actions and other events also extends to the coherence of meaning and individuality, necessity and contingency, unity and multiplicity.

This makes it clear once more what is gained by focusing our attention on the concept of 'strife.' It is the coherence of that which is irreconcilable in the sense of the pairs of concepts mentioned above and others, the coherence of that which can be neither separated nor unified but which, because of this fact, makes possible life's various forms and modalities. To take account of strife means that one rejects the simple alternatives of either-or and both.

Textual interpretation provides a model for what is here meant by freedom, one that is developed in the first chapter and to which the other chapters are orientated. A text which has taken the form of a work is the necessary play-space in which the reading and interpretation of the text takes place. Every meaningful text has many possible—and impossible—interpretations; textual interpretation as such is only innovative where it does not degenerate into capriciousness. Textual interpretation is bound to the text itself, and there it must find its way amidst the tension between originality and faithfulness, coherence and subtlety. This brings us back once again to the idea of strife.

Because textual interpretation functions as a model for the discussions of freedom and strife offered here, these interpretations for this reason alone can be described as "hermeneutic." But it would be superficial if one were to see the hermeneutic element only in the fact that texts and interpretation play a guiding role. Rather, what is decisive is the aforementioned and—as yet unclarified—relationship between contingency and necessity. In this and similar cases it is impossible to obtain ultimate and certain knowledge. Rather one remains confined within the bounds of understanding, if that is a limitation at all; understanding appears as a limitation only when one dreams the dream of ultimate foundations.

For this reason, hermeneutic philosophy is far from being a joyful or resigned skepticism, or a plea to integrate philosophy within rhetoric. Where there is something to understand, there is a sense that makes a claim upon us, and not merely an ever-expanding and spreading kaleidoscope of linguistic signs and gestures. Sense must without question be represented. When something is understood, one can neither remain solely at the level of representation, nor can that which is represented be ascertained without it. Representation is a form of strife.

When one can endure this strife and not give up the idea that sense can be experienced, the world appears less inscrutable, pluralistic, and arbitrary as some believe. Hence the term *hermeneutic* can serve to indicate that one is not prepared to participate in the game of "postmetaphysical" thinking that is today universally beloved, but rather attempts to think metaphysically and to see metaphysics as it deserves to be seen, as something differentiated and rich with tensions. Several of the chapters collected here argue that one can only do justice to modernity when it is understood metaphysically.

To understand what is here meant by metaphysics, let us turn to the author who, after Heidegger, is essentially responsible for the meaning which this term now carries:

> First then, in my judgment, we must make a distinction and ask, what is that which always is and has no becoming, and what is that which is always becoming and never is? That which is apprehended by intelligence and reason is always

in the same state, but that which is conceived by opinion with the help of sensation and without reason is always in the process of becoming and perishing and never really is. (*Timaeus*, 27d–28a)[4]

The opinion expressed in this passage is not that of Plato, but rather that of the Pythagorean Timaeus, and it is only his opinion. Whether the clean distinction between beings and "that which never is" is meant to be as emphatic as it sounds here can only be determined by a reading of Plato, but it seems clear that it is not meant in this way. A reading of Plato would confirm that being and becoming, presence and time, form, as it were, the basic strife within which Platonic thought subsists. The thinking which occurs within this basic strife is metaphysics.

This already implies that the name *metaphysics* does not designate a sharply delimited branch of philosophy; the same also holds true for aesthetics and politics. Although it is true that four chapters are devoted to each of these three areas, this merely expresses a point of emphasis. Taken together, the essays aim to express the coherence and interconnection of the political, the aesthetic, and the metaphysical.

A word on the authors to whom these these chapters are dedicated. They appear here together because they had something to say to me concerning the matters I wanted to discuss and clarify, or because, often enough, they first stirred my interest in these things. For this reason, they are not merely present when their work is being discussed; in conversations, those who are silently present are often just as important as the speaker or the addressee.

The circle of authors considered here certainly could have been broadened. Many from whom a longer contribution would have been both interesting and helpful are mentioned only briefly. However, one must keep the circle within reasonable limits, otherwise every philosophical effort points beyond itself.

The interpretations offered in this book do not subsist solely within the context of the authors spoken of and cited, but belong, both before and during their genesis and reworking, to many actual conversations. To all those who stimulated, corrected, and challenged me, I wish to say thank you. I would like to single out Hans-Georg Gadamer in particular, because without him I never would have written on hermeneutic philosophy. Therefore, without him, this book would not exist.

This holds also, but in a different way, for my parents. At one time I did not want to burden them with the usual dedication of academic texts, much of which appears clichéd, even when it is honestly meant. This is no longer the case, and I gladly take the opportunity now to do so. Both understand why.

Günter Figal
October 1993

1

On the Silence of Texts
Toward a Hermeneutic Concept of Interpretation

The dilemma involved in understanding texts was formulated decisively by Plato in the *Phaedrus*. Leaving aside the possibility that they will be corrupted as they are handed down, texts are stable linguistic units, creations of, at the very least, relative duration. Understanding appears to find a firm point of orientation in texts because we can return to the written word without any real difficulty, which is not the case with speech. Texts are a medicine for memory and wisdom: *mnémes te . . . kaì sophías phármakon* (274e).[1] But *phármakon* does not merely mean medicine, but also poison. The written word entices us to trust it in a rather problematic manner and to forget understanding altogether (275a). Worse still, he who poses questions to texts receives no answer; in their stony existence they offer us nothing unambiguous and settled (275c), but rather tempt and entreat us to interpret them. Whoever is able to read can form an opinion about texts, and no author has the power to correct his readers, to exclude certain insights or propose other, more nuanced, ones. In short, texts are stable but not ambiguous; they are accessible, but they also conceal a meaning which the movement and motility of dialogue can at least illuminate.

One should recall the discussions of the *Phaedrus* in order to appreciate the context of the position which dominates the current debate, namely, the position in which understanding is, on closer inspection, taken to be a form of interpretation. The reason behind this is that the meaning of a text is not something that possesses a stable identity, but rather every reading enters into new linguistic contexts and consequently brings with it uncontrollable displacements of meaning.[2] Those who support this thesis are mainly concerned with overturning the relationships articulated in the *Phaedrus*. Poison becomes the only medicine because the silence of the texts apparently requires interpretation. Texts, so we are told, contain nothing that could disclose or illuminate itself. The notion that the meaning of a text possesses a stable identity is a false idealization, and whoever is moved to produce his or her own articulation of a text merely produces a new text within the infinite play of linguistic signs.

The assurance that no meaning hides behind texts waiting to be drawn out or unlocked can, of course, only be made when the expectation exists that there is such a meaning. In the case that this expectation persists, we can naturally ascribe it to the enduring influence and persuasiveness of the Platonic texts and the tradition which was founded upon them. A "deconstruction" of Plato and the Platonic tradition would then merely be a matter of freeing oneself from this expectation.

But we must ask whether this is at all possible. The "solemn silence" of texts which Socrates speaks of in the *Phaedrus* (275d) proves itself to be, on closer inspection, the necessary presupposition of every interpretation. If texts were simply dumb we would not want to learn anything from them; in the silence lies the possible but reserved or withheld speech. A text is not merely an arbitrary vehicle for one's own speech, and if it were, this speech would not be interpretation. It is not possible, therefore, to interpret a text without having an expectation of what the text means.

If texts are truly silent, it appears that there is an expectation that has not been fulfilled. However, where we must engage in interpretation, we cannot hope that the text will provide an answer; rather one is compelled to speak oneself. What is expressed as a result of this process cannot be interrogated meaningfully to determine its agreement with the text; every comparison of a text and its interpretations is itself a new interpretation.

This much is certainly incontestable: no text speaks that liberating word which would confirm the interpretation that this and nothing else was meant. Whether this word would in fact be received as a liberation is not so certain, for it would mean the end of interpretation. Interpretation, therefore, depends upon the silence of texts; it arises from this silence, and the text necessarily remains silent with respect to it. Meaning which is simply given needs no interpretation.

However, even if the reserved speech of texts as their claim to meaning is taken to be the fundamental condition of interpretation, the expectation of meaning which is thereby awakened naturally could be illusory. In this case the recommendation that we should not seek anything behind the text or assume that there is anything there to be sought would be in vain, because no interpreter could follow it. But then the thesis that every linguistic utterance is merely a displacement within the open system of language would be justified. To be sure, interpretation would then begin with the expectation of meaning directed to a text, but carrying out the interpretation would not be a process of discovering meaning but rather of inventing it, and while this might appear meaningful when it is enacted, it never uncovers a coherent meaning. If one were now to say that the expectations of meaning formed by the interpreter need not have any foundation in the text, one is then admitting that the act of interpretation is akin to being caught in a necessary illusion.

To the question whether this is illuminating or not, Gadamer has rightly said that it decides "about the range and extent of hermeneutics as well as the objections of its opponents."[3] If interpretation is not, at the very least, also a discovery of meaning, we cannot say that it is a form of understanding. If interpretation were not essentially related to texts, a general elucidation of understanding, as philosophical hermeneutics understands it, would not lose merely a marginal field of application, but rather a paradigm, a model, largely by means of which it could establish its validity. It would become unbelievable as hermeneutics.

With respect to this problem, a philosophical hermeneutics in Gadamer's sense gives us no reason for worry. Within the framework of its conceptual possibilities, interpretation allows itself to be grasped as understanding, and without at the same time falsifying that which is essential about the interpretative process. In what follows I want to show that interpretation is a discovery of sense that has nothing to do with either the decoding of a text which conceals its meaning or with the freeing of a secret meaning which can only be identified by the interpretative process. Interpretation is a type of invention whose freedom is not devoid of all constraint.[4]

The particular characteristics of such an interpretative process are best seen when we do not immediately focus upon the explicative and reflective exegesis of a text, but rather upon an activity which clearly can be recognized as a kind of "interpretation," namely, the performance or presentation of a piece of music or the recitation of a work of poetry. Gadamer explores this phenomenon in the first of the two parts of *Truth and Method* devoted to the "experience of art"[5] and there emphasizes its two essential elements: constraint and freedom. It is worth considering both elements and their relationship to one another in more detail.

Superficially it is rather easy to understand what is here meant by constraint and freedom. Every interpretation that is also a representation has its virtue in its faithfulness to the work. That is to say, it should aim at nothing more than to make it possible for the work to come forth. It should not, therefore, allow its attention to the work to be diverted by the example of other, putatively more exemplary, presentations, but rather be concerned with allowing the work itself to become present. The interpreter is restrained by what the text itself prescribes. This includes musical scores, which are also texts.

However, as we know no text deprives an interpreter of all his or her decisions. Measure and phrasing cannot be determined at all exactly, to say nothing of the particular tone of a performance. In addition, if we consider the unique circumstances of every lecture and every game, then it is clear that no two performances can be completely similar to one another. Although the work is unique, its performances will always diverge from one another. That aspect of the work which remains the same and endures, whose parameters all performances must respect, becomes present by means of a performance or presentation, though each time in a different manner. The continuous presence of a work manifests itself only at a particular time. The freedom of the interpreter consists in how he gives form to this time.

If we were to say merely this, then we would not have genuinely grasped the essential freedom which belongs to every interpretation. The decisions which are required of each interpreter and are mostly not explicitly made, can be seen on closer inspection to have their basis in the fact that the work allows for these decisions in the first place. Autonomy only subsists within the play-space of the work, so that this play-space actually constitutes the freedom of the interpreter. Interpretation means to remain within the freedom of the work and in each case to allow this freedom to manifest itself in the free play of performance.

The work is the freedom of the interpreter because it discloses possibilities which are perceived in the process of interpretation. In very few cases these possibilities are laid out clearly for us, and we then can and must decide between them. More often, when the work itself says nothing, the work requires that the interpreter become autonomous. It leaves the enactment of the interpretation open by saying nothing. Whenever works appear to us as texts in that they can and must be read, then the freedom of interpretation is the silence of the texts.

For this reason the freedom of interpretation is far from being an indeterminate openness. An indeterminate openness cannot be represented. Representations are possible only when something determinate is present, which must, insofar as it is determinate, give direction to the representation. With this we have reached the point at which the thesis that interpretation is invention has its strongest support. In the end it is undeniable that there is no access to a "work in itself." Nothing can be said about a work if we ignore our own experience. No work can be understood otherwise in its determinateness than through interpretation. When the issue concerns the determinateness of a work, it is impossible to avoid interpretation.

Nevertheless, it would be a mistake to use the determinate nature of a work to define interpretation. If we think of the representative function of interpretation in the sense of a performance, we will certainly find this to be illuminating. No one would think of seriously asserting that an interpreter invents his score during a performance. And if the concept of "interpretation" is to have a controllable sense at all, we would have to object to this presupposition whenever it is a matter of more than a mere performance. The conceptually articulated and considered exegesis of a poem can also only be considered "interpretation" if it is, in its enactment, comparable with the poem as recited; the exegesis, too, must remain within the play-space of the text which allows it to manifest itself as a representation. When we speak of interpretation, it is a matter of a range of possible realizations which extend—without a qualitative leap—from simple performance to the conceptually differentiated exegesis.

Certainly this does not resolve the question of the identity of a work or of a text in general. Whenever this is contested, one clings to the—pertinent—observation that it is impossible to avoid interpretation. But then one forgets that the silence of a work is a positive experience: only that which is determinate and that which can be articulated in a determinate manner can be silent. Even if the musical score does not produce its own sound, one can only produce music with the score by referring to it and—perhaps by essaying different interpretative possibilities—also referring back to it. In the process one stands in a relation to that which "is there," to the motionless existence of signs. If the particular meaning expressed by a sign cannot be determined precisely for she who utters it through the context of its utterance and its associations, it nevertheless remains a simple fact that signs can be fixed and can be identified as fixed. The materiality of texts, their mere existence, is therefore at the very least a first criterion for their identity. Theuth, the founder of writing of whom Socrates speaks in the *Phaedrus*, invented a medicine for the memory to the extent that the fixed musical score and the stable text are things to which we can return.

In spite of this, it would be clearly insufficient if we were to ground the identity of a text solely in its material constancy; moreover, considered more precisely, it would even be false. No one who says that he is reading a particular book is referring to the copy of the book that he holds in his hands, but rather to the identical text which can be reproduced any number of times—to something, therefore, that needs to be realized materially, but whose existence does not consist essentially in this realization.

Wherein does it consist? Because it is impossible, as we have seen, to interrogate texts themselves without the mediation of interpretation, this question evidently can be answered only by appealing to interpretation itself. If interpretations can be understood only by appealing to the work as such, they must contain at least a reference to the identity of the work, so that the material existence of texts can be understood as an indication of their existence as bearers of meaning.

The indicative function of texts depends upon something which is quite obvious. Every interpretation which aims to be the representation of a work must satisfy two conditions. It must do justice to both the unity and the multiplicity of a text; superficial and vulgar interpretations are no less unsatisfying in themselves as those interpretations which lose themselves in the nuances of a text. This would not be the case if we did not expect that the multiplicity of nuances which can be discovered by an interpreter remain tied to the unity of the text, and that, conversely, the unity of the text will unfold itself in as many nuances as possible.

If these two conditions are valid for any interpretation, we are obliged, in enacting the interpretation, to take them into account. More precisely, the nuances of an interpretation must be limited by the unity of the whole. This requirement constitutes an obstacle and a challenge, just as conversely, the diversity of a text represents an obstacle and a challenge to the representation of the text's unity. To categorize a text and draw out its nuances, to unify and arrange a text, these are the aims of interpretation. What resists and challenges this process cannot stem from the force of the interpreter, but must rather be the claim of the text itself.

In this way the work itself proves to be a form of opposition and a challenge within interpretation. Interpretation is a process which is based upon a complementary tension: while the unity of the text unfolds itself, displaying its nuances, the nuances of the text seek to be made manifest as a unity. Accordingly, unity and multiplicity both play a double role in the relationship of interpretation to the text: as the claim of the text itself and as representation in the enactment of the interpretation. Both elements are doubly constrained in relationship to one another: what opposes the interpretation also makes it possible. Hence the work, in its unity, is the play-space for interpretation insofar as the latter aims to bring out the nuances of the text, while the work, in its multiplicity, is the play-space for the unifying power that is expected from interpretation. The freedom of the interpreter is, in each case, that essential characteristic of a work that both constrains the interpreter from being able to develop the work for himself and that which makes this development unnecessary. What constrains the interpreter in this manner makes its appearance by being brought forth in the enactment of a contrary interpretation. This appearance is the process of being represented, while this coming forth is representation itself.

The work constrains interpretation in a manner corresponding to the double limitation which governs the relationship between the work and interpretation. At the same time, it is not possible to establish a connection to the work as a whole by circumventing interpretation. The work is not in any sense "given" in the absence of interpretation, and for this reason it is not possible to conceive of interpretation as the discovery of something which exists prior to the interpretative process. On the contrary, to the extent that it is the task of interpretation to facilitate the representation of the work, its function is rather like invention. But it is an invention that is both autonomous and constrained—like an intelligent answer is related to a question; we must reach the answer ourselves, and yet the question precedes the answer and determines its parameters. We must have understood the question in order to be in a position to give an independent answer. The work which is to be interpreted is a double question which expects a double answer.

The interpretation of a work does not distinguish itself from the dialogue between question and answer in virtue of the fact that it is the task of an answer first to develop the question, so that the meaning of the question first appears in the answer. Rather the difference lies in the fact that the question which the work poses to the interpreter is not enunciated by the work but is posed in silence. The richness of nuances within a work is not a determinate question posed to the interpreter's ability to locate such nuances, but rather is posed to his powers of unification. Just as the unity of a work is not a determinate question posed to the interpreter's powers of unification, but rather posed to his sense for nuances. The work is not a question but is open to question, and this corresponds to the fact that interpretations are always contested. Interpretations do not portray a work in such a way that the resemblance of the original to the copy can be checked. Interpretations in this sense can never be either true or false, but can at best underestimate the complexity of a work and misjudge its unity in such a manner as to make themselves unconvincing in comparison with other interpretations. It is also true that interpretations are distinct from one another in a manner which cannot precisely be determined. Different ways of reading and their respective contexts, which no one interpreter can master, essentially elude all control. Nevertheless, interpretations are not arbitrary parts of a boundless multiplicity, but are representations. Interpretations agree in that they allow the play-space of the work to which they belong to manifest itself in a similar manner. Interpretations articulate both of the essential elements of the work by presenting the otherness and agon of the works within themselves.

The strife within the relationship between work and interpretation is the reason that interpretations are merely provisional. No interpretation, no matter how convincing it may be, is definitive; consequently, all interpretations of a work are equal in the very least in that they are all equally entitled to claim correctness. However, they all have an equal claim to correctness only because they are all equally original; every interpretation, whether good or bad, is an original representation of the work. Later interpretations are not necessarily better than earlier interpretations, and vice versa. Knowledge of earlier interpretations, as mentioned above, can even be disadvantageous for the later interpretations; they carry with themselves the danger that one is more concerned with other interpretations than in engaging the claims of the work itself.

If all interpretations of a work are equally original, then their temporal order is irrelevant with respect to the work itself. It is, or course, possible to write something like a history of interpretation, and within the domain of conceptually articulated interpretations later interpretations can refer back to earlier ones and confront them. We can compare interpretations with one another. However, this will not make it possible for us to extrapolate the true form of the work, but rather from the similarity of the interpretations we can conclude that they all belong to the same play-space. All interpretations of a work belong together in that they have their freedom within the work, the freedom of their temporally bound enactment.

This also can be expressed by saying that the work is the presence of its interpretations, while the interpretations are the temporal presence of the work. The work anticipates all its interpretations; this is shown in a constancy which is not merely the constancy of its material existence. Its constancy is rather an openness which is continually capable of being represented. The work is the constant play-space of its interpretations.

That which is written or otherwise fixed waits, as something with a material constancy, to become the play-space of a representation and to be represented as a play-space. It regards potential interpreters silently, full of anticipation, and as soon as the interpreter counters this silence and elucidates the work, she is bound by the play-space of the work, by the need to return to the work in the act of representing it. In the course of interpretation the work is experienced in a three-fold manner: in its material constancy, as the play-space of articulation and in the particular ways in which it is articulated. The work speaks to the interpreter in its constancy by promising the play-space which allows for its—the work's—articulation and thereby for its representation.

The interpreter proceeds in dual fashion from the work; it provides him with the occasion and the play-space for interpretation. The enactment of interpretation proceeds from the constancy of the work as a promise, in order to bring forth the meaning of that which continues to exist. Interpretation is the articulation of the work which both begins and ends with the work itself. We can refer to this as the anamnestic structure of interpretation, following Gadamer's many references,[6] which in turn are based upon Plato's assertion that the essence of understanding is anamnesis. As Plato represents it, anamnesis also proceeds, as it were, in the form of a circle. It arises from within sense experience and refers back to something by means of which that which is perceived is understood as that which it is. In this way it makes manifest, with respect to that which is perceived, that which allows the object of understanding to be understood at all.[7] Interpretation is thus a form of discovery, namely, it discovers the play-space of the work. However, this process of discovery within interpretation can be articulated only as something invented, because no work prescribes how its essential elements are to be represented.

To be sure, the structure of interpretation distinguishes itself from anamnesis in the Platonic sense in one essential respect: what one returns to is not something which confronts one always in the same essential way, but rather is something which exists only in a relative way as a work or artifact. Works belong to time, even to their time, and when they outlive their time they no longer speak immediately, but under favorable conditions earn that venerable appellation which Socrates associates with meaningful but uncertain silence. Of course these works are not venerable in the sense of relics from a distant period, but as material memory. Becoming and passing away are deposited in texts and works of all kinds.

Seen in this way, every interpretation that refers to a work also refers to history. That certainly does not mean that the texts and works that are interpreted are documents of what and how things were. For when history takes the form of a work, it is no longer experienced as something in the past, but rather as the play-space, the freedom, of understanding. The existence of the work is a sign of a presence that fulfills itself as the presence of interpretation. It follows then that we find ourselves in the play-space of texts and works from history, without being guided by historical representations. In the play-space of texts and works, we return to history in order to find a presence which is no longer merely temporal, the presence of a comprehending interpretation.

2

An Essay on Freedom
Ontological Considerations from a Practical Point of View[1]

It is characteristic of the concept of 'freedom' that it belongs to two different domains of philosophical inquiry. On the one hand, the concept refers to the being of human beings, and thus has an *ontological* significance. By elucidating what freedom is, we are also saying something about the way we are. On the other hand, the concept of 'freedom' is used in order to indicate how we understand ourselves and others within the context of everyday activity. This is the *practical* significance of the concept, whose ethical and political dimensions can be accentuated. If we understand someone as free, we presuppose—ethically speaking—that he is responsible for his actions. Consequently, we consider it reasonable to demand that everyone should act in accordance with this sense of responsibility. It is then consistent, politically speaking, to declare that because human beings are fundamentally responsible for their actions, corresponding rights also should be granted and guaranteed to them.

The ontological and the practical significance of the concept of freedom are fundamentally independent of one another. One could even deny that the concept of freedom has an ontological sense and at the same time be convinced that, practically speaking, it is impossible not to regard human beings as free. However, this does not mean that the ontological and the practical dimensions of freedom necessarily have nothing to do with one another. Ontological interpretations of human freedom can be used to justify the practical application of the concept of freedom, to show that we actually are the way we understand ourselves to be.

However, as the foregoing indicates, such attempts at grounding are not necessarily illuminating. It is possible to remain skeptical in relation to them and to be unwilling to accept assertions connected with them, because, for example, they are held to be "unclear" or "metaphysical."[2] Such skepticism always has the justifiable sympathy for cautious and undogmatic thinking on its side. But it would be unwise to blindly trust this skepticism. The appeal for a merely practical application of the concept of freedom is itself not immune to dogmatism.

It is not difficult to understand how a merely practical application of the concept of freedom can be dogmatic. If we accept the practical supposition of personal freedom in the sense that one is responsible for his or her actions, we have decided in favor of an interpretation of freedom that is not the only one and that is in no way obvious, most likely without even knowing we have done so. It is not necessary to take freedom to be a distinguishing characteristic of persons; this is true even when one shies away from the difficulties of saying what a person actually is. Because the conviction—none too rarely articulated by means of the concept of practical freedom—that freedom is a distinguishing characteristic of persons is so obvious, attempts to ground the concept of freedom ontologically can appear implausible from the outset when they come up against the practical conception of freedom. Here the practical conception of freedom becomes a dogma. Attempts at ontological grounding that oppose this dogma, conversely, also can motivate us to revise the practical interpretation of freedom.

In what follows I would like to offer an ontological grounding of the concept of freedom that leads to just such a revision of the dogmatic variation of the practical understanding of freedom. In addition, I would like to show that this revision also has a practical or, more precisely, a political significance. The belief that freedom is a distinguishing characteristic of persons is expressed in a political conviction whose significance for modernity is difficult to overemphasize, namely, the conviction of liberalism.[3] We can designate this politically significant proviso with respect to another as the practical application of the concept of freedom, hence also as the liberalistic dogma. The following is concerned, therefore, with overcoming this liberalistic dogma, and with the immediate goal of bringing into clearer focus what freedom actually is.

If this is successful, it follows that we should not so readily cling to the fundamental convictions of liberalism. Rather, the attempt to develop an ontological grounding of the concept of freedom leads to an ethical and political conception which is an alternative to liberalism. In spite of this, it is not necessary to renounce some essential themes of liberalism. The high esteem for human individuality that is characteristic of liberalism can be maintained within the context of the concept of freedom I would like to develop. This is clearly an advantage, because the rights of the individual in this way can be justified in the face of every totalitarian attack. The intended alternative to liberalism is, therefore, a conception in which what is most essential to liberalism is retained.

The attempt to provide an ontological grounding of the concept of freedom, as I will present it, is developed within the context of Martin Heidegger's analyses and reflections. However, because it is not a question of my engaging in a confrontation with Heidegger, I will not essay an interpretation of his texts.[4] Rather, the following reflections on the ontological grounding of the concept of freedom are meant as systematic variations on Heideggerian themes; they place these themes in a different context and with a different emphasis than Heidegger himself. Above all, this is due to the political orientation of my reflections; Heidegger never developed a political philosophy. Toward the conclusion of this chapter I indicate how a concept of the 'political' could be developed within the context of a Heideggarian conception of freedom. To aid me in this task I will briefly touch upon the social philosophy of Hannah Arendt.

2.

With respect to everyday linguistic usage it is easy to see that freedom is not necessarily a distinguishing characteristic of persons. We speak of free public spaces, free streets, and also of free positions at the workplace.[5] This use of the term *free* is thoroughly independent and not metaphorical in the sense that it could be traced back to the practical application of the concept of freedom. If we speak of free places or streets, this has nothing at all to do with the responsibility of human beings for their actions; rather, these expressions mean that places or streets are readily accessible and open to traffic. Freedom here means "accessibility."

Not much is immediately gained by means of this reference to the application of the term *free*. For at first glance it is certainly not clear how the understanding of freedom as accessibility can be related to the freedom of persons; and only when this is possible can this reference be productive for an ontological grounding of the concept of freedom.

In order to understand the connection between freedom as accessibility and the freedom of persons, it is advisable to make a slight detour. We will first need to consider a quite clearly classical interpretation of the freedom of persons: to be free and responsible for one's actions is equivalent to being able to act otherwise. Only where one has the choice between different courses of action is it necessary to choose between them, and if need be to justify this decision.

Understood completely within the context of a practical concept of freedom, this interpretation provides no grounding for the claim that we are truly free as opposed to simply understanding ourselves as free. For an objection can be raised against the assertion that every free agent must possess a choice between several possible courses of action that is no less classical than the interpretation of the freedom of action sketched above. According to this objection, although we see ourselves confronted with several possible courses of action prior to acting and it appears to be the case that we are able to freely choose between them, it is by no means clear that the decision is in fact free. It can even be the case that afterwards we are able to grasp the dependency of our own action, which necessarily remains hidden to us in the moment of decision. But then the freedom of action only consists in the requirement that we understand ourselves as free in the moment of decision, whereas we can retrospectively see that we were not free at all. Freedom of action is then a kind of epistemological indeterminacy.[6]

The thesis of epistemological indeterminacy certainly can only satisfy us if we limit our consideration of the freedom of action to the person who acts. But possibilities of action are not solely a circumstance of the actor, but also of the world in which the actor finds himself and within which he acts. Every action enters a context and alters it in one way or another; with every act we reveal particular world possibilities. Even in those cases where we follow the courses of action laid down by others, it is a matter of possibilities that have actually been opened up. The world of acting persons is therefore accessible to them as a domain of possibilities; things in the world allow themselves to be used or altered, while persons of the world mutually determine possible courses of action for themselves. Possibilities of action are also always possibilities of the world in which we find ourselves; the world allows us to comport ourselves in a multiplicity of ways within it.

The possibility character of the world is not restricted to the moment of decision, but also remains in existence whenever a possibility that had been decided upon is, or has been, realized. It is not merely the case that unchosen possibilities of action for the most part continue to be present while an action is performed, but every phase of an action is the more or less new discovery of possibilities that are then opened up to it. The possibility character of the world is continuously confirmed in action. And finally, as a sphere of possibilities the world overshadows every genuine act by opening the view to actions which can be commenced after the conclusion of a particular action. We always can do more than we actually do; only within the space of possibilities that present themselves to us are there wishes and intentions, hopes and fears, and all these views to what is possible are not merely the "subjective" concern of the person who acts, rather it is only from within them that we experience the world as a sphere of possibilities. In a particularly pregnant manner we experience how we understand and judge actions always within the context of possibilities, rather than in isolation. It is only within the sphere of such possibilities that our actions have the context which lets them be meaningful.

Actions, therefore, are only possible within a world. But with respect to such a world the distinction between the way in which we are and our understanding of ourselves is no longer plausible: we cannot justifiably doubt that the world is actually a context of possibilities which makes action possible. The assertion to the contrary, which can merely be assumed, is contradicted by every genuine action. One might now be inclined to assert that even if it is undeniable that the experience of the world is that of a context of possibilities, nevertheless the path we take through this context is always determined, and that this kind of determination is one in which we would continually experience freedom and therefore would no longer be incompatible with it. On the contrary, because we are in a world that we can fundamentally only experience in its freedom, it is difficult to say precisely how we ought to understand the determinateness of our action; it is as though we are here thinking of pathological limitations of world openness, which as exceptions only serve to confirm the rule.

It is, therefore, freedom in the sense of accessibility which grounds the freedom of action. We are free because all of our actions necessarily belong to a world that freely releases actions and that cannot be exhausted by any single action. We are free in that we open ourselves in the world to the possibilities that are accessible to us. We are open to the open possibilities of the world. This openness, which Heidegger in *Being and Time* designated with the concept of 'disclosedness' [*Erschlossenheit*], is our way of being.

If we attempt, on the basis of this outline, to determine more precisely the most important aspects of the concept of freedom as openness, we need to attend to the relationship of the world to being-in-the-world. The world is not open because we understand it as such; it is not open because openness is characteristic of our ability to act. Rather, the openness of the world *shows itself* in our respective openness. What shows itself is essential to him through whom and for whom it can show itself. But it is not constituted by someone through whom and for whom it shows itself. It is how it is in itself. And we must say, therefore, that our freedom is actually the openness of the world, whereas we are so constituted that the openness of the world shows itself through us and for us. This has consequences for the practical concept of freedom. It is apposite now to consider them.

3.

To begin with, if the ontological concept of freedom outlined above truly is convincing, it will no longer be possible to defend a merely practical concept of freedom by citing trifling arguments to the contrary. Not only has this thesis lost its plausibility because it provides no basis for our knowing whether we are actually free or not and merely assumes that we are, but even if this thesis is not ontological, it nevertheless almost necessarily assumes an ontological form. For if one says that beings, which we understand as free on the basis of merely practical grounds, are persons, this can still be interpreted as a statement of convention; the concept of a 'person' merely displays our practical assumptions. But the beings designated as persons are nevertheless the only instances in which the assumption of freedom makes itself concrete and can be interpreted; we can only speak about how freedom shows itself by saying something about persons. This brings about a complete reversal of the practical assumption: if beings that we understand as free are persons, then freedom is a characteristic of persons. That, however, is the heart of the dogma of liberalism, and for this reason liberalism, with its adherence to a merely practical concept of freedom, loses its plausibility.

In liberalism a practical assumption of freedom is therefore bound up together with an image of what persons are. This shows itself most prominently in the view that the fulfillment of an individual life is guided by the goal of self-realization and that every individual, as a person, is given the task of finding his or her own way of life. Such an image is also compatible with the conviction that there is no universally binding articulation of a common good life which could serve as a point of orientation for individuals. As beings for whom self-realization is a requirement, persons are the final authorities on understanding human life.

However, the fact that we must see ourselves and one another as free and therefore as responsible for our actions does not, taken by itself, exclude being bound together by a common conception of the good life; on the contrary, this thought can even work against the isolation of persons insofar as it it is directed to the responsibility of persons for their actions and thereby to duties which we have toward one another. Certainly, it is to be doubted that this reference to the responsibility for one's own actions is sufficient to counter the liberalistic isolation of persons. The rights of others correspond to duties toward others; but if we attribute to those with such rights merely the possibility of self-realization, then we remain caught within liberalistic dogma, with the result that individuals or persons are the final authorities on human life.

If we understand freedom as openness, we need not oppose the thought of individual self-realization by merely referring to a common conception of the good life. This is of considerable benefit, for such a reference would itself be in danger of dogmatism: there is not merely *one* common conception of life, and every one that is considered to be good by its advocates is not, for this reason alone, necessarily good. If we were to consider them valid simply because they are considered to be good by their advocates, we would be acting just as dogmatically as they. A universal pluralism of common ways of life is groundless, exactly as groundless as a universal pluralism of persons and their self-realization.

Against this the thought of freedom as openness offers a criterion for evaluating different conceptions of the good life. A conception of the good life conforms to this criterion when it takes into account that being in a world includes being together with others just as much as individuality. As a sphere of possibilities a world is binding when it inaugurates communality and opens up the possibility of individuality. We ought to consider this more closely, so as to understand the binding force of a world in the interplay of its two elements.

The world binds first in that it is a *particular* world and as such fixes particular possibilities of action. The requirements are inaugurated for these determinate possibilities alone; only such determinate possibilities, or those similar to the possibilities that have already been exercised, are known. The determinateness of a world divides itself into the determinateness of activities, social roles, and determinate models of self-understanding.

It is probably unnecessary to emphasize that this binding power of the world ought not to be confused with a slavish devotion to predetermined models: to act in a world always means to be able to act otherwise because the prescriptions of a world have the character of possibilities. For this reason, it is always a question of modifying what is stipulated or combining it in a different way in order to come to new solutions. It is not merely the case that a possibility is always situated within a context of alternative possibilities, but for every possibility there is some degree of openness as to how it can be realized. From this perspective a world is comparable to a game whose rules are established so that there are always multiple ways for them to be followed.

But now the binding power of the world comes into view in another respect. The world binds not only in that it generally stipulates a particular frame of action or comportment, but a world is also binding for comportment in its individuality: every action and form of self-understanding is particular and perhaps also unmistakable in that it takes up and actualizes given models and patterns in a particular manner, just as a pianist performs a sonata that has been played countless times before in a unique and unrepeatable manner. This individuality arises out of the fact that the models and patterns of a world are only real in their respective actualizations, but never have a definitive reality. The respective actualizations do not simply carry the possibilities of the world into reality, but they themselves remain possibilities. Every actualization of a possibility is particular in that it is always also an indeterminate modification with respect to other actualizations. In leaving open just how it can be realized, a possibility is a free-space, the freedom of individual action. Individual action is only possible in a world.

The relationship of given possibilities and individual actions can be determined by saying that the possibilities of a world are *represented* in particular actions. Individuality, which reveals itself in action and more generally in how one lives one's life, is only possible in a determinate world that is open in its determinateness. Conversely, the actuality of such a world requires the individual, because the actuality of a world has the character of representation.

The world and the action that takes place in the world belong together within representation in a specific manner. Actions, which represent the particular possibilities of a world, are understood in light of these possibilities. This means that with regard to its sense an action is identical with the possibilities represented by means of it. But at the same time it is necessary to distinguish actions from the possibilities which allow them to take place, if only for the reason that no possibility allows only one particular action. Every possibility in the world can be represented in a multiplicity of ways. The distinctness of an action from the possibility which allows it constitutes the particularity or individuality of an action. In other words, the individuality of an action is everything that cannot be understood in terms of the possibility that gives the action its sense.

Both elements, identity and distinctness, are equally important for representation: without the identity of an action with the possibility which allows it, the action would be incomprehensible, for what is understood in action and with respect to actions are the ever-open possibilities. In the absence of a distinction between an action and its underlying possibilities, the possibility could have no actuality and nevertheless continue to exist. Once again we can see quite clearly how the actuality of an action cannot be grasped in the absence of the possibilities which allow it to take place. Similarly, it is apparent that the possibilities of a world are only efficacious by allowing themselves to be realized. The actual of the possible is free where the possible is not exhausted in it and where the actual is characterized by its individuality with respect to the possible. Under the supposition that we can refer to this unity of identity and distinctness as "difference," the representation of the possible in a truly existing individual can be understood as the difference of freedom.

The relationship of the actual and the possible, as it is here sketched using the model of an action and the possibility which allows it, is encountered in everyday life, mostly in more complex forms. What we experience as the actual is not individual, isolated actions, but acting persons. What we designate as a person expresses itself in action, in that actions are coordinated and performed in a more or less clear continuity. In this sense persons, too, do not represent individual possibilities, but clusters of possibilities. And, correspondingly, persons find their commonality in the fact that they recognize one another as representatives of a cluster of possibilities that is understood as a unity.

Persons, therefore, are not entities. Their essence is the difference of freedom, namely, that they are open to the space of possibility within which they function as representatives. The more clearly persons can be recognized as actors and show themselves in their actuality, the more faded becomes the cluster of possibilities which allows them to come into being; and the more clearly this cluster is experienced as something shared, the more its representatives return to it. Accordingly, the freedom of a world is an interplay of commonality and individuality in which the relationship between the two interacting elements never reaches a fixed and final state. The interplay is a strife in which neither of the two elements is what it is without its counterpart; and each of the elements can only have an effect at the expense of the element with which it is in conflict. The freedom of a world consists of nothing other than this strife. It is within this strife that we play the difference of freedom.

Moreover, the foregoing indicates what kind of claim is made upon us here: we can only be the way we are when we allow commonality and individuality to be equally efficacious, by understanding our respective being and doing in its interrelationship with that of others in a world and, in similar fashion, by recognizing and even esteeming the individuality of others.

The question of how we can satisfy this claim is generally quickly answered, namely, by understanding that we are in a world that is ours and within which we represent its possibilities in a particular way. In this way we can be persons without isolating ourselves in a liberalistic manner. However, the experience of this common world is not so easily guaranteed. The common space created by the representation of individual clusters of possibilities is partial; in their action every person represents a more or less clearly circumscribed cluster which is not identical with the cluster of the world—there are possibilities that belong to a world which we do not observe whilst we are acting, and often do not want to observe, but which nevertheless belong to the space of our own action. There are persons who belong to a world with whom we have nothing to do, either directly or indirectly, but without whom the space of possibility within which we act would not be what it is.

For this reason a world can only manifest itself as a community. The community is an obligating reason for limiting egoism and group interests of all kinds, and for letting solidarity be recognized when it does not lie within individual action. However, there can be a community only insofar as a world as such can be experienced. Under the presupposition that a world has the character of the possible and the possible of the type of a world has its actuality solely in representations, the experience of a world as a community is bound together with representations. The world as such must be represented so that it can be experienced explicitly as this particular world. Then we are not merely representatives *in* a world, but we also are representatives *of a* world, namely, ours.

Even in the absence of an explanation as to how it should be conceived, it is quite clear that the representation of a world differs from representations of particular possibilities or particular clusters of possibilities in a world. No representation in a world reveals exactly one possibility or precisely this cluster of possibilities, but also points, more or less clearly and more or less explicitly, to other possibilities. In every action the context within with the action takes place is present along with it; even the particular cluster of possibilities points beyond itself. However, it is not the aim of actions to make this further context explicit; it is always represented with the action, but it is not itself the object of representation. For this reason, representing a context as such is part of the representation of a world. Because we are concerned here with a particular type of representation, it would do well to give it a specific name. In this sense we can refer to the explicit representation of a context as a *representation*.[7]

Within the context of a theoretical elucidation the question arises *how* we can be representatives of a world, and here difficulties present themselves that are actually already present within the concept of a particular world itself. No one is able to fix the limits of a world with certainty. Worlds are not unities that can be definitively separated from one another. Rather worlds are altered by the life and action that takes place within them. It is normal and for the most part desirable that a form of exchange take place between worlds, and this in turn is possible only when there are discoverable commonalities between them. Why should we not then adopt an all-encompassing perspective, speak of a single communal world, and accept the task of uncovering enough commonalities so that in the end the communal world of all persons is recognized?

It would be hasty, however, to want to bring a swift end to the many diverse worlds. If we consider the discovery of commonalities between worlds to be a worthwhile goal, we must not merely presuppose in a trivial manner that there are different worlds, but we must also make it clear that a world can only incorporate other, foreign worlds opposed to it by virtue of its determinateness and particularity. Every discovery of a commonality between our own world and the foreign one is a translation or an integration that is made possible by our own world. Accordingly, the attempt to abandon our world would at the same time diminish our own possibilities of translation and integration. Only despair or self-hatred could support such a renunciation. And even if a communal world that could get along without such possibilities of translation and integration were possible, the image of this world is more akin to a nightmare than to a friendly vision; it is the image of life that has been completely leveled, in which the possibilities of action and understanding have been reduced to stereotypes.

Nonetheless, it is difficult and, in the end, impossible to measure the limits of our own world. We experience our own world for the most part inexplicitly, in that we act and orientate ourselves within the space of its possibilities; occasionally the world thrusts itself upon us, when in the foreign world we become aware of the limits of our own. But when it is necessary to act not merely in our own world but also in the sense of this world, it must become explicit. This requires a *representation*, and therefore we need to be representatives of our world without our being able to possess the world itself in any way. The *representation* of a world is also subordinate to the difference of freedom, and in a particularly radical manner. Nothing that is open in a world can be realized by the *representation* of a world in its totality; the *representation* of a world is different from the world as it is experienced. However, the world in its totality is the same as its *representation*. The world is only made manifest in its *representation*, which is a reversal of the situation with respect to the possible. Whereas a possibility that is open in the world is confirmed by means of its *representation*, the *representation* of a world lets it first be recognized. This most particular variation of freedom deserves a closer look.

-------------------------------- **4.** --------------------------------

The representations of a world distinguish themselves from the *representations* in a world in that they are necessarily explicit; that is to say, they are only understood correctly when they are understood as *representations*. By explicitly presenting itself, the world can first be experienced as a totality, as a *space* of possibilities. Freedom becomes explicit in a public manner by means of *representation*, and thereby first becomes public freedom.

The *representations* of a world can be of the most diverse kinds; symbolic actions, particular buildings or sculptures can serve to let a world become explicit. However, symbolic actions and works of art only clearly fulfill the role given to them when they are understood in their role. Whoever understands them must be able to elucidate them in accordance with their sense. And when this is possible, it involves reference to the world as portrayed. The interpretation of a *representation* is itself a *representation* whenever it allows the world to become explicit; it is even the primary *representation* in contrast with those that require interpretation. A world becomes explicit, therefore, primarily in that it becomes the subject of discourse. A world must be discussed and reported upon. It must be able to appear *as* a world in myth or history, so that its other symbolic *representations* can be understood.

It is not our intention here to give a precise account of how myth differs from history. As narrative forms, both are able to cross over imperceptibly into one another. One distinguishing characteristic between them is the treatment of figures and events as types in myth as opposed to the focus on individuals in history; just as the role played by repetition in myth corresponds to that of development in history. History plays itself out in an explicitly temporal schema, while this is of secondary importance for myth. The distinction between myth and history would be more significant if history could be proven to be the truth of myth. However, this is not the case. Historical figures and events can have a thoroughly mythical quality.

Myth and history do not represent a world under all circumstances, but only when they are actually understood and accepted as *representations*. A myth that has lost its ability to convince, history that has become inconsequential, no longer allow the binding commonality of the world to appear. It is therefore crucial that if a myth is still transmitted and if history is recounted anew, that we intend the narration to be an articulation of ourselves in a world. Not least of all, it is decisive that the *representation* of a world is shared by as many as possible who belong to this world. Only in this way can a myth or a history be binding—history that has become a specialization of academic historians no longer represents a world. If myth and history are to be binding, they must, in spite of all the differentiations and variants, be concerned with a *single* history and a *single* myth. Only in this way can a world as a totality be discussed.

By means of the successful *representation* of its world, a community manifests what Hannah Arendt in *The Human Condition* designated as "power."[8] Power is here the capacity for communality, and for this reason is not already given through action but rather first by means of the commonality of a history in which a cluster of diverse actions, their sense, is fashioned into a whole. Power in this sense can be a political factor; indeed, it is even the presupposition of political efficacy. But it is certainly hardly convincing to consider power by itself, with Arendt, as the basic phenomenon of the political. Power first becomes political when it is articulated in the form of a state, or at least is connected to this form. The state is the determining unity of the political.

A world that is the object of communal *representation* need not be constituted as a state, but it is suited to such a structure insofar as it is only within its parameters that the problems of a community can be decided and overcome. For this reason the political unity of the state is also essentially distinct from communal *representation* of a world in myth or history in that it has its own actuality in decision and action, not in linguistic articulation.

This decision and action is also fundamentally a form of *representation*. Whoever is engaged in state business, irrespective of the office or the capacity, acts neither as a private individual nor as a representative of the interests of a party or group, but rather in the name of the politically constituted community. We assume that this, at the very least, ought to be the case whenever we criticize corruption or the stubborn pursuit of special interests in the political domain.

For this reason political action as a form of *representation* has to establish itself primarily in action, namely, that actors reliably carry out their duties, that what they do is done in the sense of the community and its preservation. Certainly such reliability can be articulated only with regard to the mythical or historical *representations* in which the community has its actuality. Crises of political reliability are for this reason also often crises of the ability of the community to produce *representations*; there are crises that arise when a world can no longer be discussed in a convincing manner.

Crises of this kind ought naturally to be a challenge for a political community. As such they certainly can be confronted only when they are experienced neither as a type of natural catastrophe nor with the conviction that it is necessary to find the optimal organization of political relationships in order to rule out crises of this kind once and for all. There are no quick fixes precisely because crises arise under particular circumstances. It is necessary to have the judgment to diagnose them and to consider suitable solutions for the particular case.

However, a merely pragmatic engagement remains limited when it is bound up with the refusal to be clear about the particular composition of the political and its presuppositions. If the thoughts developed here are illuminating, it is due to the attempt to understand the structure of representation and *representation*. But the structure of both is the difference of freedom in which commonality and individuality are bound up with one another in an adversarial manner. The tension between them is the liveliness of cultural and political life, and for this reason we should not attempt to remove it. Political strife lives upon the fact that we expect our opponents to ignore what is most important to us. Correctly understood, however, strife causes one-sided solutions to lose their credibility. For it is clear that a community is equally endangered by an overdeveloped individualism as by an overdeveloped communality. Both endanger the representations and *representations* within which freedom takes place.

3

The Intensity of the Political
Carl Schmitt's Phenomenology of Enmity and the End of the Ideological World Civil War

"The political world," writes Carl Schmitt in chapter 6 of *The Concept of the Political*, "is a pluriverse, not a universe."[1] One need not be a particularly acute observer to recognize that the historical events of recent years have confirmed this proposition. The collapse of the Soviet empire has allowed the political world to become more particularized. The conviction that the end of the cold war would bring the world community closer to the "idyllic goal of complete and final depoliticization" (54/54) has proven to be mistaken as hardly any other. It has also become apparent that where the "pluralism of the world of states" is newly discovered and practiced, we find "the real possibility of the enemy" confirmed. What is here confirmed is the concept of the 'political,' which is to say, the "specific political distinction to which political actions and motives can be reduced" (26/26), the distinction between friend and enemy.

However, it is not primarily the tendency toward a particularization of political relationships that occasions a new or renewed interest in Carl Schmitt. Similarly, Schmitt's reflections on the concept of the political do not deserve attention for the sole reason that they accord a central role to the category of the enemy. Rather, what should arouse our greatest interest is the manner in which Schmitt determines the particular relationships of the political. A series of contemporary conflicts plainly appear to be perfect examples of this definition. Schmitt writes,

> The political can derive its energy from the most varied human endeavors, from the religious, economic, moral, and other antitheses. It does not describe its own domain, but only the *intensity* of an association or dissociation of human beings whose motives can be religious, national (in the ethnic or cultural sense) economic, or of another kind and can effect at different times different coalitions and separations. The real friend-enemy grouping is existentially so strong and decisive that the nonpolitical antithesis, at precisely the moment at which it brings about this grouping, pushes aside its hitherto 'purely' religious, 'purely' economic, 'purely' cultural criteria and motives and subordinates them to the completely new, singular conditions and conclusions of the political situation at hand, which, from the perspective of that "purely" religious, "purely" economic and other "pure" points of departure, often seem to be rather inconsistent and "irrational." (38–39/38)[2]

This definition of the political is attractive if only because it takes account of the ubiquitous phenomenon of *politicization*. If the concept of the political is understood as an "intensity" rather than as a particular domain of human life, it is unnecessary to stipulate that certain political antitheses and conflicts must be distinguished, once and for all, from those that are unpolitical. Schmitt's concept of the political takes into account the dynamic on the basis of which the situations and forms of human life can suddenly appear in a new light. However, this flexibility within Schmitt's concept of the political also constitutes a difficultly: if nothing is fundamentally protected from becoming political, in the end nothing can be said to be essentially political. It appears that Schmitt's conception does not allow the political to have an institutional dimension.

This brings about a further and more significant difficultly: when the political is nothing more than an intensity of antitheses and conflicts, then the political evidently takes on the character of a fact that resists all evaluation. If it is a question of distinguishing between friends and enemies, religious, moral, and economic criteria fall by the wayside. With respect to the political, the question is always only, as Schmitt puts it, whether "or not [it] is actually present or at least potentially possible" (36/36).

However, this, too, has another and not unattractive side: If religious, moral, and economic criteria are inadequate means of evaluating the political, the possibility exists that political antitheses and conflicts can be kept free of religious, moral, and economic evaluations and in this manner their further intensification can be avoided. Religious, moral, and economic relationships and evaluations are finally what increase to the intensity of the political and are altered by it. Hence the attempt to combat their religious, moral, and economic dimension can merely further polarize them and drive them deeper into conflict.

According to this sketch, the plausible and problematic aspects of Schmitt's concept of the political appear to cancel out one another. The illuminating emphasis on the political dynamic is purchased at the the cost of ignoring political institutions, particularly that of the state. The separation of the political from religious, moral, and economic criteria evidently can be obtained only at the price of reducing the political to the status of a mere fact. Furthermore, it cannot ultimately be established if this fact is merely an intensity of religious, moral, or economic antitheses and conflicts. To consistently represent Schmitt's concept of the political, we must be able to maintain the singularity of the political without at the same time giving up the idea of intensity. We must be able to show how the factual status of the political both necessitates and sets in motion its own, essential ways of coming to terms with it.

In what follows I will attempt to argue along these lines. I am not, however, concerned with a detailed reconstruction of the entirety of Schmitt's thought, nor of giving an account of Schmitt's place in the context of his time. Rather I will take this opportunity to investigate whether Schmitt's conception of the political can be elucidated and developed like a classical philosophical theory, without being reduced to the reconstructed intentions of the author or related to the historical circumstances in which he lived.[3]

The course of my reflections is determined by the following problematics. First I will pursue the question of whether Schmitt's concept of the political can be defended against the objection that it ignores institutional aspects of the political. Then I will discuss the nature of the factual character of the political and the different ways of coming to terms with it. The discussion of these two questions only makes sense in this order. After interrogating these possibilities which belong to the fact of the political, it is necessary to ask whether political understanding and action are not already determined by making reference to particular institutions or whether, on the contrary, these institutions must be understood as instantiations of particular forms of action.

With regard to the first question, we can begin with Schmitt's remark that the distinction between friend and enemy merely provides the political with "a definition in the sense of a criterion and not as an exhaustive definition or one indicative of substantial content" (26/26). Schmitt certainly does not mean that the distinction between friend and enemy denotes only one aspect of the political, but rather that every aspect of the political can be recognized only if it has an essential connection to this distinction. By no means does Schmitt think that an adequate concept of the political must be composed of various, equally constitutive elements of which the distinction between friend and enemy is merely one among many. These qualifying remarks need not mean that Schmitt contradicts the opening sentence of his text, according to which "the concept of the state presupposes the concept of the political" (20/20). Rather, they are clearly meant to give some indication as to how the principle of the priority of the political can be understood with respect to the state. The distinction between friend and enemy certainly does not exhaustively determine the state. However, we would do well to keep in mind that a state can only be determined and distinguished from other, nonpolitical institutions by recourse to the distinction between friend and enemy. The reason for this is that the distinction between friend and enemy essentially reflects the constitution of the state. The political is the essence of the state, and to this extent the concept of the 'state' presupposes that of the political.

If the political is the *essence* of the state, then the state is equally the *essentially political institution* or, as Schmitt puts it, "the authoritative entity" (44/44). Other groups or institutions also can become political, and to this extent it is plausible to say that the political is not confined to the state. However, because the state is the essentially political institution, the politicization of nonstate institutions is shown predominantly in the fact that these institutions take the state to be their enemy or declare themselves to be enemies of the state, and the state accepts this declaration of enmity rather than merely criminalizing the institutions that oppose it. The state determines whether a violent group is merely criminal or is an enemy of the state. The political distinction between between friend and enemy is therefore a distinction made by the state, without it thereby being exclusive to the state. Conversely, it is for this reason that the state should be understood on the basis of this distinction, although in actuality it is not reserved for it alone.

The foregoing definition clearly needs to be supplemented in one respect: The state is an essentially political institution in that it demands that its citizens unconditionally relinquish the right to distinguish between friend and enemy and hence to make decisions regarding friendship and enmity. Aside from this, the state can also demand from the citizens—and this is of great importance for Schmitt—that they bear responsibility, along with the state, for the state's decisions. In this respect, the distinction between friend and enemy can be understood as the point of departure from which to comprehend the particularly political assent of the members of a state to this decision. This distinction allows us to understand what other theoreticians of the political wish to explain with the idea of a contract. We can only understand ourselves as citizens of a state when we are prepared to approve, in principle, the defense of the state against its enemies. One component of this is that we accept "the ever present possibility of conflict" (32/32).

If we consider both of the foregoing points—the determination of the state as the decisive entity and the dependence of citizens upon the friend-enemy distinctions of the state—it becomes clear that Schmitt's concept of the political by no means excludes the institutional element of the political. For Schmitt it is solely a question of grasping these aspects in the context of an event and, correspondingly, of understanding the institutions from the perspective of their actions within an event. States, for Schmitt, are in their essence stages of decision and action. To the degree that the concept of the political sets their decisions and actions within a system of decision and action which extends beyond their parameters, the concept of the state assumes the concept of the political. The concept of the political is the concept of a particular kind of decision making and action that is fashioned, as it were, on the basis of the state, without realizing itself exclusively in the state.

With respect to political action, it is important to remember that Schmitt did not want the definition of the political that accompanies the distinction between friend and enemy to be understood in terms of "war or militarism" (33/33). The justification for this is simple. To the extent that diplomacy is concerned with regulating precarious relationships to other states, to the degree that, with respect to internal politics, the aim is to preserve the peace, the goal is to hinder armed confrontation, and it is precisely here that political activity stands under the shadow of the distinction between friend and enemy. It stands under the shadow of the "extreme case" (35/35), which, if we follow Schmitt, can be true in varying degrees. Every "concrete antagonism," writes Schmitt, "becomes that much more political the closer it approaches the most extreme point, that of the friend-enemy grouping" (29/29). It is not only conflicts that are political in which the "real possibility" of violent resolution is quite clear, to say nothing of when their actuality is already immanent. In situations of this kind, what political action is fundamentally about merely becomes explicit. In Schmitt's sense, what is political is neither violent confrontation considered in itself nor its avoidance, but rather the essential coherence of both. The mere condition of civilization and of communal peace is not political, neither is war or civil war; rather what is political is peace with full knowledge of its fragility—the maintenance of peace and war for the sake of peace. The case of war is not the rule; it occurs, as Schmitt explicitly says, only as "an exception" (35/35). But the rule coheres with this very exception, because otherwise the rule could not be grasped as a rule and obeyed. Hence the essence of the political is not war but strife, or more precisely, the agonistic coherence of opposites. And the particular pathos which dominates Schmitt's essay can be understood in the context of this coherence: the text raises objections against the overestimation of conditions of security in order to provoke a serious consideration of how they are established and maintained, without fostering illusions about the stability of peaceful conditions.

If the foregoing reflections have elucidated Schmitt's concept of the political, it remains necessary to comprehend more clearly his understanding of the political as an intensity. For it is precisely when the political is not understood as a particular field of knowledge that the specificity of political actions can be grasped; these are actions that are part of the agonistic coherence of war and peace and are required by them. Actions of this sort can in fact become necessary within the context of every "field of knowledge," and to this extent they cannot by themselves constitute a field of knowledge that would be equal to the others. Moreover, if we once more consider Schmitt's description of the state as the "authoritative entity," it becomes clear that the definition of the political as an intensity in no way equates the state with other groupings or communities, even if it belongs together with such things in a conflict-laden field of diverse antitheses.

In spite of this, the crucial difficulty of Schmitt's thesis is not overcome. Rather, it first shows itself most clearly once the essential role of governmental decision making and action in determining the political has been understood. If political antitheses and conflicts are nothing more than an intensity of religious, moral, and economic tensions, then political action appears in the end to be merely the playing out of such tensions. Political activities do not then serve merely to conserve governmental existence and independence (cf. 46), nor do they merely serve to conserve or create peace within the state. Rather the essentially political institution of the state loses its priority over other groupings, so it appears, precisely whenever it settles religious, moral, or economic problems in the intensity of the political. The nonpolitical, or the not-yet-political, activity embedded in political institutions becomes political by way of intensification. In order to clarify how this occurs, let us turn to Schmitt's more precise determination of political enmity.

Schmitt's text here presents an ambiguous picture. On the one hand, we read that the "highpoints of great politics" are "the moments in which the enemy is, in concrete clarity, recognized as the enemy" (67/67). As an illustration of this thesis Schmitt can point to Cromwell's speech in which the Spanish appear as the providential enemy of the Protestant English. On the other hand, Schmitt can also speak of "unusually intense and inhuman wars," which, *transcending the limits of the political,* simultaneously degrade the enemy into moral and other categories and are forced to make of him a monster that must not only be defeated, but also utterly *destroyed.* In other words, he is *an enemy who no longer must be compelled to retreat into his borders only"* (37/36; emphasis in original). The thesis that the political is an intensity appears not merely to countenance the "highpoints of great politics," but clearly to aim at its apotheosis. What is the religious conflict that increases to the point of a decision between being or nonbeing supposed to be if not a model of intensity? If one accepts this and declares, accordingly, that the talk of the suprapolitical degradation of the enemy is a gesture of mere pacification,[4] then more than just this formulation ceases to be valid. It follows from this that Schmitt has elucidated his conception of the enemy in a completely erroneous way, and one is forced to give up the essential elements of this conception as not having been meant seriously by the author. It is not a question of the distinction between political enmity and nonpolitical opposition, but rather that the moral and religious opponent or the economic competitor would also appear under the guise of the political enemy. The problem, therefore, touches the core of Schmitt's conception of the political, and for this reason alone it deserves particular attention. The question is whether, following Schmitt, we can arrive at a convincing concept of the political.

At first glance the characterization of the enemy, as Schmitt presents it in the course of introducing the concept, appears to justify the reference to the example of Cromwell. The enemy, says Schmitt, "is precisely the Other, the stranger, and it is sufficient for his nature that he is, in a particularly intense way, existentially something different and foreign, so that in the extreme case conflicts with him are possible. These can be decided neither by a previously determined general norm, nor by the judgment of a 'disinterested' and therefore 'neutral' third party" (27/27). For Cromwell, the papist Spanish are other and foreign "in a particularly intense way" insofar as they threaten the existence of the English Protestants and, due to their religion, cannot simply be driven back within their borders. "With France," Schmitt paraphrases Cromwell, "one can make peace, but not with Spain, because it is a Papist state and the Pope maintains peace only as long as he wishes" (67/68). Accordingly, only the religious interpretation can account for the malevolence of the Spanish, and if this is the case, then political enmity can really no longer be distinguished from religious opposition. Papist Spain, to employ Hobbes' formulation, is "the Kingdome of Darknesse."[5]

However, Schmitt undoubtedly relativizes interpretations of this kind when he distinguishes between the "psychological expression" of such interpretations and the "autonomy of such distinctions" (28/27–28): "Psychologically, the enemy is easily treated as being evil and ugly, because every distinction, most of all the political, as the strongest and most intense of the distinctions and categorizations, draws upon the other distinctions for support" (27–28/27). If it is permissible to apply this analysis to Cromwell's religious interpretation, we see that it does not get to the heart of the political relationship; it is nothing more than an—eventually comprehensible, but factually inadequate—*articulation* of the political antithesis, which obscures the autonomy of the political emphasized by Schmitt.

However, the consequence of this insight must be an appeal for the denial of religious, moral, and other kinds of political enemies. The political enemy would in fact be the Other, the stranger who, as Schmitt says, "threatens one's own form of existence" (27/27), one's own form of life, and loses his political significance when the threat is no longer a "real possibility." The standards of one's own form of life make it impossible to vouchsafe an interpretation to the Other, the stranger, though it is the case that one is compelled to secure an interpretation and articulation of one's own form of life in relation to him as the Other and the stranger. The enemy would be the Other—and not the Other of myself. The political settlement of enmity would mark a caesura in the enactment of the self-interpretation that is carried out in terms of the interpretation of the stranger; the intensity of the political would then be equivalent to a fundamentally new kind of conflict. One would then rightly distinguish political conflicts from conflicts of other kinds, even when they arise out of nonpolitical conflicts; one could then do justice to the diversity of the ways in which such conflicts are settled. The political resolution of enmity, the securing and defending of one's own form of life against threats, would be no solution to the problem of self-understanding and one's understanding of what is foreign. Nevertheless, it does at least represent a liberation from the agony of this understanding, which consists in a fixation of the proper [*das Eigene*] upon the foreign [*das Fremde*]. For if it is the case the one cannot experience oneself without the foreign, that one becomes what one is by interpreting the foreign and translating it into the proper, it is then precisely here that the fixation upon the Other in the process of definition proves itself to be a form of unfreedom. One can neither let the Other be nor expressly experience it; one rejects the Other and must nevertheless orientate oneself to him. The chains of negative dependence are dissolved when one lets the Other be and is politically mindful to protect the border and, in the extreme case, one's own life.

However much these thoughts might correspond to Schmitt's conception of the "inherently objective nature and autonomy of the political" (28/27), it remains appropriate to doubt whether they actually correspond to Schmitt's meaning or to that of his text on the concept of the political. For when it is not a question of combating the *position* of an enemy but rather of merely reacting to his possible or actual attack, political enmity has a neutralizing effect. It neutralizes the position of the antitheses, and when one considers what disastrous effect Schmitt ascribes to such neutralization, it then appears that one does him no favors by defending the autonomy of the political. Instead one moves closer to a suspicion which Leo Strauss has formulated against Schmitt from a critical and challenging perspective, namely, the suspicion that with the affirmation of the political a particular type of liberal conviction is expressed:

> Whoever affirms the political as such respects all who are willing to fight; he is just as tolerant as the liberals, but with the opposite intention. Whereas the liberal respects and tolerates all 'honestly held' convictions, so long as these respect the legal order and acknowledge the sanctity of *peace*, whoever affirms the political as such, respects and tolerates all 'serious' convictions, in other words, all decisions leading up to the real possibility of *war*. Thus the affirmation of the political as such proves to be liberalism with completely reversed premises.[6]

Naturally Strauss is aware that this does not correspond to Schmitt's own opinion. This becomes evident with all the clarity one might wish for from Schmitt's "Address on the Age of Neutralization,"[7] to which Strauss also makes reference[8] and without which one cannot actually grasp Schmitt's conception of the political. It is not for nothing that Schmitt published this address together with his text on the concept of the political.

At the heart of Schmitt's address is a critique of liberalism. In this historical-philosophical sketch Schmitt describes a progressive leveling of authoritative systems which have, at the very least, reached a provisional end in the "faith in technology that is widespread today" (AN, 89). The belief that "all peoples and nations, all classes and denominations, people of all ages and generations" could "with equal obviousness enjoy the advantages and conveniences of technical comfort" essentially assumes that—liberal—faith in a comprehensive "sphere of peace, understanding and reconciliation" (AN, 90), which is synonymous with the loss of the ability to make political decisions. However, this faith has, according to Schmitt's diagnosis, the character of a fateful deception: the Bolshevik revolution in Russia has "put into effect the anti-religion of technicity" and established a state "that is more and more intensively governmental than any state of the most absolute sovereign" (AN, 80).

Schmitt's critique of the liberal desire for peace, of the trust in universal understanding and reconciliation, would be apolitical if it did not have its foundation in the existence of the Bolshevik state. With respect to this state it is, as Schmitt thinks, naive and dangerous to blind oneself to the necessity of political decision making, so that liberalism, with its universalistic dream, is seen only as the inability to practice politics. There is a distinction between friend and enemy, only the liberals have not yet become aware of it. They are prevented from perceiving this distinction because in their way of thinking no allowances are made for the distinction—and for the decision that accompanies it. The liberals and all those who subscribe to "an oppressive religion of technicity" (AN, 94) are not in a position to see that the technical organization of the world is no solution, but rather represents a problem that can only be solved by political means.

The "intellectual sense" of the century—here Schmitt summarizes these thoughts—"first emerges when it reveals what kind of politics is strong enough to seize control of the new technology and grasp the genuine groupings of friends and enemies growing upon the new ground" (AN, 94). The intellectual sense of the century stands in clear relief once the fronts of the world civil war have assumed a clear form. The intellectual sense of the century emerges when clarity rules over victory and defeat in the world civil war.

Without being hasty one can say that this clarity has since been created. But one will hardly want to assert that Schmitt's diagnosis of his time has been confirmed; rather its main point has become a matter of historical interest. One has known for many years who the vanquished are; however, it is equally clear that there there is no univocal victor who has successfully seized "control of the new technology." And with regard to the "groupings of friends and enemies" that have grown upon the new ground, it is certainly not possible to doubt their existence. However, it would be difficult to designate one or even some of them as "genuine."

This is of decisive importance for Schmitt's understanding of the political as an intensity. Only on the assumption of a secular confrontation for "ultimate meaning" can we comprehend why Schmitt understands the intensity of the political as the radical expression of "intellectual" positions which confront one another: the nationalized and militant antireligion of technology and that position said to emerge out of "the power of an synthesizing knowledge," whose purpose is to allow for the creation of "an order of human things" (AN, 95). When it is a question of the "ultimate meaning" of the century, one can, with respect to the political, think of a constellation which is an analog to that of Protestant England and papist Spain.

With the end of the world civil war between East and West there is no longer any evidence for a single hostile position. There is no longer a position in the sense of "great politics," a position which would be opposed by only one other. Politics no longer contains a single, dramatic alternative where what is at issue is the meaning of the century, perhaps even the meaning of history itself. In this sense the enemy has also lost its "concrete clarity."

However, this is not true for the category of the enemy as such. On the contrary, Schmitt's insight that the political world is a pluriverse and not a universe can now frankly be brought to the fore through the question of the ultimate meaning of the century. The political can now clearly be understood as a means of neutralizing different ideological positions without the danger of being mistaken for the good intentioned—but only good intentioned—liberalism of universal understanding. Where what is at issue is the political neutralization of the positional element, we no longer speak of universalism, but rather of a 'pluriversalism' or simply of 'pluralism' whose political import, for the sake of its own possibility, must be limited. Openness, tolerance, and liberality come up against a barrier, namely, when something becomes an existential threat to one's own existence. What is threatening is, as has been noted, not the foreign as such. Rather a great deal of that which is superficially considered to be part of the proper can, on closer inspection, be proven to be foreign. What is truly threatening is only what reveals itself to be hostile, and hence politically foreign, by mounting an actual attack on one's own form of life. What this means for a free, constitutional state probably does not need to be elucidated in detail.

Hence the conception of the political that is possible within the scope of Schmitt's definition is also not identical with Leo Strauss's conception of a liberalism of conflict. By incorporating the notion of neutrality into Schmitt's conception as a result of which all possibly or actually antagonistic positions must be accorded equal rights, Strauss explicitly wants to bring into sharper focus the positional character of this conception. However, if we consider it more closely, the liberalism of conflict or war is an abstraction. Strauss intentionally underplays what Schmitt, with regard to the distinction between friend and enemy explicitly observes, that the "possibility of correct recognition and understanding" is here "granted only by means of actual participation and collaboration" (27/27). The actual distinction between friend and enemy is always a practical one; it belongs to a particular situation and can be understood only from the perspective of experience and action. Whether others also bear this decision, whether others make similar decisions or not, are not questions of universal tolerance, but rather questions that are of importance only when they concern the circumstances of political action and thus one's own political action. The only move is how one's own form of life can be represented politically in the face of threats.

This means, however, that political action is perspectival. The political radically illustrates that, as Nietzsche has remarked, we cannot "see around our own corner."[9] And we should not attempt to do so. For where it is a question of the existence of one's own form of life, nothing is more neutral, nothing appears more in another light than one's own actual, particularly constituted existence. Seen in this way, politics is the art of communal survival—and nothing more.

One can find this disappointing, regrettable, and false. However, this is the price of recognizing the autonomy of the political. The picture becomes decisively richer if one considers the many aspects upon which forms of life are constructed and develop; it becomes richer when one considers that the forms of cultural life do not retain their vivacity when they do not test themselves, in numerous interpretations and translations, against the Other, the foreign. Without the foreign, the proper does not develop, just as in the absence of a particular perspective the foreign cannot be interpreted and, in this sense, understood. The proper and the foreign cohere because they can neither be reduced to one another, nor can they definitively be reconciled with one another. They cohere because only in conflict with one another are they what they are. However, as a result of this antagonistic coherence of the proper and the foreign, the political articulation of their conflict can only have disastrous consequences. Like the distinction between friend and enemy, it would then consist in the limitation of the proper and the exclusion of the foreign, which, from the perspective of culture, could no longer be distinguished from the conflict between foreignness and properness. This leads to the agony of negative determination, to that pale twilight of understanding and nonunderstanding that recognizes neither political contours nor cultural translations.

In order not to fall into such a twilight, it is good if political decisions are made without concern for the appeal or even the truth of the Other or the foreign. However, it is likewise good when one is clearly aware, within the intensity of the political, of the limited nature of the proper. The alternative to a particular culture is a not a universal culture, but none at all. But when it is a question of the survival of particular cultures which develop within the context of their own tradition and history, they cannot eschew the possibility of the political. This is also true of a liberal or, more felicitously, a hermeneutic culture of interpretation which must, if necessary, affirm and assert the autonomy of the political against fundamentalism of different varieties. To the degree that the political is an intensity of the cultural conflict between the proper and the foreign, the concept of the political assumes the concept of culture. However, political intensity has a quality of its own. This does not immediately bear upon the life of a culture, but affects its preservation in a twofold sense: in the sense of its actual existence and in the sense of its preservation in the face of the unfreedom of understanding. To this extent one also has to say that the concept of culture needs the concept of the political.

4

Public Freedom—the Strife of Power and Violence
On Hannah Arendt's Concept of the Political

Whoever develops a philosophy of the political in this century and in the process makes essential reference to the structure of the Greek *polis* has actually already done everything necessary to arouse skepticism and opposition. For no matter how much sympathy one might have for the Greeks, there is general agreement that the political circumstances of classical Greece actually have very little to do with the modern world. Why that should be the case can be said with equal speed: in order to grasp the Greek context there is no need for the distinction between state and society that is constitutive for the modern world. And what belongs together with this: the classical Greek understanding of politics is not oriented around the thought of persons determined by freedom of action and rationality, which is the case with at least a whole series of modern theories. In other words, the classical Greek understanding of politics is neither a philosophy of the state and a theory of society, nor liberalism.

Whoever nevertheless develops a concept of the political that is oriented to the Greek *polis* and, like Hannah Arendt, is obviously familiar with the modern theories, certainly will have to reckon with skepticism and opposition, and will probably even have consciously counted on it. The usual mode of access to the political then has the character of a conscious provocation. However, provocations are only successful if they shed light on what is otherwise hidden, if they bring into view what one normally does not see or does not wish to see. Provocations are successful only if they indicate a lack in commonly accepted convictions; this, conversely, provokes another objection against them, but it also brings them sympathy and agreement.

Ultimately, provocations are not necessarily convincing. Their persuasive power is even more strongly endangered than that of positions which are carefully thought out, differentiated, and consider all aspects and nuances of the matter, because they are one-sided; in order to demonstrate the deficiencies of accepted convictions they overemphasize some things and exclude others or, as a consequence of their engagement with the issue, adopt a more abbreviated and sharper perspective. But one cannot adequately accept such provocations if one immediately calculates their one-sidedness and criticizes their limited view of things. One will only do justice to provocations that are to be taken seriously intellectually by taking what they identify as the deficiencies of accepted convictions as one's starting point and then asking whether their one-sidedness and sharp focus is really the expression of a selective view of the phenomena. If that is not the case, then the one-sidedness only leads to a new and better starting point for a consideration of the entire phenomenal domain.

In what follows, I want to show that Arendt's conception of the political, which is oriented to the *polis*, can be understood in exactly this way. The provocative sharpness with which this conception is formulated ought, I believe, not be considered a sign of narrowness with regard to the matter at hand. It can be corrected, and by presenting and elucidating Hannah Arendt's conception of the political, I will recommend a correction in this sense.

What has irritated readers again and again about Arendt's conception is that the structures and phenomena upon which she focuses in *The Human Condition*[1] appear, for a selective determination of the political, to produce as good as nothing in return. The political, one is led to believe, is the space of appearance[2] of human action. It is, as Arendt says, that "space where I appear to others as others appear to me, where men exist not merely like other living or inanimate things but make their appearance explicitly" (192/198–99). The possibility, to represent one another reciprocally, is political. What is "political" about this possibility is not clear, at least not without further explanation.

In order to understand the definition sketched above, one should consider its two aspects more closely. First of all, Arendt insists on the the distinction between a mere appearance and something coming-into-appearance. It is not sufficient simply to be there for the others, rather it is a question of explicitly presenting oneself before them. If this is a political action, then political action does not merely consist in doing something for another in a manner that is accessible, but rather first in *wanting* to be accessible to others with one's own actions.

One also could express this by saying that political action is, in an emphatic sense of this word, *public*. Something is not already public if it occurs openly, without secrecy. What is not concealed is thereby not yet public. Rather, an action is public when it is performed for the sake of being accessible.

Action and speech, following Arendt, can be public in this sense. But it follows from this interpretation of the public that, conversely, not every action and speech is also public. An action is public, then, if it is *explicitly* performed in front of others. A speech is not already public if others can listen to it, but rather first becomes public if its meaning is the audience.

Even this does not yet make the definition of public action clearly unambiguous. For by the publicity of an action or a speech one cannot mean that action or speech are meaningful when done before others. Emphatic publicity, that is, publicity that in its true form is understood politically, consists rather in the fact that action and speech are *in the sense* of those others before whom they are enacted. The publicity of action, understood politically, consists in the fact it is performed *before* and *for* others.[3]

When one acts in this way, one is clearly not simply connected to others through one's actions without otherwise having anything to do with them. Acting or speaking before and for others rather allows one to recognize that one forms part of them. Acting or speaking publicly includes one in the public realm, namely, without expressly needing to underscore this yet again. For one acts or speaks under the presupposition of publicity. One is already in the public realm and is able, simply for this reason, also to publicly act and speak.

This leads to the second aspect of Arendt's definition of the political which one ought to consider more closely. In the terminology of *The Human Condition*, to be in the public realm is to be in the space of appearance of the political. The concept of the space of appearance does not here designate anything which simply exists. Rather it is, as Arendt says in the formulation already cited above, "the space where I appear to others and others appear to me," or more precisely, "where men . . . make their appearance explicitly." It is not completely clear how this is meant. For the idea that a space arises by something appearing in it sounds barely plausible. One could at best say that the space manifests itself thereby and can be experienced as a space. The space is the *condition* for the appearance, and if one reflects upon this, one can also make it more comprehensible how the appearance in action or speech and the space of appearance cohere. The appearance in action or speech must be *permitted* by the others. This permission should not be understood in the sense of an explicit action. Rather it occurs willy-nilly in that one is *open* to the fact that others make their appearance. Acting and speaking belong to this openness, just as, conversely, this openness becomes manifest through the acting and speaking proper to it.

The openness to the action and speech of others is what binds us together before all cooperation in action and before all the agreement and accord that is possible in speech. For before communal action, before agreement in dispute and conversation, before the possibility to bring others closer to a particular conviction by means of speech, speech and action as such must be permitted and one must be admitted into this permitted openness. How one acts in particular and what one says in particular ultimately depend upon how one *wishes* to make one's appearance. It stands open, but it can only stand open in the openness of the space of appearance. And then the actual freedom of action and speech is the space of appearance in its openness, the free-space in which alone this action and speech can be enacted. In action and speech this is perceived as freedom, understood as a free-space. One perceives and understands it, and in action and speech, one allows it to manifest itself.[4]

Now the two aspects of Arendt's definition elucidated above can be related to one another. If political action and speech are enacted before and for others of whom one is oneself a part, it is then enacted in the public realm and for the public realm. The public realm, however, is the space of appearance; it is the free-space which is authentic freedom. And then an action or a speech is political which is enacted in freedom for the sake of freedom. Insofar as what is at stake in action and speech is freedom, political action and speech are free in a particular, and particularly intensive and explicit way.[5]

These reflections are certainly still quite formal. However, their formal character was necessary in order to give the fundamental definitions of the political in Arendt's work as sharp a contour as possible. And proceeding in this formal way a decisive point already stands out: the concept of the political, as it has hitherto appeared, is *descriptive* to the extent that it names the decisive condition of political action and speech. At the same time, however, this makes the concept *normative*: in a basic sense what is political are, to use a formulation of Jürgen Habermas, "the structures of an unimpaired subjectivity"[6]—in other words, the structures of authentic freedom sketched above. Certainly the normative character of the conception developed above could easily provide the incentive to call into question its descriptive possibilities or at least to cautiously evaluate them. In order to decide whether this is justified or not, one must probe these possibilities and see how Arendt interprets political action in detail in its coherence with the space of appearance of freedom.

Now it is just this which at first glance appears to be so greatly marked by a nostalgic veneration of the Greeks and a highly idiosyncratic accentuation that the persuasive power of the entire conception could come into question. Arendt orients herself to the *polis* in order to understand the political space of appearance more precisely. The *polis*, for Arendt, is a place of remembrance in the most precise meaning of the term. Or, as she herself says, "the *polis* was supposed to multiply the occasions to win 'immortal fame', that is, to multiply the chances for everyone to distinguish himself, to show in deed and word who he was in his unique distinctiveness, and so emancipate action, as it were, from its dependence upon the productive and poetic arts (190/197). It ought not depend on the poets whether the works and deeds of a worthy life are to be preserved in memory. For aside from the fact that this is a highly unreliable form of preservation—how much passes away without being captured by a poet, how few things make a poet a hero?—the poetic representation of works and deeds is problematic because it is a form of production and not a form of action; it remains external to political action and only provides a copy of it.

Arendt immediately concedes that this idea naturally has nothing to do "with the historical causes for the rise of the Greek city-state." But she adds that the understanding of the *polis* as a place of remembrance follows "what the Greeks themselves thought of it" (190/197). As proof of this, she refers to the famous speech of Pericles to the memory of those killed in the first year of the Peloponnesian War. At the decisive point in Thucydides' text Pericles says that Athens needs no Homer in order to announce its military glory; rather "we have everywhere left imperishable monuments of our good and bad deeds behind us."[7]

While it appears audacious to want to understand the essence of the *polis* on the basis of sentences such as this one, one need only grasp what is at issue here in general terms in order to see how far removed it is from the imputation of irrelevancy. What Pericles means is that Athens has made history and this history will be present for as long as the *polis* exists. Political action is historical because it is enacted on the basis of its continued presence in the public realm. And the public realm, in turn, can itself be grasped only in that one articulates it through the telling of stories. The political space of appearance is the space of presence for the history that is enacted and preserved within it. As event and narrative, history belongs in this space of presence, and this space of presence obtains its particular form through history. It is actual only by means of what is presented in it. The essence of the political lies in the freedom to history which is perceived in history as event and narrative.

What is clearly convincing about this idea is that political communities cannot be understood without history. Political communities are, in their essence, not pragmatic alliances for the purpose of economic preservation, and they also do not exist insofar as their members carry out particular cultural achievements. In Arendt's terminology, political communities have their essence neither in work, nor in production. They are, one ought also to add, also not dependent upon whether all their members speak the same language, practice the same religion, or even exhibit the same ethnic ancestry. In that case it is essentially more enlightening to see the identity of political communities in the fact that they have a single history which they can recount and carry on, in the fact that, as Arendt puts it, "the reality of the world is guaranteed by the presence of a world-with-others in which one and the same world appears in the most diverse perspectives" (192–93).[8]

Certainly one could still doubt that the essence of the political is adequately grasped in this way. It is hardly plausible simply to identify history, in the sense elucidated above, and politics. But this is not at all what Arendt has in mind. History is present in the free-space of the world-with-others, and this free-space itself, together with history, only has a political character when it is experienced as *power*. 'Power' is the central concept in Arendt's conception of the political. Accordingly, everything depends upon grasping what the term *power* here means as precisely as possible.

It may be that Arendt also took this concept over from Thucydides. In his speech Pericles speaks of the *dynamis tes poleos*, the power of the city (II, 41), and he means by the expression not merely the ability to be successful in war, but rather the excellent manner in which the Athenians construct a *polis*. The *polis* first demonstrates the excellence of individuals, and accordingly Pericles can proudly say that Athens owes its successes not to a calculation of advantages, but rather to a trust in the freedom of its citizens (II, 40). Whether Arendt's concept of power is inspired by this or not, her interpretation, in any case, seamlessly corresponds to the understanding of it sketched above. Power, she says, is "that which holds a political body together . . . and what first undermines and then kills political communities is loss of power and finally impotence" (193/200).

This, in turn, can now be related to the relationship of the political to history. The cohesion of a political community exists only where it succeeds in recounting history in such a manner that a meaningful context for action is constructed, which is nothing other than the historically determined free-space of this action. Power is the successful interplay of *epos* and *ergon*, of narration and deed. A community, which no longer presents itself as the free-space of action *in the sense* of the free-space, can no longer count on actions of this type. The excellence of the individual and the *polis* cohere like deed and narration. Where the space of appearance and appearance, the free-space and action and the way of being present and history accord with one another and hence increase into an intensity, power occurs. Power is an intensity of historical freedom.[9]

The particular meaning of this concept of power emerges more clearly if one considers that power is not dependent upon institutions, in particular not upon the institution of the state. Therein lies the provocation of Arendt's political philosophy discussed at the outset, on the basis of which one can doubt whether this political philosophy contains a productive concept of the political at all. A space of appearance or free-space is essentially held together only by power. It comes into being, as Arendt says, "wherever men are together in the manner of speech and action and therefore predates and precedes all formal constitution of the public realm and the various forms of government" (193/199). In its essence it is not determined by institutions. One must understand why this should be the case before one can speak of the limitations or weaknesses of this conception.

In the first place, a concept of the political that does not identify the political with the state has the clear advantage that it allows for an unbiased understanding of political life. No one would seriously contest the political character of a civil rights movement or a popular uprising, the struggles of a colony to achieve independence, a revolutionary cell, or an opposition group. And as one could easily demonstrate, what holds together communities of this kind and eventually makes them convincing is nothing other than power in the sense in which it is interpreted above. All of these communities are meaningful constructions of their historical freedom.

These examples clearly also show that here power is, in one way or another, related to the state and the state organization. Revolution and political opposition aim at a displacement of the state organization in favor of another one, uprisings are directed against states, civil rights movements bring suit against the state on behalf of the rights of citizens who are being discriminated against. Communities of this kind, we can therefore assume, are termed "political" because they are related, in one way or another, to the institution of the state.

But Arendt does not want to contest this either. Her provocation would be futile if she wanted to attempt to exclude the state and its organizational forms from the determination of the political. She merely wants to contest that the state is the essence of the political, not deny the political significance of the state. The pivotal point can be formulated as follows: power is the liveliness, the soul of the political, while the state and every other prestate organizational form or organization otherwise related to the state are its outward form, its body. And while the body might still exist for a while after the soul has withdrawn from it, while it may even be conserved with all sorts of devices, it can for all that at best simulate this liveliness for the superficial observer. That states nevertheless ultimately decline goes together, as Arendt says, with the particular nature of the public realm, which, "because it ultimately resides on action and speech, never altogether loses its potential character" (193/200).

The experience that political institutions can lose their life and become empty need not be regarded as strange. In order to be able to actually have this experience one need merely accept, explicitly or implicitly, what Arendt underscores, that the state is not the soul of the political. Conversely, the soul of the political clearly manifests itself in the outward form of the state or in a competing organization connected to the state, and Arendt is fully aware of how necessary this is. She emphatically points out that the space of the appearance of the political needs to be established externally and that this is primarily provided by laws. But the laws and consequently also all of the institutions bound up with them are not authentically political. They are, "like the wall around the city . . . not results of action but products of making" (187/194). Arendt here rightly refers to Aristotle, who distinguishes the activity of the legislator from authentically political actions, the *politeusthai*.[10] The legislator, she thinks, provides only the necessary, but not the adequate conditions for the political.

Next to the understanding of the *polis* as a place of remembrance, it is this idea of an authentically political activity and the distinction between politics and legislation which belongs together with it that makes the orientation to the Greeks so attractive for Arendt. For here she finds the basis and foundation upon which she can diagnose and criticize all the problematic aspects of political life, particularly of modern political life. As they are carried out, diagnosis and critique prove themselves to be variations of a fundamental theme. Precisely because it does not constitute a form of genuinely political activity, everything which concerns the establishment and formation of political institutions stands in danger of becoming autonomous. It can attract attention to itself in an inappropriate manner, so that the impression arises that the problems of the political must be solved in this sphere. Arendt criticizes Plato and Aristotle already on this point. They withdrew their attention from authentically political activity and its space of appearance and devoted themselves to the problem of the production and institutionalization of political spaces. This change in orientation first clearly becomes dangerous for the political where it has practical consequences and leads to the autonomy of institutions, to the detriment, even destruction, of the authentically political. Where individuals or groups dominate the institutions and isolate them from the citizens, political power vanishes under the manifestation of *violence*, which, in Hannah Arendt's sense, is the capacity for an isolated tyranny outside of the political free-space. It is the capacity to realize goals without, and even against, the free-space of the political. Ancient tyranny is already an example of this (197/202). However, just how fatal is the autonomy of the institutional sphere is first demonstrated when it has led to a thoroughgoing privatization of the citizens; and a citizenry that has been made impotent in this way can be demagogically mobilized, violently organized, and supervised. While privatization already is achieved with the repression of the political by the economic, the "mobilization of the depoliticized masses"[11] was reserved for the totalitarian systems of this century. Whether one willingly hears it or not, according to Arendt's diagnosis, modern liberalism, where the human being is degraded from a *homo politicus* to an *animal laborans et consumens*, is a necessary condition of totalitarianism.

All the more important is the question of whether and to what extent the presupposition of this diagnosis, the distinction between authentically political activity in the free-space of the political and the establishing and organizing arts of legislation and governing, is convincing. At issue here, as stated at the outset, are not fundamental doubts regarding Arendt's conception, but rather the presentation of some corrections and changes in emphasis.

When Arendt compares the laws of a community with the walls of a city, she makes it clear enough how little she undervalues the activity of the legislators. The laws are nothing less than the establishment and the securing of historical freedom. However, when she designates this establishment and securing as "prepolitical" (188/195), she arouses the impression that everything has been accomplished with this single erection of the wall of law. The legislator, like the architect, withdraws as soon as the city is ready to be occupied. Unfortunately, this is not the case. Repairs are necessary too often for this to be so. Plato and Aristotle were so very interested in questions of legislation not because they "wished to turn against action" (188/195), but rather because of the instability within the domain of political action. Their political philosophy is meant therapeutically.

Arendt knows very well how great the instability of the political is and how quickly the power of a community vanishes. This is already indicated by her remark that power fails to lose its potential power "even in the most stable seeming situations." In view of this, however, it is in keeping with the meaning of Arendt's conception that a greater significance be given not merely to the establishment but also to the preservation of political free-spaces than she herself allows, especially since it does not contradict her intention to see the essence of the political in the historical freedom of the community. Everything which contributes to the preservation of this freedom presupposes this freedom. It remains related to this freedom like the activity of the doctor or the therapist is related to health.

Precisely because of its latent character, the political cannot be thought without being actualized in institutions, and because of its instability it remains directed toward an institutional reality, toward therapy with laws. Where it is a question of the actuality of the political, one can even say that it cannot be understood otherwise than institutionally. The laws and the constitution, which is articulated by means of laws, constitute the actuality of a merely possible political freedom; just as it certainly remains true that this actuality can, like a deserted house, only simulate life. Where history no longer occurs and is no longer recounted, the house comprised of law and a constitution becomes a ghost house.

The relationship of politics and institutions can be determined more precisely if one considers that securing political freedom institutionally is not possible without violence, be it through the threat or exercise of violence. Violence is then not merely a phenomenon of antipolitical caprice, but it is rather connected to the domain of the political. It is lawmaking and law preserving, without being exclusively used for this purpose.[12] One is therefore confronted with the particular state of affairs that the political freedom of violence, understood as power, requires an external capacity for domination and tyranny in order for it to be able to occur. And in this way the political presents itself as the indissoluble, but also irreconcilable, relationship of power and violence.

One also could express this by naming power and violence "agonistic," and designating their relationship as a form of strife. Because they are *in conflict*, power and violence exclude one another, and because they exist only in conflict, one cannot exist without the other. Their relationship, therefore, cannot adequately be defined in terms of a logic of "either-or" or "this as well as that." Above all, however, their relationship never can be definitively determined. The power of historical freedom cannot, on the basis of itself alone, achieve a genuinely stable existence, but rather remains bound to violence. Violence and the institutional reality which it contains, either actually or in the form of a threat, are never justified on the basis of themselves alone, but are bound to power as their Other. Yet power, once again, can never actually be the basis for the meaning of violence, because it is its Other, its absolute Other. And because that is the case, violence will have a tendency to remain threatening to power when it comes forward to preserve it. It is like a weapon that is capable of killing those whom it should protect. For the same reason, a tendency always lies within historical freedom to disdain violence and, moreover, to disengage power from violence and to constitute its existence on the basis of its own resources. The ultimate impossibility of this occasionally is evoked by a contempt for power in favor of violence and the institutions which it establishes and preserves.

Arendt precisely analyzed this strife of power and violence from the perspective of their dissimilarity, and in the process she drew attention, again and again, to the fragility of political power in the face of violence. She pointed out that tyranny "prevents the development of power" (197/202) and consequently can be defined as a "combination of force and powerlessness" (196/202). Tyranny is the earliest example of a politics directed against the political, a perversion of the political which is enacted in an opposition of the outward form against the essence. Correspondingly, using the phenomenon of "passive resistance" and its political power (194–95/201), Arendt underscored the essential nonviolent character of the political and so in passing one could say she thereby helped the revolution of 1989 to be understood as an authentic form of the political.

However, she paid too little attention to the interplay of power and violence. And this is the case even though her point of departure fully offered her this possibility, even required it. The theorist of political power remains at a distance from the state because of its potential for violence, and thus the institution of the state really only comes into view as a presupposition and threat to the political. However, this only takes into account half the phenomenon. Hannah Arendt ignores that the state, as the external, institutional reality of the political, can be imbued with the political, and only then, when it is, does it correspond to its definition. Certainly the precariousness of the institution lies in the danger that it will become soulless, but it also belongs to the possibility character of the political to allow the institution to be seen to be the outward form of the play-space of political freedom. Seen in this way, the perversion of the political does not lie solely in the hindrance or destruction of power by violence. It also belongs to the perversion of the political that the violence which hinders and destroys power should also serve to protect and preserve it. National Socialist Germany and Bolshevik Russia are perversions of the state and not its logical expression.

In her lengthy investigation of *The Origins of Totalitarianism*,[13] Arendt comes close to this assessment again and again. She emphatically indicates here that totalitarian tyrants are not tyrants in the traditional sense and, correspondingly, that totalitarian systems are not a possible form of tyranny. Rather, the totalitarian system is characterized by a destruction of positive law radically distinct from the lawlessness of the tyrant, which is motivated by self-interest and the desire to preserve sovereign authority. In the totalitarian system, laws and the institutions which are connected with them do not constitute the external reality of the political, nor do they any longer constitute its autonomous form. Rather the fact that they have in a sense become dynamic is what destroys the essence of law itself. Instead of stabilizing a political space or merely constituting its more or less autonomous external form, laws in the totalitarian system are "laws of movement." Now the injury to positive law takes place by means of the fact that it is "forced to become continually fluid: what was regarded as law yesterday is today surpassed and considered wrong" (707). As Arendt adds, in this way every law becomes a decree.

The totalitarian system—to summarize these and the other observations and analyses made by Arendt—no longer merely represents the hindrance or destruction of political power through violence, but rather the destruction of the entire framework of power and violence which, in the interplay of historical freedom and institutional reality, constitutes politics. For this reason, Arendt rightly can say that the gas chambers of the Third Reich and the concentration camps of the Soviet Union have "disrupted the continuity of Western history" (704). In view of this, it is certainly not logical, with respect to totalitarianism, to speak of the establishment of a new type of state and thereby to articulate, in rudimentary form, the reservations against institutions and violence which are so characteristic of *The Human Condition*. On the contrary, after the experience of totalitarianism and its continuing possibility there remains the task, which can be solved only with great difficulty, of understanding oneself within the horizon of the Western history and its political traditions without denying the break in history and tradition.

That is the task that Arendt set for her conception of the political, and if that is the task, then the orientation to the model of the *polis* cannot be transcended. Arendt emphasized the historical character of her orientation so decisively and recounted the history of the political with such a lack of compromise as a history of decline, that one ought not to attribute to her a more or less endearing anachronism or an ahistorical Grecophilia. But history is not merely just the past; it is also that which is comprehensible today. Historical is what has occurred previously, but which, at the same time, is not understood as something that is merely decrepit. In this sense, the "bare existence of the Periclean age" (199)[14] cannot be normative, but the understanding of this existence can be. Where the *polis* is understood as a historical free-space, a type of freedom is implied which is not exhausted by being a quality of isolated subjects. A community is brought into play in which individuals cohere, because the freedom which becomes manifest though their actions is common to them. A type of communitarianism is here sketched which retains the best of the liberal tradition, the great respect for individuals, and for this reason is superior to liberalism. And where the free-space of the political is, at the same time, thought as the space within which history comes to presence, we see how a community owes its particularity to its ability to maintain the past in the present. The particularity of a political community is always historical, and correspondingly, a relationship to the community cannot merely be a relationship to the outward form of its constitution. Patriotism, in its essence, is never merely a constitutional patriotism. Where the constitution alone is to constitute the particularity of a community, this only reveals a lack of historical freedom. Nevertheless, the outward form of the community, which is an expression of constitutional patriotism, can be a challenge to imbue this form, once again and more explicitly, with political life. In this way the strife between power and violence emerges once again; it reveals how the unstable relationship of historical freedom and institutions is not only the danger, but also the opportunity of the political.

5

The Intermediate Time of Modernity
History and Nihilism, Europe and Fatherlands, in Nietzsche's Perspective

In aphorism 245 of *Beyond Good and Evil* Nietzsche sketches a short but pregnant picture of the physiognomy of Europe, which also serves as a vivid reminder of a past age. This is the picture:

> The "good old time" is gone, in Mozart we hear its swan song:—How fortunate we are that his rococo still speaks to us, that his "good company," his tender enthusiasms, his childlike delight in Chinese touches and curlicues, his courtesy of the heart, his longing for the graceful, those in love, those dancing, those easily moved to tears, his faith in the south, may still appeal to some *residue* in us. Alas, some day all this will be gone!—but who may doubt that the understanding and taste for Beethoven will go long before that! Beethoven was, after all, merely the final chord of a transition and break in style and *not*, like Mozart, the last chord of a centuries-old great European taste. Beethoven is the interlude of a mellow old soul that continually breaks and an over-young future soul that continually *comes*; on his music lies that intermediate time of eternal losing and eternal extravagant hoping—the same light in which Europe was bathed when it dreamed with

Rousseau, danced around the freedom tree of the revolution, and finally almost worshiped before Napoleon. But how quickly *this* feeling pales now; how difficult is mere *knowledge* of this feeling even today—how strange to our ears the language of Rousseau, Schiller, Shelly, Byron sounds, in whom, taken *together*, the same fate of Europe found its way into words that in Beethoven knew how to sing!—Whatever German music came after that belongs to romanticism, a movement that was, viewed historically, still briefer, still more fleeting, still more superficial than that great entr'acte, that transition of Europe from Rousseau to Napoleon and to the rise of democracy.[1]

The period of which Nietzsche here writes, with ironically playful wistfulness, has subsequently been frequently investigated; it is the transitional period of the historians of modernity. Above all, however, it is the age of European self-understanding, and to this extent it cannot merely be "viewed historically." This age may be gone, a short "interlude," a "great entr'acte" which followed the "the last chord of a centuries-old great European taste," and came before the "still briefer, still more fleeting, still more superficial movement" of romanticism filled the stage with life. It may be a time whose language sounded foreign to Nietzsche the diagnostician. Likewise, it is a time to which we find ourselves suddenly transported when we inquire into something like Europe's physiognomy from a historical perspective. The aftereffects of this mode of self-understanding shaped by the transitional period have been felt for quite some time.

This is evident, so it appears, not least of all in the gesture of the diagnostician himself: he listens to the final chord, which he hears in Mozart's music, and thereby reveals himself to be a "mellow old soul that continually breaks," because what touches him is perceived to be merely an epilogue.[2] And when we read a little later in the same chapter, "Peoples and Fatherlands," that the genuine "European problem [is] the cultivation of a new caste that will rule Europe" (*BGE*, 251)—a theme that is sounded frequently in this text—it appears that Nietzsche transforms himself into a somewhat dubious, but rather "over-young future soul that continually comes" by inadvertently expressing his hopes. In the obituary penned by Nietzsche, all appearances also point to "that intermediate time of eternal losing and eternal extravagant hoping." The intermediate time of European history as played out in that great entr'acte.

What distinguishes the diagnostician of this history from those whose self-understanding it has shaped—those who dreamed with Rousseau, danced around the freedom tree of the French revolution, and almost worshipped before Napoleon—is the certainty that all this is nothing more than a masquerade, a masquerade which one has drawn from "history . . . the storehouse of costumes" (*BGE*, 224). A costume from this storehouse also represents an admiration for that "great taste" and the hope of a new European perspicacity. The diagnostician of European history therefore knows that the epilogue is just as much a costume as the prologue; above all he knows that history is the pattern for all costumes of this kind.

Masks and costumes create confusion, at least at first, so long as we do not yet recognize the costumed person, and perhaps thereafter as well, namely, when we ask ourselves why the person presents himself to us wearing a particular costume. With regard to the diagnostician of history, this question is not difficult to answer, for the text cited above immediately provides us with a clear answer: the historical masquerade gives him the opportunity to cast a glance at the other costumes. The glance back to the past allows him to recognize what is not proper or suitable to him, because in this retrospective glance the historical masquerade reveals itself. The peculiar character of historical thought is that it is able to enter into a relationship with itself. The historical age can also be considered historically. The peculiar character of historical thought reveals itself in historical meditation.

The peculiar character of the historical consists in its neglect of the present. We hold onto what has been just as much as onto what lies in the future and disregard what is. This holds true for some more than for others, but it is evidently and fundamentally true for each and every German: "They belong to the day before yesterday and the day after tomorrow—*as yet they have no today*" (*BGE*, 240). To the extent that Nietzsche's epilogue makes this quite clear, his historical perspective on history is homeopathic. In *Beyond Good and Evil* as in the second of the *Untimely Meditations*, Nietzsche opposes the "historical sickness," above all that of the Germans.[3]

The historical costume and masquerade as such can clearly only become explicit and consciously displayed to the extent that—to pump Nietzsche's metaphor yet again—it is not one's everyday dress. In other words, the schema of historical thought itself is only explicit and can be explicitly employed only to the extent that one is not caught within it. Nietzsche's epilogue to the historical age and his prologue to a new act of history presuppose—if they are masquerades—a position outside of history. For it is only from such a vantage point that the basis for the interest in history can be revealed.

I would like now to assert the following: the basis for the interest in history is modernity, and *Europe* for Nietzsche is merely another word for culture under the banner of modernity. However, modernity is a characteristic form of being present. It is the way of being present which is essentially not an intermediate time between the past and the future, but, at the same time, contains the tendency toward such an intermediate interpretation within it. Modernity is the essentially, historically interpretable way of being present of understanding, which does not actually subsist in time, but is rather the play-space for the presence of what has been and the future, the presence of remembrance and desire. For this reason, it belongs to modernity—in a characteristic reversal of the way of being present and the making present—to be able to take up remembrance and desire and thereby to appear to be a way of being present. To put it yet another way: modernity is the present of historical consciousness, which, in so being, is constantly in danger of historically relativizing itself. Nietzsche, I want to assert, is the philosopher of modernity in this sense. His epilogue to the intermediate time of eternal losing and eternal extravagant hoping is spoken in the play-space of a perspicuous modernity, and it is as a result of this play-space that it is able to assume an external position with respect to the schema of history. For this reason, this play-space is also the place of the play of masks with the schema of history.

In order to clarify the concept of modernity as the play-space of historical meditation sketched above, I want, once again, to make reference to the particular character of the intermediate time described by Nietzsche. What is at issue here is a permanent intermediate time. The "interlude" named "Beethoven," as Nietzsche describes it, is the interlude of a "mellow old soul that *continually* breaks and an over-young future soul that *continually* comes; on his music lies that intermediate time of *eternal* losing and *eternal* extravagant hoping" (my italics). When one's self-understanding is framed by this intermediate time, the loss remains unconquerable and the hope unfulfilled, because one has laid everything on loss and hope rather than lamenting a particular loss or nursing a particular hope. However, it is precisely for this reason that the feelings of loss and hope can abate; the understanding framed by this intermediate time and with it, the intermediate time itself, can fade with time and then become subordinate to historical meditation. Historical meditation then appears in contrast to that which it has supplanted; this is, as can be inferred from *Beyond Good and Evil*, the age of the "European hybrid," who gets his costumes from the storehouse of history only to find that none of them fits him properly.

Whoever does this for some time undergoes a particular experience. He comes to know an array of costumes, that is to say, an array of "moralities, articles of faith, artistic tastes and religions," for "again and again a new piece of prehistory or a foreign country is tried on, put on, taken off, packed away, and above all *studied*" (*BGE*, 223). Everything is elevated into the present of representation with no particular order; it "flows into us 'modern souls,' our instincts now retreat in every direction, we ourselves are a kind of chaos" (*BGE*, 224). However, this chaos has the character of a way of being present. Whoever seeks to understand each and every thing that is past in the end understands nothing any more because he no longer understands himself. Moreover, he no longer understands himself on the basis of the past in relation to the future. He has entered the way of being present, namely, the way of being present of "nihilism."

In the game of hide and seek which constitutes *Beyond Good and Evil*, this diagnosis of the "historical sense" is not made explicit. However, an entry from Nietzsche's unpublished notebooks, which probably was written a good year later, makes explicit what is implicitly said in the account from *Beyond Good and Evil* and hence provides grounds for thinking that it was consciously excluded from that text. The modern human being, writes Nietzsche, "experimentally believes now in this value, now in that value, and then drops it; the circle of values that have been outgrown and discarded becomes ever larger, and the *emptiness* and *poverty of values* is felt more and more."[4] Where what has been becomes part of the circle of "discarded values" together with all that is useless for self-understanding, it nevertheless remains present; the present poverty of self-understanding becomes visible in the present abundance of what is left over: "One of the symbols of places without a history is refuse. Space is menaced by garbage. Waste is no longer coped with as in refined cultures; it outgrows the structures. When a ship founders, the wreckage drifts ashore. The mast and the planks are used for building shacks or as fuel. People live on and from the refuse—among garbage heaps that they exploit."[5]

The nihilistic poverty of self-understanding is not the antithesis of the "historical sense," but merely its consequence. If one allows oneself to be led by the historical sense long enough, then one unavoidably falls into nihilism, because that which is considered historically is already made distant and, for the most part, loses its hold on us much too quickly. Thus the self-understanding framed by the intermediate time of eternal losing and eternal extravagant hoping also leads to nihilism, and for this reason it can, "considered historically," only be an entr'acte. The experience of nihilism is already contained within the self-understanding framed by the intermediate time, because here one is focused already upon that which is lost. This orientation follows the more or less determinate expectation of future possible orientations. Where the past no longer speaks to us because it already has been pushed to the side, one falls victim to the principle of hope, which, for its part, can only draw upon that which is known to us historically. When this reversal occurs a number of times and thereby becomes explicit, the youthfully hopeful escape route into the future is also displaced. Nothing which the historical sense hopefully inspires can be adequate to it, and as the number of costumes that do not fit increases, the probability grows ever greater that none will ever do so. At some point this probability becomes a certainty; everything that has been handed down remains there, but loss and hope are powerless. At the same time, a way of being present emerges in which the historical sense had also kept itself ready, as it understood itself within the frame of the intermediate time. The nihilistic poverty of self-understanding is, on the one hand, the consequence of the historical sense. On the other hand, however, it is the experience of the play-space in which the historical sense continually maintains itself.

The nihilistic way of being present, "a type of chaos" Nietzsche calls it, succeeds the intermediate time of historical understanding and can, in this manner, open up a space for a retrospective look at this intermediate time. At the same time, the intermediate time itself becomes something foreign, which no longer corresponds to, or is adequate to, itself. The schema of historical mediation itself belongs to the values that have fallen by the wayside, and for this reason it is no longer possible for one to understand oneself from within it. One should not let oneself be deceived about this by Nietzsche's diagnostic and prefatory masquerade.

However, as we observed above, the nihilistic way of being present does not merely succeed the intermediate time of historical understanding. With it a way of being present emerges which opens up the space for an interest in history. Every history is an interpretation of the present, and the present becomes the present of modernity when it has within itself a tendency for historical interpretation. However, when what is recalled and wished for emerge as things of no use, their way of being present makes clear at the same time that one can only have believed to be able to understand oneself *historically* on this basis; in a period of historical change, one can only have *understood* oneself on this basis because it was present. The gesture of eternal loss was therefore just as inadequate to the present within memory, as the gesture of dissolute hope was to that which had its present in this wishful conception. The recalled belongs in the play-space of a way of being present; the hoped for and the wished for can only actually be what they are. Within the intermediate time one actually devalues the present.

Nietzsche also considered this self-misunderstanding in a posthumous note, which, not without good reason, is furnished with the title "Overall Insight." It runs as follows:

> the *ambiguous* character of our *modern world*—the very same symptoms could point to *decline* and to *strength*. And the signs of strength, of an attained maturity, could be **misconstrued** as *weakness* on the basis of traditional (*residual*) emotional devaluations. In short, our *feelings, as value feelings, are not up to date.*

> *To generalize: value feelings are always* **behind the times**;
> they express conditions of preservation and growth that be-
> long to times long gone by; they resist new conditions of exis-
> tence from which they have not emerged and which they
> necessarily misunderstand and instruct others to view mis-
> trustfully, and so on: they arouse suspicion against what is
> new. (*KSA* 12:10 [23])

If we follow this note, the "modern world" is ambiguous only insofar as the "signs of strength" could be *misconstrued* as weakness.
This expresses nothing less than the conviction that a critical, or
better, a deprecating view of the modern world in all cases is inadequate. We always can devalue our own present for the sake of
the day before yesterday or the day after tomorrow and thus turn
against ourselves. Hope and loss project a standard based on the
present upon which the present is then wrecked.

Regardless of whether it orientates itself principally to the past
or to the present, the devaluation of the modern world always
arises out of an accustomed orientation to a "much earlier time."
This devaluation arises out of the habit of historical thought
which can only offer what has been or familiar representations as
frames of orientation, and if the present fails to be understood
within this framework, it struggles "against new conditions of existence." To be sure, if our "value feelings" are, as Nietzsche says,
always behind the times, always trapped within the schema of
history, then the modern world cannot evaluate itself. One can already sense this in the chaos of nihilistic arbitrariness. However,
nihilism is still historical in that it is permeated by the actual impossibility of evaluation. It therefore remains fixated on the past
possibility of evaluation and is for this reason always in danger of
being transformed into an interpretation of the present framed by
the intermediate time. When the familiar values cease to be credible, we become resigned and become susceptible to values which
appear to be new. Perhaps we become susceptible to them merely
because it is not so easy to remain openly nihilistic. We become
enthusiastic for goals and values which we know that we do not
actually believe in. When what is fashionable becomes universal,
that is a sure sign of nihilism.

Nevertheless, nihilism and the historical consciousness which
belongs with it are not the only experiential possibilities of the

"modern world." The way of being present which had constituted the play-space of memory and desire can also emerge as "the authentic modernity." In a posthumous fragment from 1887, Nietzsche explains how this idea can be more precisely understood: "authentic modernity" is "the sense for and delight in nuances" (*KSA* 12:7 [7]). It is, therefore, first and foremost a sense for details and degrees of difference in the "storehouse of costumes," which is to say, a sense for the chaos which the historical sense leaves behind and within which it finds itself. At the same time, however, it is also the *delight* in this chaos, and it is this that first allows Nietzsche, in the note cited above, to speak of "authentic" modernity: the intermediate temporality of the historical sense, of nihilism, understood as the agony of the historical sense—that is also modernity, but not "authentic" modernity. The present of understanding is displaced by the intermediate time and the disgust with the values that have fallen by the wayside remains bound up with it. Nihilism is the historical sense which cannot articulate itself from within the intermediate time and knows no other articulations of self-understanding. Freedom from the schema of history is only won by means of the historical storeroom's delight in chaos. Only by means of this delight have we left the intermediate time for good.

However, it is initially unclear what has thereby been achieved. The historical storehouse's delight in chaos is not, by itself, able to guarantee what the historical sense at least brought with it as a promise and maintained, however problematically, in the schema of intermediate time. The delight in chaos is not able to guarantee that we understand ourselves now in its way of being present. But according to Nietzsche, the delight in nuances should not be considered alone. It coheres in an agonistic relation with another drive, "which delights and excels in grasping the typical" (*KSA* 12:7 [7]).

The agonistic coherence of both forms of delight can be understood in the following way: the one is made possible only when actively opposed to the other, when it conflicts with it. Delight produces the chaos of details and degrees of difference only to the extent that it appears as something that can be overcome and subjugated; on the other hand, this process of subjugation only produces delight where it can prove itself against the details and degrees of difference. The more developed the delight in nuances, the more it provokes the drive to grasp the typical, and the stronger the drive to grasp the typical, the more it needs the delight in nuances in order to develop itself further. However, if the delight in nuances is made possible only by means of the drive to grasp the typical, then it must also belong to "authentic modernity." It, too, must have emerged from a way of being present that is not part of the intermediate time.

With regard to this it is surprising that Nietzsche compares the drive to grasp the typical with "the Greek taste of the best period." For it does not belong to the present but to the past, which we can only relate to as the "day before yesterday." Even the idea of giving form to one's own present evidently cannot dispense with the schema of historical thought.

That is undeniable, just as it was undeniable that the glance at the intermediate time of historical self-understanding can be made only by means of historical spectacles. However, the reference to the Greek taste of the best time does not stand under the sign of eternal loss. Rather, it can even intensify the delight and talent for grasping the typical by showing how this once was possible. When a fundamental characteristic of "authentic modernity" is elucidated by a reference to classical culture, Nietzsche's earlier conception of a type of history in the service of life reveals itself. "Monumental" history is grounded in the conviction "that the greatness which existed at one time was, in any case, *possible* once and may thus be possible yet again" (HL, 2). Its maxim is "That which once was able to expand the concept 'human being' and make it more beautiful, must exist eternally, so as to be eternally capable of doing this again" (HL, 2).

But what "exists eternally" cannot easily be understood as something historical. We can only do justice to this conception from within our own way of being present, and in this respect the reference to classical culture serves only to allow this way of being present to be understood within a historical schema. Classical culture is the historical conception of what is timeless. The present is recognized in what has been; the way of being present articulates itself historically, rather than allowing itself to be determined by the schema of history. The reference to classical culture indicates that the attempt to understand ourselves *in* history, that is to say, within the framework of intermediate time, does not necessarily lead us to misunderstand ourselves. We can also understand history, and through it, understand ourselves. Our own present is formed in the process of understanding. Where the understanding of history is an instance of self-understanding which conforms to our way of being present, it is a successful typification.

For a life in the sense of "authentic modernity," successful typifications alone are certainly not sufficient. It is not enough to retrieve what has been and what is still present into the way of being present, for then the interpretation of the present will not be clear as an interpretation. Rather, for this to be possible the two agonistic elements of "authentic modernity" must both come into play unencumbered. The failure of their conflict to reach a resolution can obscure the fact that the understanding of what has been actually belongs to the present, in that what is understood becomes independent and conceals the articulation of understanding. In addition, other problematic asymmetries appear just as quickly.

Nietzsche again expresses his reservations about such asymmetrical formations by voicing doubt about the observed typifications and, in so doing, focuses attention upon the delight in nuances. He expresses the same reservations with a different emphasis with respect to chaos by indicting the successful typification and concurrently making typifications of his own. Nietzsche's diagnosis of his own present constantly uncovers the two sides of the present by revealing the agonistic "attunement"[6] of modernity, its "authentic modernity."

What is revealed in this way is the physiognomy of Europe. However, if Nietzsche refers to the chaos in which the historical sense finds itself, this must be understood together with the claim that with the chaotic historical sense a new type of human being is being developed at the same time, the type of the "European hybrid." His development is the "slow emergence of an essentially supranational and nomadic type of human being, which, physiologically speaking, possesses a maximum of the art and power of adaptation as its typical distinction" (*BGE*, 242). Even when one attends to every nuance, there, too, a power is at work, the power not to let oneself be deceived. But it is a power which "does not make possible the *powerfulness* of the type" (*BGE*, 242), if it remains caught within the manifold and merely seeks an equilibrium which it considers desirable within the framework of "modern ideas" (*BGE*, 222). In an "age of disintegration" the "most profound desire of a human being" is

> that the war he *is* should come to an end. Happiness appears to them, in agreement with a tranquilizing (for example, Epicurean or Christian) medicine and way of thought, pre-eminently as the happiness of resting, of not being disturbed, of satiety, of finally attained unity, as the "sabbath of sabbaths," to speak with the holy rhetorician Augustine who was himself such a human being. (*BGE*, 200)

In this passage we can recognize a description of the contemporary, hedonistic cultural tourism, which dreams of a great cultural universality to which people everywhere immediately and directly belong. The mistake of this way of thinking is clear: we dream up a state in which everyone can be together because we do not want to go to the trouble of coming to a more limited understanding. We imagine a world without difficulties and transform the entire dump into an amusement park.

The weakness of the "European hybrid" which Nietzsche speaks of here consists in the fact that he thinks unhistorically and historically at the same time. The eternal losing and eternal hoping, as it is expressed in Beethoven's music, has been left behind like an ill-fitting costume. Nevertheless, the "European hybrid" steels himself with his dreams in the shadows of the intermediate time. The past knew the values which separated people and the obligatory, limited forms of life; that is the way it was, but it now belongs to the past. The present is the transitional period to a situation in which everything belongs together with everything else. When one reacts to this fanatically, drawing arbitrary and brutal divisions among people, once again igniting tribal thinking, the situation becomes worse still and often ends up being fatal. One way or another the "European hybrid" does an injustice to his own present; he is not in a position to experience his modernity as "authentic." He does not want to prosecute the war that he is or endure the strife of authentic modernity. That appears to be reserved for the strong, the "higher human beings."

However much Nietzsche praises and admires the powerful, in the end he knows better. "Human beings such as Napoleon,

Goethe, Beethoven, Stendhal, Heinrich Heine, Schopenhauer," and Richard Wagner "experimentally [anticipate] the European of the future" (*BGE*, 256). They are "tyrants" in the "spiritual" sense, strong human beings who need slaves "in the subtlest sense," the European hybrids (*BGE*, 242). They belong to that "type of higher human beings who had to teach their century—and it is the century of the *crowd!*—the concept of 'higher human being' (*BGE*, 256). However, we have heard as much about the problematic nature of the adoration of Napoleon as about the temporally intermediate nature of Beethoven's music. And when we read of Wagner that "his entire manner, his self-apostolate could perfect itself only when he saw the model of the French socialists" (*BGE*, 256), it is clear that he, too, lived according to those "modern ideas" which promoted the amusement park on the great dump and led to solutions which were in no way consistent with it. The modernity of the higher human beings is, therefore, also not to be trusted; the weakness shines through their strength. Their attempts at integration cannot accomplish what they promised. They could never accomplish it.

The strength to be found in the modern world is of a different order as that displayed in the examples of the "higher human beings." It is the strength of the seeker of knowledge, who "forces his spirit to recognize things *against* the inclination of the spirit, and often enough also against the wishes of his heart, namely, by saying no where he would like to say yes, love and adore, and thus acts as an artist and transfigurer of cruelty" (*BGE*, 229).

The "inclination of the spirit" which Nietzsche speaks of here is the "will to mere appearance, to simplification, to masks, to cloaks, in short, to the surface." This will, the text continues, acts *"against* that sublime inclination of the seeker of knowledge, who sees things profoundly, complexly and thoroughly, and *wants* to see them in this way" (*BGE*, 230). It is not difficult to recognize the opposed "attunement" of modernity once more; at the same time, "grasping the typical" is defined more precisely as the "will to simplification." This will is opposed by the "sublime inclination" to multiplicity, the delight in nuances, and the context makes it clear how little what is at issue here are two simply disparate forces opposed to one another. The inclination of the seeker of knowledge is clearly an articulation of the same spirit, which is also determined through the will to simplification. And further still: the inclination of the seeker of knowledge to multiplicity can only express itself through the will to simplification: "Everything that is profound loves masks" (*BGE*, 40). It needs simplification, a limited horizon (*BGE*, 230), in order to be able to make room for the delight in nuances within its borders; at the same time, however, the delight in nuances is boundless and puts every limited horizon into question.

The self-understanding of authentic modernity is therefore neither a resigned nor a joyful pluralism; it is also not a search for the triumphal unity of ultimate answers. It is only possible where "opposition and war . . . [act] like one *more* charm and incentive of life" and in addition to "the powerful and irreconcilable drives, a real mastery and subtlety in waging war against oneself, in other words, self-control and self-outwitting, has been inherited and cultivated" (*BGE*, 200). It is only possible when one who has mastered himself does not succumb to the seduction of self-understanding framed by intermediate time and instead experiences the multiplicity of the present as a stimulus. However, because the multiplicity of the present leads us to grasp the typical, we clearly must outwit ourselves and follow the "will to mere appearance" if we are to do justice to it; limited horizons are unavoidable.

On the basis of this diagnosis, we can only conclude that for Nietzsche the self-understanding of the moderns also has the character of that unremitting experimentalism which is often attributed to him. This is only correct to the extent that no horizon can ever be closed definitively. We can only secure the completeness of our own horizon by experiencing it within the context of change; the simplification which this horizon represents cannot simply exist, but rather must be constructed ever anew.

But in this sense the horizon has always already been formed. It is only possible for the horizon to correspond to the provocative multiplicity if the horizon has always already been drawn and the determinate generated by means of simplification. However, even if the simplification may change in virtue of the fact that it can be constructed anew, it must already exist so that it can be constructed. Correspondingly, it cannot be so altered that it becomes something utterly different, because it would then cease to be a type.

In addition, every type remains a simplification, and for this reason the provocative multiplicity never allows itself to be completely integrated within a horizon. By remaining in existence, it releases the dynamic of synthetic understanding ever anew. In conflict both elements remain perspicuous to one another: typological simplifications should correspond to the multiplicity, and for this reason they must be understood as forms of appearance. However, the multiplicity can be corresponded to only by being simplified and, in spite of this, appearing as a multiplicity.

The agonistic "attunement" of simplification and refinement also forms the presupposition for Nietzsche's diagnosis of Europe's political character. At first glance this is not immediately clear. For in *Beyond Good and Evil* "fatherlandishness" is criticized with all the clarity that one could wish for, and the last aphorism of the chapter on "Peoples and Fatherlands" proclaims with equal clarity "that *Europe wants to become one*" (*BGE*, 256). One of the most "unequivocal portents" of this is the European character of the "more profound and comprehensive men of this century," whose goal is "to prepare the way for this new *synthesis* and to anticipate experimentally the Europeans of the future" (*BGE*, 256)—naturally not the "European hybrids," but rather those tyrants of the spiritual sort we considered above. We also noted the reservations Nietzsche has with respect to the "profound and comprehensive men." Although one could explain Nietzsche's reservations in the present context by recognizing that here the Europeans of the future are only anticipated in an experimental manner, his perspective with regard to the future remains fundamentally questionable. As Nietzsche makes clear at the end of the aphorism, the European tendency toward unity has hardly any prospects of succeeding, for "the strangest" creation of that anticipatory man of the future named Richard Wagner, the figure of Siegfried, is "perhaps inaccessible, inimitable, and beyond the feeling of the whole, so mature, Latin race, not only for today, but forever" (*BGE*, 256). Whoever wants to deflect the suspicion of national chauvinism in this statement must allow himself to have the nasty, sarcastic comments on the Germans and the exuberant praise of the "Latin races" in the chapter on "Peoples and Fatherlands" pointed out to him. There is but one unspoken consequence of this diagnosis: should the unification of Europe not exhaust itself in a nihilistic leveling of differences as it escapes from the historical sense, it cannot be thought otherwise than in the opposed "attunement" of modernity. We must not then understand ourselves from within history, but rather must attempt to understand history. That, in turn, is not possible in the absence of the particularity of perspectives, with the result that the proper remains separated from the foreign. However, the proper needs the foreign so as not to become ossified. And the foreign requires the proper, because it needs to be translated into the proper, so that it does not become merely the arena of a nihilistic cultural tourism. However, one should just as little forget that "the proper" is a simplification. Perhaps we are closest to the unification of Europe when we see through modernity's precarious modes of representation and translation.

6

Type and Nuance
Unlimited and Limited Aesthetics with Nietzsche

Aesthetic experience is known to be a complex phenomenon. Whoever attempts to understand it conceptually must ask himself how the relaxed feelings and thoughts experienced while walking through a park are comparable with the concentrated playing of a piano or the interpretation of a "dark" poem. In addition, there appear to be few, if any, commonalities between the experiences involved in producing a work of art and those relating to its reception. Philosophical attempts to determine aesthetic experience often enough end up being equally vapid. The definitions essayed by philosophers are perhaps no worse than any other, but in their formal poverty they more obviously remain far behind the richness of what is experienced.

This situation appears more awkward when we consider that in most cases aesthetic theories are bound not only to the nature of their subject, but also to the philosophical interests of their authors. For this reason we should not, at the outset, trust any of the theories that have been worked out, but rather attempt to identify something that is common to all aesthetic theories. What comes to light by means of such a process might, by all appearances, merely be a determination completely devoid of all content. But in spite of the differences, even disparity, between aesthetic theories, we nevertheless have a good chance of hitting upon the essence of the phenomenon: it is less likely that all theories of aesthetic experience misconstrue their subject. If we encounter the most general determination of a thing by confronting each of its forms, and if the most general determinations run through the entire range of phenomena, then yet another series of determinations will result which can be read and understood in relation to them. Less general determinations of a thing are interpretations, commentaries, and specifications of the more general.

With regard to a general determination of aesthetic experience, we can say that it is a matter of an interplay [*Zusammenspiel*] of sense and contingency, unity and multiplicity. In fact, one could hardly put things any more generally and, so it appears, with any less content. For what experience, even if we do not call it aesthetic, is not an interplay of unity and multiplicity? In spite of this, the determination is not trivial, for it is unclear. Above all, it is a matter of saying more precisely what we here understand by 'interplay'. And if it is genuinely a question of a single determination which captures what is common to all philosophical theories of aesthetic experience, then we can presume that the theories themselves cannot finally, perhaps even not essentially, be distinguished by the fact that they develop distinct interpretations of what is here designated as "interplay."

If one pursues different interpretations or merely types of interpretation of the interplay between unity and multiplicity, it will quickly become clear that they are neither on equal footing, nor do they simply have a neutral relationship to one another. Rather one could say, once again in a quite general way, that an interpretation which aims at a *reconciliation* of unity and multiplicity ultimately misconstrues the phenomenon of aesthetic experience in precisely the same way as does an interpretation which emphasizes the *disjunction* between them, assuming, naturally, that the talk of their interplay is adequate to the subject at hand.[1] But that it is in fact adequate is inadvertently confirmed by the varieties of reconciliation aesthetics as by the varieties of disjunctive aesthetics: just as harmony cannot be described without recourse to the difference of the harmonic elements, so dissociation cannot be expressed without the idea that the distinct elements belong together. Thus in each case it is necessary to consider the coherence of both elements as well as their difference, and aesthetic experience as a whole cannot be understood as either a process of unification or dissociation. The harmony of the various elements in a unified whole does not then constitute the kernel of aesthetic experience, nor are the impressions of unity found within it put into question by the fact that the elements of multiplicity and contingency assert their rights in opposition to them. The essence of the aesthetic consists neither in the fact that multiplicity and contingency are bound together within a meaningful whole, nor does it lie in a distance from meaningful experiential contexts, and is, accordingly, to be understood as a form of sovereignty or independence. In its essence aesthetic experience is neither the enactment of human existence in the unified abundance of its disparate aspects, nor the enactment of reflective freedom—neither the experience of the "total human being" in the sense of Schiller's letters on aesthetic education, nor the stamp of romantic irony.

What then is aesthetic experience? If we take the unity of its two elements just as seriously as the impossibility of their reconciliation, then we can at least say that it is the productive or receptive experience of meaning under the explicit condition of contingency, the productive or receptive experience of unity with respect to the irreducibility of the manifold. The more decisively contingency appears as a condition of aesthetic experience, and the more clearly the irreducibility of the manifold determines the experience, the more the experience becomes aesthetic. For then the coherence of the meaningful element, the unity of a context or affairs without which there is no experience, can be experienced and thought only in the interplay between contingency and the manifold. Every positive revaluation of aesthetic experience also positively revaluates contingency and the manifold, but certainly without affirming its dominance. And this positive revaluation can occur only if we have not assumed from the outset that these two elements will become subordinate to coherence and unity. Aesthetic experience is a phenomenon exceedingly filled with tension.

Aesthetic experience in this sense was a central theme of Nietzsche. Like no other, Nietzsche had stressed that aesthetic experience itself was a type of strife. The element of reconciliation, of unity, which belongs to aesthetic experience is itself merely an element of the strife which characterizes experience as a whole. Taken by itself, this assertion is already worthy of serious consideration, but it is not Nietzsche's only point. Rather, the agonistic nature of aesthetic experience is, for Nietzsche, the nature of life itself. No one before Nietzsche had so radically wanted to understand the experience of life as aesthetic experience and aesthetic experience, in turn, as the experience of life. Not least of all, this thought has made Nietzsche a central figure of contemporary philosophical debates. Whoever wants to make aesthetics the fundamental discipline of philosophy has in Nietzsche, so it appears, a suitable ally and appropriate authority.

Now the program of an "unlimited aesthetics"[2] is certainly not unproblematic. It is problematic from both of the perspectives which are dominant in contemporary aesthetics. If one remains within the tradition of Kant's *Critique of Judgment* and does not essentially tie aesthetic experience to art, then one must object against the program that aesthetic experience merely "emerges from the background of cognitive experience, though without any knowledge to deliver."[3] Then, however, freeing aesthetics from its limits could only appear as an affirmation in that condition of joyful or enforced joyful delusion indicated by the formula "aesthestization of the life world." Unlimited aesthetic experience would then be tantamount to the loss of practical and theoretical knowledge under the spell of a long-running carnival. However, if one remains in the Hegelian tradition—which is not particularly prominent today—and understands philosophical aesthetics essentially as the philosophy of art, then the program appears no less problematic. That all experience of life is artistic or is an analog of art is certainly not intelligible without further explanation. If we want to indicate Nietzsche's place in this debate, we can say that he adopts the second difficulty so as to meet the first objection mentioned above. Nietzsche would object to the distinction between aesthetic and cognitive experience and say that aesthetics actually delivers what we, with misplaced emphasis, call "knowledge," precisely when it is artistic. All experience is, more or less transparently, either dependent upon artistic forms or is itself a form of artistic experience. However, the more decisively the experience becomes artistic, then the more it will be enacted in a profitable and enlightening manner, and the more one also knows what one actually is doing, when one has experiences.

If this is Nietzsche's position, then we might ask whether the orientation to art as a model here actually accomplishes what it is supposed to accomplish: to produce the concept of an experience that is perspicuous to itself. I do not believe that this question can be answered with a simple yes or no. In what follows I would like to show that in one respect Nietzsche's position is illuminating; Nietzsche presents an impressive and largely illuminating theory of experience in view of a positive revaluation of contingency, and it is therefore understandable that for this purpose he looks to art for a model. To be sure, Nietzsche pays a considerable price for his accomplishment. Because artistic creation becomes a model for an authentic form of life, an essential aspect of art and its experience no longer allow themselves to be properly considered, namely, that art must manifest itself in works. In order for art to become a model for life, Nietzsche must understand artistic creation without granting a particularly important place to its results. That alone might be problematic; however, in addition to this, the orientation to the model of artistic production excludes the possibility of an adequate understanding of the reception of art. This weakness in Nietzsche's position is also not without diagnostic force. By repressing the need for art to express itself in works in order to emphasize the artistic character of life, he privileges an essential element of modern or, more precisely, avant-garde art, thereby allowing us to better understand the aporia characteristic of avant-garde art.

In order to develop my thesis I will focus upon an unpublished note from Nietzsche's posthumous writings. The notes bears the title "Physiology of Art" and runs as follows:

A sense for and a delight in nuances (authentic *modernity*), in that which is *not* general, runs counter to the drive that delights in, and is able to, grasp the *typical*: like the Greek taste of the best period. There is an overpowering of the fullness of life in it; measure becomes master; at bottom there is that *calm* of the strong soul that moves slowly and feels repugnance toward what is too lively. The general rule, the law, is *honored* and *emphasized*: the exception, conversely, is set aside, the nuance obliterated. The firm, powerful, solid, the life that reposes broad and majestic and conceals its strength—that is what *"pleases;"* i.e. that corresponds to what one thinks of oneself. (*KSA* 12:7 [7])

To begin with, it is not difficult to recognize that the sense for and delight in nuances and the delight and ability to grasp the typical are formulations of Nietzsche's versions of multiplicity and unity, contingency and coherence. Their interplay is here understood as agonistic, which is fully in keeping with the sense of the anticipatory remarks made above. But the agon is accentuated in such a way that the dominance of one element over the other is emphasized: measure becomes master, and the nuance is obliterated.

Taken by itself this formulation certainly suggests that something odd is afoot. In the second part of the note, Nietzsche describes a deficient form of aesthetic experience: when the law is honored and emphasized a delight in grasping the typical in the work is also likely to be found, but certainly this has nothing to do with the manifestation of an ability. The honoring of the law, measure, of what is firm, powerful and solid presupposes a successfully enacted typification; in the honoring of results and works an insignificant pleasure is at work that "corresponds" to what one thinks of oneself. The successful typification, the successful emergence of coherence and meaning, can be taken as a symbol of the successful integration and unity of life, which one happily claims for himself—all the more gladly the less it is a product of a form of life governed by self-understanding. The less it bears the integrating stamp of coherence and sense, all the more decisively must the nuances be obliterated. The orientation to the works of art is thereby decisively devalued. However, it is still early to consider that. The structure of the experience described by Nietzsche has not yet been sufficiently clarified.

If one does not do justice to the sense for nuances when one orients oneself to the aforementioned process of integration, then the sense for nuances must, conversely, be able to manifest itself when the integrating stamp of coherence and sense is actually enacted. Only when the sense for multiplicity, for what is not general, manifests itself can grasping the typical conversely express itself as a force—force cannot be experienced without opposition. The sense for nuances is therefore not merely an adversary of the ability[4] to grasp the typical, but rather is united with it as its provocation.

Conversely, it is equally the case that the delight in nuances, in multiplicity, cannot make itself manifest without the opposition of typification; what is not general does not ultimately delight because it puts those generalizations which have lost their power to compel into question. It delights because the typifications which already exist within the multiplicity prove their worth in an unforeseeable manner and so are able to appear in a new light. The delight in nuances and the delight in grasping the typical stand in an agonistic "attunement"[5] to one another; between them is conflict, the father of all things, and for this reason they are together only as opposed elements in a "confrontation."[6]

It is only in light of these considerations that a closer determination of both elements and their relationship to one another becomes possible. If the aforementioned characteristics are to constitute aesthetic experience as such, it is clear that the interpretation of their relationship is not satisfactory; what is missing is an account of what qualifies the agonistic interplay between differentiation and typification as *aesthetic* experience. To determine this we must first consider what it means for both elements themselves to be opposed to one another in this agonistic fashion.

This brings us back to the second part of Nietzsche's note. When typification, the mark of the general, remains tied to the experience of the nongeneral, there is no longer a danger it will coalesce and become independent. Every successful typification, every successful attempt to make parts or aspects of a phenomenon cohere and produce a unified entity, is put into question by the fact that new details come to our attention which require a new attempt to fashion a coherent entity from them. However, in Nietzsche's view this does not lead to an unavoidable relativizing of previously obtained meanings. According to the note cited above, what delights us and is not merely an object of sterile admiration is the *enactment* of typification, and it follows from this that it is essential for every event to be capable of being overtaken by another. The will to typify is decisively more important than each type itself.

Nietzsche formulated this thought in another posthumous note. There we read that

the satisfaction of the will is *not* the cause of pleasure: I want to fight this most superficial theory in particular. The

absurd psychological counterfeiting of the nearest things—
rather the will wants to advance and continually become
master over what stands in its way. The feeling of pleasure
lies precisely in the dissatisfaction of the will, in the fact that
the will is never satisfied unless it has limitations and resistance—. (*KSA* 13:11 [75])

This sounds perhaps like that expansionistic dynamic of domination Heidegger sees in the structure of the will to power, which
is what is at issue here. However, if we relate what Nietzsche says
here to the unity of typification and differentiation, then another
picture emerges. The point of the sentences cited above lies precisely in the fact that the will to typify is—and must be—the
conduit to its agonistic other, in order for it to be capable of manifesting itself. What can here be called "the will" only allows itself
to be understood on the basis of a totality, a "momentary coalescence of all the drives constituting us" (*KSA* 12:1 [61]), as Nietzsche says at one point. The ability to grasp the typical emerges
from a contingency, which it then reacts to and to which it remains indebted. Understood properly, the transparent will to typify must in itself be the affirmation of the totality evident in every
detail, which renders it, as the will to typify, possible and puts it
into question at the same time. But it is precisely this which
makes the actualization of typification "aesthetic" for Nietzsche.

Perhaps this can be seen best if we next attempt to clarify once
more the unreasonable expectation that is bound up with the idea
of an act aimed at grasping the typical. Here it is a question of allowing, for the sake of the act itself, the typification that has been
achieved to be put into question once more. To call this an unreasonable expectation may be blamed on the "absurd psychological
counterfeiting" of teleological conceptions of action; however, the
act of typification, even when it is said to be more important than
the realized type, cannot be thought at all without an acknowl-
edgement of teleology. If *grasping* the typical also constitutes genuine delight, the *typical* must be grasped; in the process of
grasping, the typical must be brought into prominence, if we want
to give any kind of account of what occurs here. The typical that
has been grasped must, if it is a question of the dynamic of grasping, be just as provisional as it must be binding from the perspective of its intentional definiteness. Both belong together in that

the type, the coherence of the manifold that is produced which becomes a meaningful whole, has the character of *appearance*.

What the term *appearance* means in this context was expressed by Nietzsche in a note from the spring of 1888, which was later included in *Twilight of the Idols* after some minor revisions. The note reads as follows: "The world divided into a 'true' world and an 'apparent' world is a suggestion of decadence:—to value *appearance* more than *reality*, as the artist does, is no objection against this assertion. For appearance is merely this reality once again, as a selection, an intensification, a correction" (*KSA* 13:14 [168].[7] In this passage we find two meanings of the term *appearance* subtly combined with one another and contrasted with a third meaning. Nietzsche uses the expression in relation to the artist in the sense of something showing itself; appearance is reality once again. To be sure, this formulation is not univocal, and because of this we also need to also consider the meaning from which Nietzsche wants to distance himself; "appearance," properly understood, is no mere copy of something that we have access to other than in appearance, as the distinction between a "true" and an "apparent" world suggests. This understanding of appearance is meaningless with respect to the world, because the world as a whole cannot subsist alongside putative images which have been made of it. We misunderstand the meaning of a portrait if we presume to pass judgment upon it by inquiring into its "similarity" with the person whom it represents. Every successful portrait allows us to see something that we would be unable to see without it, so that in the end the person is understood by means of the portrait rather than the reverse. Appearance, therefore, is not "reality once again" in the sense that it is reality's double. Rather, appearance is fabricated reality, reality to the extent that it is expressed as a selection, an intensification, and a correction. In one sense this definition of appearance collapses into the first definition given above. Reality can appear only in the form of a fabricated representation, for the fabricated representation constitutes the perception and knowledge of reality, the act of discovery for which and in which there is something to be discovered at all.

However, here another meaning of appearance comes into play. On the one hand, a representation only qualifies as a representation if it can be distinguished from that which is represented. On the other hand, this does not in any way lead us back to an understanding of appearance as a doubling of its subject. The represented can be distinguished from the representation solely in virtue of the fact that we assume its superior richness when compared with the representation. This assumption is confirmed by the possibility of further representations and is indicated by the representation itself in that we refer to it as a compendium of the original. In summary, therefore, we can say that appearance is the showing itself of something in a detailed representation, which is "merely" a representation due to that fact that it is a compendium and is relativized in relation to further representations. However, multiple representations, if they are sufficiently complex, acquire the character of "reality" in that they foster a new representation, which, in turn, typifies them.

The play of representation, as it has been sketched here, is familiarly the play of perspectivism, in which the world, as Nietzsche says in aphorism 374 of *The Gay Science*, has "once more become 'infinite' for us, inasmuch as we cannot reject the possibility that *it may contain infinite interpretations.*" Again and again Nietzsche goes to pains to draw attention to the richness inherent in this idea, a richness to which one could only be adequate by having a sense for nuances. And if this richness is truly what is at stake, it cannot be for the purpose of exposing as nonbinding the enacted typification or successful interpretation one holds at any given time. The binding force of each enacted interpretation cannot be rejected if only for the reason that it cannot be relativized with respect to other interpretations. To relativize an interpretation in this way would amount to a new enactment of an interpretation that is binding when it is enacted. Different interpretations can be described and understood only in an interpretation, which, when it is enacted, cannot be the object of an interpretation from the same perspective. Nevertheless, it should be regarded as an interpretation, namely, on the basis of the agonistic "attunement" of differentiation and typification from which it arises. As "mere" appearance, each context reveals in that moment the multiplicity, which, when experienced, makes possible the typifying interpretation. The multiplicity emerges in the process of interpretation. The binding force of each interpretation is due to the fact that it is an appearance which now cannot be relativized; it is mere interpretation in its contingency, in the fact that as an interpretation it is the appearance of that which is itself contingent, the appearance of what could also appear in a different form. But the binding force of the contingent can be understood as the essence of the aesthetic.

In this sense the aesthetic does not represent a release from the agonistic character of life, but is its manifestation. Life, as Nietzsche understands it, must always express itself in the "attunement" of meaning which is conditioned by contingent and transitory states of affairs. The "attunement" of meaning opens the way for the appearance of multiplicity and contingency, which, in turn, relativizes its own appearance, by only appearing in an abridged form. What appears in appearance is that which the form of its appearance holds in suspension, as it were, and in this sense every appearance opens up another form of appearance. The thought of the aesthetic character of every meaningful context makes it possible for Nietzsche to understand them as having been formed in order to subject their coalescence and dogmatic tendencies to criticism. Such contexts are artifacts, and only when that is understood can we make our way adequately in them. We recognize that they are subject to change, that they can be expanded, revised, and translated into one another, but do not view this as a reason to declare them devoid of binding force. The heart of the program of an "unlimited aesthetics" is thus the idea of a transparent and hence changeable representation, which, when enacted, nevertheless remains binding upon us. An act of discovery is authentic whenever its binding force coheres with its dynamic character. That is the authenticity of the aesthetic.

If one wanted to call representations, as Nietzsche understands them, "aesthetic" on the grounds that they are appearances, it is certainly necessary to consider that the concept of the 'aesthetic' is not being used in a manner consistent with its usual meaning. Here the concept stands neither for the coherence of contemplation and reflection, which is the basis for Kant's determination of aesthetic judgment, nor for art in a more restrictive sense. Rather one should think of the transparency of a representative context, as it is expressed quite differently, but nevertheless comparably, in the allegorical sequence from Plato's *Republic*.[8] That the enactment of a representation is expressed in works of the type that are usually identified as works of art is, for Nietzsche, peripheral to an act of representation. The will to typification does not find its fulfillment in the completion of a work, and the manifestation of the act of representation in the work even has the problematic aspect of having an unburdening effect, because one now finds a coherent context, rather than forming it oneself. However, we should not assume that for Nietzsche the experience of works of art can be thought only in the sense of this problematic unburdening. If we consider the note on the physiology of art, we might have reason to say that the experience of works of art is interpretation, grasping the typical, which has its foundation in the contingent aspect of the work. But this, too, leads us once more to a concept of 'interpretation' that ultimately does not do justice to the experience of works of art.

In order to show why this is the case, it first should be admitted openly that for an interpreter of a work of art it is in fact probably the sense for nuances that brings her to essay an interpretation. What needs to be interpreted in works of art and challenges us to interpret them is probably not in fact something general. However, one would hardly be willing to understand the interpretation of works of art in general as typification, which is equal to the context and the type of the work. This is only the case when the interpretation of a work of art is itself a work of art, for example, when a novel is interpreted in another novel, when a painting is copied, or also in the case of musical variations. Otherwise it is characteristic of interpretations of works of art that they remain within the play-space of the work and do not put it at their disposal without altering their status. Recognizing this certainly does not lead directly to the reverence of developed form, whose questionableness Nietzsche emphasizes. Between this form of interpretation and the interpretation which itself typifies, there is a third possibility, and every interpretative experience of a work of art is guided by it, namely, being addressed by the harmony of a work. Here we do not subordinate ourselves to any putatively authoritative determination of meaning, if only for the reason that the harmony of the work which addresses us is not univocal. It allows the multiplicity of the work to shine through and, in this manner, provokes us to reflect and elucidate the work for ourselves. In short, it provokes us to interpretation. However, before this occurs the harmony of the work fosters experiences, such as reading, hearing, thinking, or strolling, which measure and actualize the play-space of the work and which cannot abandon the play-space of the work without losing their foundation.

Because the manifold which provokes us to interpretation can only appear in a particular manner, the play-space of the work is binding for the interpretation of what appears in a particular manner. With the manifold and the contingent one engages in a particular unity and bindingness, which, as the play-space of experience, avoids being directly grasped, just as it wishes to be understood. The experience of works, therefore, is also in itself agonistic, strolling through a garden designed by Peter Joseph Lenné, no less than reading a poem by Paul Celan. Unity and multiplicity, harmony and contingency, equally determine the experience of works of art in that a conceptually but not ultimately determinate unity is necessary for the work of art to be interpreted in detail. Only a unity which eludes strict determination can be a play-space for interpretations—for interpretations which ultimately are not like appearances, because they cannot simply reproduce the unity within which they are enacted. Here Nietzsche's model turns upon itself: not the construction of unity but the binding force of unity is what is crucial in the experience of works of art. Not merely the manifold, but also unity needs to be represented. The work would not be mere appearance here, but rather the interpretation, which can only articulate the experienced harmony under the proviso that it is merely apparent. When one understands the work as mere appearance, as only a possible representation, it is no longer interpreted, but is rather robbed of its binding force.

To be sure, there are works in which the expectation of a harmony which addresses us is disappointed and, correspondingly, the intentions of the creator are also disappointed. While works of art in just this sense are unsuccessful from the perspective of an unlimited interpretative dynamic, they appear to lead us back to the idea of a universally established aesthetic experience. It is these works that are mostly taken to be characteristic of modern art and appear to confirm Nietzsche's emphasis upon the enactment of experience at the expense of completion. Certainly they confirm in a more or less explicit radicalness Nietzsche's idea, according to which the sense for the nongeneral is the "true modernity." True modernity can be understood as a way of being present under the dominance of the contingent, a way of being present in which we have to see ourselves challenged to assist the contingent in achieving an adequate presence and articulation.

There is at least one person who knew how to determine modernity with respect to art and who, in the process, hit upon formulations which in a remarkable manner recall Nietzsche's remarks in his note on the physiology of art. This person is Charles Baudelaire, whom Nietzsche, in *Ecce Homo*, describes as "that typical decadent in whom a whole tribe of artists recognized themselves."[9] In his essay "The Painter of Modern Life," Baudelaire says that modernity "is the transitory, the fugitive, the contingent, one half of art of which the other half is the eternal and the immutable" [*La modernité, c'est le transitoire, le fugitif, le contingent, la moitié de l'art, dont l'autre moitié est l'éternel et l'immuable*].[10] Where the eternal and the immutable, as one-half of art, can be distinguished from their modernity in this way, it is certainly nothing more than the purely formal aspect of artistic creation. And when Baudelaire says that the aim of modernity "is to extract the eternal from the transitory" [*Il s'agit . . . de tirer l'éternel du l'immutable*],[11] what he means is that the artist should help the transitory and the contingent achieve an enduring presence in the work by means of the representative possibilities at his disposal. If Baudelaire had known the later work of Monet, he would have been much better able to illustrate his thoughts than with Constantin Guys, the hero of the essay "The Painter of Modern Life." Certainly he then would have been able to uncover indications of how little self-evident his classicism is with respect to artistic form. Monet's series of cathedrals, haystacks, and poplars make clear how an art which places itself completely in the service of the transitory is forced to relativize the compositionally fully formed presence of the individual work.

As is well known, this tendency of modern art radicalized itself and became the principle of avant-gardism. An art can be called "avant-garde" which seeks to put established forms of representation artistically into question and to transcend them. As part of this process of putting into question avant-garde art values the particular and the contingent: it destroys once successful typifications by bringing together what, according to established representations, does not belong together, and by rejecting representation altogether or reducing representative forms to such a degree that new nuances come into relief.

However, avant-gardism is not something that belongs to art itself, such as the change of styles. Whether it is playful or imbued with life-reformatory or socially revolutionary seriousness, the artistic avant-garde have always argued for the transcendence of boundaries between art and life, and have thereby repeated Nietzsche's point in their own way. The goal of their efforts at transcendence was an authentic, transformed experience without art as such, participation in practices which aim to change society, or also simply the expansion of aesthetic engagement with the banal objects of everyday life. The products of artistic activity thereby are reduced to catalysts or stimulants of aesthetic experience. This holds equally true for Duchamp's bottle dryer and a didactic piece by Brecht. The "ready made" tells us to experience any old thing aesthetically, and whoever adapts one of Brecht's didactic pieces to the current conditions of political struggle is, in the opinion of the author, fully justified. The credo of Joseph Beuys is the consequence of the avant-garde: every person is an artist.

It is certainly easy to see that all this is extraneous to an art which manifests itself in completely formed works. The relics of Beuys' actions owe their place in museums solely to the fact that they are essentially treated like a sculpture by Rodin. One can pointedly say that the artistic character of avant-garde products lies in the involuntary conservatism and involuntary classicism of their recipients. Avant-gardism is a countermovement and as such is aporetic.

For aesthetic experience, as Nietzsche describes it, something quite similar holds true. The model by means of which it is developed does not allow artistic creation to be understood in light of the ability to grasp the typical operative within it without this ability manifesting itself in such a way that makes it comparable to Greek taste in its best period. The more decisively authentic modernity makes itself felt, the more urgently it must be overcome in an authentic classicism, in a process of giving form to the contingent, whose binding force does not lie solely in its enactment, but rather in its forms. Nietzsche himself saw this, and in the note on the physiology of art he attempted to articulate this idea by considering the characteristic presence of the work as an impediment to the enactment of its experience—without, however, giving up his orientation to the model of artistic performance itself. The alternative to the meaningless admiration of the completion of the work remains for him the "excitement of the artistically creative state" produced by works of art (*KSA* 13:14 [47]).

Meanwhile, at least one motivation for this assertion is clear: the suspicion against the liberating character of an experience that is given over to the works themselves. If this suspicion is not compelling, then the avant-garde side of a theory of art developed with Nietzsche ceases to be convincing, and so does avant-gardism itself. The situation is somewhat different with the universalization of artistic creation: its motivation is intelligible, and, as the aporia of avant-gardism illustrates, its result is all the more intelligible the less one is orientated to the paradigm of art. It is precisely the program of a universalization of aesthetics that confirms that one should trust the type of aesthetic experience only conditionally and instead practice the sense for nuances. Nietzsche's "liberation" of the aesthetic from its boundaries compels us yet again to draw a boundary between art and life.

7

Stereoscopic Experience
Ernst Jünger's Poetics of
The Adventurous Heart

Literature is represented experience, and a literary work is the representation of its experiential content. A work that is not based upon experiences is not a work of art, but at best an artistic fragment. However, when experiences are not represented in a pregnant manner, when experiences, therefore, are not made present by giving form to their presence, their communication remains documentary. The claim of art is not adequately met.

When the representation of experiences has the character of a work of art, the experiences give rise to the experiential content of a work. The experiences are now worked up and staged in such a way that new experiences are made possible: the experiences of the reader. The experience of reading is an experience with staged experiences. Texts which make experiences possible in this way are, in the words of Hans-Georg Gadamer, "eminent texts" (TI, 248/38). The eminent text is not merely "a phase in the execution of the communicative event" (TI, 245/35), a genre which aims at producing a better understanding, but rather the play-space within which one has experiences in accordance with its standard.

These experiences are possible on different levels. In some cases they can be directed toward the language of a work or consist in the fact that we anxiously follow the narrative of story. They can also be expressed by means of a more or less explicit comparison of our own experiences which those that appear in the work or reflect our own experience to such a degree that in the experiences incorporated into the work we, as it were, see the author over our shoulder. Generally speaking, the experience of reading plays itself out concurrently on at least some of these levels.

Interpretation, too, is an experience of reading. The explicit question of the experiential content of a work and its principle of representation begins with the text. This question only exists within the play-space of the text, and correspondingly it should be a part of the attempt to grasp the play-space of the text conceptually. Interpretation should be the conceptually intensified experience of reading, otherwise it becomes less interesting for the reader and becomes an autonomous scholarly ritual.

To be sure, no interpretation can reproduce the experience of reading. In the best case, the experience of the interpreter is still to be gleaned from his text in which determinations, interpretations, and citations become fixed. However, that is not a disadvantage. Interpreters do not want to put their own experiences into play—or when they do this they cease being interpreters—but rather they want to focus attention on the experiential content of a work. In this way interpretations can be a key which opens the space of a work. Each person must then enter for himself.

For many it remains quite difficult to enter the work of Ernst Jünger, and not because this work confronts the reader with extraordinary barriers to understanding. Ernst Jünger is not an author who, like Joyce or Proust, is more often praised than read; rather he is still viewed by many as "controversial." This remarkable word mainly suggests that the rank of an author is not seriously to be questioned, but one is not prepared, at least not immediately, to acknowledge his rank. The motives for this attitude seldom have anything directly to do with the work and sometimes constitute, as in the case of Jünger, a strange mixture of resentment, ignorance, and self-righteousness. There are signs that the attitude toward the almost one-hundred-year-old author[1] is becoming more moderate. Here and there it might also be dawning on some that for quite a while in Italy and France it has been possible to make a fool of oneself by being coy and pig-headed with respect to Jünger's work.

The reference to the "controversy" surrounding Jünger would merely be a footnote to the particularities of the self-proclaimed, intellectually righteous milieu in Germany, and thus not worth pursuing, if it did not contribute to the task of illuminating the genuine challenge of Jünger's work. Like almost no one else, Jünger has tested the degree to which the catastrophes of this century can be represented in literary form, and he has always avoided furnishing his representations with moral assurances and has refrained from pessimistically repudiating this century in its entirety because of its catastrophes. If the possibilities of literature are realized not in passing judgment, but in representation, then both cohere. Then again, some would rather that Jünger's work be avoided altogether, and sometimes the unwillingness or inability to enter into a confrontation with it is dressed up in cheap convictions. However, by adopting this attitude the opportunity to better understand our own century is lost—to understand it as it is made accessible in the play-space of literature alone, in the play-space of this work alone.[2]

Among the books of Ernst Jünger, *The Adventurous Heart* occupies a particular place. It is not merely the most concentrated of this books; its short prose pieces unite the genres which Jünger favors, the story, the diary, the aphorism, and the essay, and in this way realizes rather unique representative possibilities. The precise dreamlike prose of this book is comparable, in German literature, only to the images created by Walter Benjamin. In addition, the book mirrors its method of representation, so that it contains its own poetics and in this way exhibits the poetics of Jünger's work as a whole. And finally, Jünger published two versions of *The Adventurous Heart* which differ substantially from one another and, as two versions of the same book, also interestingly make reference to one another. The experiential content of both versions is fundamentally different: the anarchistic and national-revolutionary style of the first version (first edition, 1929) contrasts with the second version (first edition, 1938), with its stoical defense of the "lost outpost" against barbarism.[3]

Although the accents in the two versions are clearly different, their experiential content essentially remains the same. The illuminating power of the book does not show itself primarily in the fact that in it the particular circumstances of the period are depicted from the determinate perspective of the involved and affected parties. Rather the book elucidates a fundamental characteristic of this century by attempting to come to terms with it artistically. In this manner the book's experiential content and its principle of representation cohere.

In what follows I want to show more precisely what this means, and for the sake of clarity I will identify the two central concepts of my analysis in advance: The experiential content of *The Adventurous Heart* is that of the *poverty of experience*; its representational principle is *stereoscopy*. Although it is a problematic abstraction with respect to the work itself to initially interpret its experiential content in isolation, it has the advantage of making the inner logic of the work more perspicuous. Moreover, the abstraction is not unjustified to the extent that the experiences which make up the content of a work do not belong to the author alone; otherwise every work would remain foreign to its readers and, more to the point, a work would be unable to tell us anything about its time. Within the play-space of a work we often experience explicitly what we already implicitly knew; we recognize something without being able to confirm that it was something that we already understood. A work sheds light upon something which, in this light, we first come to know as something that we could recognize again. In this way the work elucidates its time.

Already in the first part of the first version of the text this claim is made for *The Adventurous Heart*. The author of "Sketches Made by Day and Night"[4] is himself certain

> that my fundamental experience, just that which expressed itself through the process of life, is the typical experience of my generation: a variation on the theme of the age, or perhaps a peculiar species, which in no way falls outside the parameters of what distinguishes that type. From within this consciousness I mean, if I am concerned with myself, not really me, but rather what lies at the bottom of this phenomenon, which every other person can therefore claim for themselves in its most authentic sense, free from all contingency. (*AH* 1, *SW* 9:33–34)

That is doubtless true of the poverty of experience. Walter Benjamin, born three years earlier than Jünger, claimed this for himself in such a decisive way that he saw in it the fundamental characteristic of his epoch. In his essay "Experience and Poverty," published in 1933, Benjamin observes that experience has "fallen in value, and that in a generation which, in the years 1914–1918, had one of the most monstrous experiences in world history." Benjamin continues:

> Perhaps that is not as strange as it appears. Could we not have made the observation then that people returned dumb from the battlefield? Not richer, but poorer in experience that could be shared with others. What was then poured out ten years later in the flood of war books was everything but experience, which rushed from mouth to ear. No, that was not strange. For experiences are never more fundamentally exposed as lies than the strategic during trench warfare, the economic during inflation, the bodily during hunger, the moral during dictatorship. A generation which still traveled to school on streetcars pulled by horse stood in the open air upon a landscape in which nothing remained unchanged except the clouds, and in the middle, in a force field of destructive streams and explosions, the trifling, fragile human body. (*GS*, 2.1:214)

The poverty of experience: that does not, therefore, mean that nothing is experienced, but that too much rather than too little is experienced. On the contrary, the poverty of experience means that what is experienced can no longer be understood in a context which can be taken for granted, taken over from the previous generation and passed on to the subsequent one. The poverty of experience is the loss of a continuity which reached beyond the circumstances of one's own life, it is the loss of history which can be recounted in stories, the loss of judgments and evaluations which can be shared directly with others, and can, in this manner, be communicated directly.

In the first version of *The Adventurous Heart*, Jünger, above all, sketches a picture of his time which agrees in its essentials with Benjamin's, and therefore reveals itself in fact as "a variation on the theme of the age." The following passage demonstrates this in a particularly pregnant manner:

> For some years we worked hard, nihilistically, with dynamite, and forgoing the most insignificant pretense of a genuine questioning, we shot up the very foundations of the nineteenth century and ourselves with it. Only just at the very end did the means and men of the twentieth suggest themselves. We declared war against Europe—as good Europeans, united with the others who gathered around the roulette wheel with but a single color, that of zero, which assures that the bank will win under any circumstances. We Germans have given Europe no chance to lose. But because we offered no chance to lose, so we also, quite essentially, gave nothing to be won; we played against the bank with its own money. (*AH* 1, *SW* 9:133)

The parallels are obvious. However, as much as Jünger and Benjamin agree in their fundamental experience, they differ in how they evaluate its symptoms. Benjamin, whose picture we should first sketch more precisely, points to the somnambulism and delusory character of the present, and he remarks that in both cases there will be compensation for the loss of experience. Benjamin speaks of the resourcefulness of diverse sects and life-reform movements, which arises out of a strangling wretchedness, and adds:

> one need only think of the marvelous paintings of Ensor in which a spookiness fills the streets of the large cites: small minded citizens disguised in festive dress, wearing caricatural masks dusted with flour and gaudy crowns on their heads, wallow aimlessly along the street. These paintings are perhaps nothing more than the picture of a ghastly and chaotic renaissance, upon which so many pinned their hopes. (*GS*, 2.1:215)

On the whole, however, Benjamin's essay is a brief for "technical engineers," who understand how "to begin anew," to construct the world in a new manner from its elements, perhaps as the cubists displayed in their return to stereometric forms (*GS*, 2.1:215). It is not by chance that at the very beginning Benjamin cites Descartes, a technical engineer *qua* father of modernity, "who above all wanted nothing more for his entire philosophy than a single certainty," that of a self-certain subject (*GS*, 2.1:215).[5] Benjamin celebrates the beginning of a culture of engineers, free from the constraints of the nineteenth century. The image of *The Adventurous Heart* picks up on similar elements and is nevertheless of a completely different type:

> We stride there upon glassy floors, and the dreams come to us without interruption; they enclose our cities like stone islands and penetrate into their coldest districts. Nothing is real, yet everything is an expression of reality. Admist the howling of the storm and the patter of the rain we perceive a hidden meaning, and even the most sober among us cannot listen to the slamming of a door in a solitary house without a trace of mistrust. The consciousness of being threatened, which continuously accompanied us like an invisible shadow, made itself felt in a very puzzling sense of dizziness and, as Pascal correctly observed, even the great mathematician who stands before an abyss in an completely secure position would not be able to avoid backing away. (*AH* 1, *SW* 9:148)

In the face of the loss of certainty depicted here, no search for a new foundation upon which to construct the world is any longer credible: Pascal confronts Descartes. It is sufficient merely to point out how dominant and creative the images of dizziness and intimidation are in both versions of *The Adventurous Heart* in order to underscore that in these images the book expresses its primary experiential content. The poverty experienced in the sense of *The Adventurous Heart* is not that of a *tabula rasa*, which would be favorable to the new beginning, but rather the poverty of accessible and secure life possibilities in a world—the uncanny loss of worldly certainty.

Nevertheless, Jünger does not merely sketch the picture of a catastrophic decline. The author of *The Adventurous Heart* certainly belongs among the "best minds" who, Benjamin says, began "to focus their verse upon the things themselves: they are distinguished by unreservedly affirming their age despite having a total absence of illusion with respect to it" (*GS*, 2.1:216). In the first version both the lack of illusion and the unreserved affirmation are heightened to the intensity of two agonistic moods: the images of the city offer "slices of a violent, demonic uprising whose surface fills the lonely equally with ravenous desire and stifling angst" (GS, 2.1:216). This passage speaks of the frantic movement of life, which for Jünger first manifests itself in the fierce battles of World War I. It is "the cold, insatiable fury" figured equally in technology, which accelerates all life processes, and the related challenge of ever-new forms of energy. Although the texts of The Adventurous Heart seek, again and again, to elucidate the essence of this frantic movement anew, it is no accident that it resists being understood as something determinate. For what is meant here is a dynamic of life itself which undermines all determinateness, that which Nietzsche in The Birth of Tragedy named "the Dionysian," which "is brought home to us most intimately by the analogy with intoxication."[6]

Within narrow limits, one might allow oneself to engage the celebration of the Dionysian, especially if one believes oneself capable of organizing and taming these vitalistic eruptions of a rapturous philologist. However, when Jünger writes of the destructive processes of the technical age, particularly its wars, that they are imbued with "such a degree of necessity that they can only be followed with the greatest interest, especially when one loves the fact that life expresses itself in strange and dangerous situations" (AH 1, SW 9:80), here we approach what, for many, is the limit of what is bearable. These limits will have been crossed when Jünger writes of having sympathy for the "attitude of the battle leader," who sees change behind the cremation of the dead, which is described as the peak of a "magnificent ruthlessness" (AH 1, SW 9:113). The provocation cannot be mediated by the desire to identify it with the revolutionary spirit of the first version. Although the revolutionary perspective is forsaken in the second version, the same figures can be found there as well.

To be sure, we do an injustice to the first version if we consider the meditation on the meaning of destruction in isolation. This meditation is here presented in the form of an image which makes its context clear:

During my usual walk I caught sight of a beautiful image in the thick undergrowth behind the dune which astonished me by its richness: the large leaf of an aspen in which was broken a circular hole. On closer inspection, a dark green fringe appeared to hang down, which turned out to be a formation composed of a series of tiny caterpillars, holding on to the leaf's edge by their jaws alone. A nest of butterfly eggs must have recently hatched here. The young brood had stretched itself out like a flame of life upon its source of food. The rarity of this image consisted in the almost total painlessness of destruction which it simulated; the fringe produced the impression of threads hanging down from the leaf itself, so that nothing of substance appeared to be lost. Here it was so obvious how life's double entry bookkeeping remained in balance. I had to think of the solace which Condés gave to Mazarin, weeping for the six thousand who died in the battle near Freiburg: "Ah, more people are born in a single night in Paris than this operation has cost." (*AH* 1, *SW* 9:112–13)[7]

What is at issue here is the *simulation* of painlessness in "life's double entry bookkeeping." The caterpillars and the leaf from which they draw sustenance appear to be a unified formation, "so that nothing of substance appeared to be lost." To be sure, this also accounts for "the rarity of this image": innovation and destruction, profit and loss, the maintenance of life and pain or death rarely appear so seamless. However, they only appear to be seamless, without in truth being so. This makes the solace offered by Condé questionable.

The two versions are distinguished by the way in which they express this questionableness. The first version asserts the coherence of life and pain in order to underscore the weight of responsibility that ought to accompany violent, aggressive behavior: "One needs to feel the knives of pain upon one's own body if one wants to handle them coldbloodedly and with confidence; one needs to be familiar with the coin with which one pays" (*AH* 1, *SW* 9:114). This is contrasted to a politics which provides "mouseholes of irresponsibility" and propagates and justifies violence without a proper knowledge of the knives of pain. What is at stake is the contrast between the authentic situation of one who acts immediately, the authentic revolutionary, and the perspective of the ideologue: the seriousness of the act versus the cheap phrase.

In the circumstances of battle, life affirmation and destruction are too clearly interconnected for one to make a casual reference to life's double entry bookkeeping.

Nevertheless, the first version still wants to give the impression that, under the weight of responsibility, it is still possible to be "caterpillar and leaf at the same time" (*AH* 1, *SW* 9:113). The "heroic temperament" openly bears the coherence of life affirmation and destruction, and for this reason "the secret seals of pain so often fall upon the heroic warriors which the sculptor and the founder have preserved for us" (*AH* 1, *SW* 9:114). Here the second version is fundamentally more precise and radical. That caterpillar and leaf can never be united or reconciled becomes clear when we read that the image of life in all its fullness, including destruction, allows "us to forget the secret sign of pain which separates both sides of the equation" (*AH* 2, *SW* 9:229). That is to say, every "confidence in life . . . that does not know emptiness" remains on the surface (*AH* 2, *SW* 9:229); to the extent that the intensity of battle is replete with such confidence, the seals of pain have no meaning for it.

This can be generalized in the following way: whenever a historical event is experienced as something meaningful, the victims who have suffered as a result must be neglected. When they are thought of, either the meaning of the historical event escapes from view or it must be the case that the victims were, at the very least, fundamentally justified. Whoever wants to affirm the achievements of the French Revolution, for example, cannot take the side of its victims. History destroys history. There can be no developments without the neglect, the suppression, or even the destruction of another history. Every story of the victory of a power, the adoption of a principle, the reform of a state or a way of life is made possible by the fact that countless other histories, life stories, were more or less brutally interrupted and violently broken off.

However, one cannot do justice to this insight by renouncing the desire to experience history as meaningful and articulating this position by means of corresponding narratives. That would be equivalent to renouncing a particular form of life and thus tantamount to handing life over to senselessness. Stories of success and of suffering cannot be reconciled. Whoever wanted to eliminate the conflict between them would either fall prey to the pure cynicism of a history seen from the perspective of the victors or, as the exclusive supporter of a history of suffering, be forced to deceive themselves that they are part of a successfully constituted form of life.

Senselessness and meaning therefore cohere. The continuity of history does not merely exist as such, but is constituted in the enactment of life itself; it is projected as the determinate play-space and in action strengthened, tested, explored, and represented. This leads to new situations of which the project of history, as it undergoes modifications, must from time to time take account. However, the project is not put into question essentially through those actions which are comprehensible, meaningful, and therefore possible only within its parameters. Rather, what puts history into question are the ceasures, the breaks, and the impediments: particular goals are reached, particular possibilities closed off, previously open perspectives upset by chance or the twists of fate. In this case, even an individual life history must then be retold. It is solely because life is discontinuous that we must continuously enact it. Meaninglessness shines through the glassy floor of meaning.

This is by no means clear in a life that is continuous or one that seeks continuity. For what is discontinuity and what is meaninglessness here always stand in the light of continuity, whether merely as its disturbance or as a stimulus to the construction of continuity. The light of continuity is the light of a confidence in life that does not know the empty spaces and does not actually wish to know them—and, in the end, cannot know them. In this light the signs of destruction already have transformed themselves into symptoms of the new.

The matter is quite different for the attitude which, in the second version of *The Adventurous Heart*, is designated as "intuitive skepticism." From the perspective of a continuous life this is a superfluous insight, which "perhaps is only possible because nature does not cut the garments sharply enough which it forces upon life." So "we make superfluous observations in situations, such as plunging into an abyss, in which we would perhaps prefer to be unconscious." At the same time there is "a degree of astonishment which suppresses the fear—in this state a fine veil that almost always covers the world is lifted" (*AH* 2, *SW* 9:253). Intuitive skepticism arises together with the loss of experience; one slips out of the continuity of an experiential context and now remains at a distance from possible new forms of experience. Rather than merely appearing to be the basis for the construction of a new world, the loss of an immediately comprehensible form of experience opens up the possibility for intuitive skepticism to experience for itself the agonistic interplay of groundlessness and the construction of continuity: "Whenever the world is out of joint, fissures are formed through which we can divine the secrets of the architecture which are usually hidden from us" (*AH* 2, *SW* 9:255).

This is presented with the memory of a battle. The cries of the victims after the end of the fighting were, we read, "like the belated protest of life against the still smoking historical machinery which indifferently rolled over flesh and blood" (*AH* 2, *SW* 9:254). Out of this caesura in the furious and deadly events arises a genuinely placeless and intentionless perception, to which the "historical machinery" becomes visible:

> It was a curious expression of disorientation which was written upon their faces—as if behind fiery stage sets, made to disappear by some unexplained means, the perplexing solution appeared to a riddle which one had long sought to solve. Before the weary inner eye the contrasting colors of a glowing and sparkling illusion glimmered which fed upon the oppressiveness of the dream and upon a passion which bordered on madness.
>
> That the world is a giant madhouse, but that behind the madness, method, perhaps even malice, lay hidden—that one has taken part in a play as an improvising walk-on under the direction of a famous director, while one could not think of whose, and whose image one only now consciously retrieves and freezes before—that one has spoken Prussian in the highest sense, that one was on duty—all this is sensed in an unthinking state, with a mixture of exhaustion and cleverness, and a nose made more acute by the closeness of death. (*AH* 2, *SW* 9:254)

In this state of unintentionally heightened attention the agonistic truth of life reveals itself in that the real appears as an illusion, a dream, and the view through the glassy foundation of the real appears as the solution to the riddle. Intuitive skepticism clings to the point of indifference between abyss and the continuity of life and can, in this way, be the undissimulated experience of both.

The first version was, at bottom, also concerned with this question. Only there the indifference of the abyss and the continuity of life, of senselessness and sense, was identified with the destructive dynamic of the technical world and the annihilating and constructive movement between one form of life and another possible one. This movement possessed the wish "that for the longest time it be in search of symbols which were genuinely its own": "for as the most certain destroyer of the idyll, of the old styled landscape, of geniality and of the historical Biedermeier style, it will fulfill this task more thoroughly the later it lets itself be caught up in a new world of values and allows itself to be incorporated within it" (*AH* 1, *SW* 9:154). The identification with the destructive "flame of a new life" previously had been declared to be a necessary consequence of the poverty of experience: "He who lost the most appears to have won the most. All human beings and things of this age press on toward a magical nadir. To pass through it means to be at the mercy of the flame of a new life; to have passed through it means to be a part of the flame" (*AH* 1, *SW* 9:116). In the second version the certainty with regard to the passage through the nadir has disappeared. The perspective of *The Adventurous Heart* no longer is identified with a revolutionary outlook. From within an intuitive skepticism it transforms itself into the magic of the nadir and also, for this reason, can be an undisguised aesthetic perspective.

The aesthetic perspective is watchful and thoughtful in a manner that, from the point of view of life's practicalities, is superfluous and perhaps even disruptive—one meditates while plunging into the abyss. On the other hand, the aesthetic observations and meditations remain bound to the course of each person's life. They are not valid like philosophical meditations in the traditional sense which correspond to the harmonious totality of the world or the cosmos, but rather accompany the course of each particular life, bound to a particular perspective, without being subordinate to it. The aesthetic perspective incorporates a distance from itself and, in this way, is an intensified experience of life. This is expressed already in the opening section of the first version:

I have this feeling—which I only seldom lose, even in the
most confused moments—as if an attentively watchful point
from an eccentric, distant place controlled and observed the
secret mechanism. Yes, it appears to me very often as if in
very human moments, like those moments of angst, there
above something takes place which could be perhaps compared to a sarcastic laugh. But also other signs—sadness,
compassion, pride—I thought I recognized from time to time,
like signs of an inner optic focused upon that fixed point
which I am inclined to call a second, finer and impersonal
consciousness. Seen from this perspective, life is accompanied by more than thoughts, sensations and feelings, its values are appraised yet again, as it were, like a metal which,
in spite of having already been certified, receives a second
hallmark from a special governing body. Seen from this perspective, this activity now takes on a more gripping fascina-
tion than that which is possible within the domain of a
self-conscious vitality. (*AH* 1, *SW* 9:33)

The "second hallmark" which life receives from the aesthetic doubling of perspective is neither an ordering of one's own life in accordance with an all-encompassing idea, nor a self-critical or
approving attitude arrived at by reflection. The first would be
comparable with making oneself an object of scientific description,
and the view from the eccentric, distant place would be like a view
through a microscope; the other would have the character of an
idea that had become part of the management of one's life and
would therefore belong to practical wisdom. The "second hallmark" is rather the appraisal of one's own life, to the extent that
it allows the agonistic character of life itself to come into view. If,
in the aesthetic perspective, life contains more gripping fascina-
tion than that which is possible within the domain of a self-conscious vitality, that is due to the fact that one experiences oneself
differently than from an administrative perspective of life; one experiences how one's own life *happens*, without at the same time
feeling merely overwhelmed by chance or fate.

Jünger formulated this thought in an almost programmatic
manner in a later book which adopts the style of *The Adventurous
Heart*: "Freedom, even sovereignty, is hidden within reflection. To
the extent that a person succeeds in 'representing' his situation to

himself, to make it an object of his meditative intellect, he removes himself from the situation and raises himself above it" (*Sgraffiti*, *SW* 9:415). The essence of the aesthetic perspective is the fact that the objectifying meditation upon one's own life is a representation; only where the meditation makes itself explicit does it endure in the face of the dynamic of life to the same extent that it remains independent of life's conventional forms. The representation can even be the residue of human dignity, by raising perhaps the only possible protest against the fatefully or contingently overpowering events of life: "When the world appears to be impenetrable to profound meditation, the agony takes on frightful and overpowering qualities." The "unrepresentable" must for this reason be regarded "as the mark of hell" (*Sgraffiti*, *SW* 9:415). The aesthetic protest is far from being an empty gesture of opposition; its freedom is that of the gift. Where the aesthetic perspective is made explicit and has an effect, a sovereignty is thereby expressed which exists when the possibilities of action are closed off. The work of art arises and emerges out of historical events; it constitutes a free-space which is not governed by the rules of historical action and events and can, therefore, allow the historical to appear. Through art sovereign experiences of history are possible.

Representation allows the freedom of aesthetic reflection to be expressed. Only by means of representation can that magic of the nadir which is characteristic of *The Adventurous Heart* also be pursued. The ambivalence of continuity and the abyss requires an artistic form, so that one does not perish in the abysmal and the self-conscious continuity of life is not diminished. This form is created through stereoscopy.

In *The Adventurous Heart* the term *stereoscopic* principally denotes a sensuous perception which can "concurrently derive two sensuous qualities from one and the same object and in fact—this is the essential point—by means of a single sense organ." The text continues:

This is only possible in such a way that one sense exceeds its own function and assumes the function of another. The red, redolent carnation: that is not a stereoscopic perception. By contrast, one stereoscopically perceives the velvety-red carnation, one stereoscopically perceives the cinnamon scent of the carnation, whereby not only is the sense of smell stimulated by an aromatic quality, but at the same time the sense of taste is stimulated by a spicy quality. The salty aroma of the sea also acts stereoscopically; it is mediated by the sense of smell, although both the wetness and the saltiness of the water are scentless. (*AH* 1, *SW* 9:83f).[8]

The stereoscopic is not, however, limited to perceptions of this kind. There is, we read, also an "intellectual stereoscopy," and this "seizes the unity within the inner contradiction" (*AH* 1, *SW* 9:86). In accordance with the singularity of stereoscopic perception, this cannot mean that two opposed elements are united or brought together under a single unity comprising them both. Rather, in an intellectual engagement something must emerge that becomes visible or is illuminated together with the opposing element. In this way the opposing element shows itself in that which it opposes.

By following the individual themes and motifs of *The Adventurous Heart* we can see just what this means. There we find over and over again botanically exact descriptions, whose structures are also meant to reveal those of the historical world. The attempt to reveal history in nature and nature in history is not intended to blur the distinction between them, but rather to place their singularity in clear view: "Consider the animal as if it were a human being, and the human being as a special animal."[9] That is one way to obtain insight by means of the tension of opposed elements. Others are named in the following passage:

> Consider life as a dream and every dream as a particular elucidation of reality. You can do all this if you make use of the magic key. For the true life discloses itself in these forms: those in which it splits apart, so that it can become conscious of itself in the manifold, and those in which it swallows itself, so that it can satisfy itself on itself. The day feeds on the treasures of the night, which for its part receives the day in its dark jaws. The human being feeds on the animal until he is given over to the animal as its booty. Every order carries the dreams in its belly which contain the seeds of its ruin, and every dream sprouts into crystal clear orders. The images are deeper than their reflection, which is thrown back and forth between the silver and the steel mirrors. (*AH* 1, *SW* 9:130)

However, with respect to the experience of stereoscopy, these passages from *The Adventurous Heart* are not the most crucial passages in which the experience is elucidated. For the text itself is stereoscopic insofar as it communicates a sense of the abyss in its conceptually driven passages to the same degree that it situates its dark dream images in the brilliance of precise description. This makes the text into an "eminent text" in that it not only makes reference to experiences, but rather makes other experiences possible. That, in turn, is grounded in the experiences which the text represents. As experiences within an aesthetic perspective they are aesthetic, that is to say, artistically articulated. In a work that proves itself to be artistically successful by being capable of becoming a free-space of experiences, the experiential content and the representative principle cohere indissolubly.

8

Aesthetic Experience of Time
Adorno's Avant-gardism and Benjamin's Correction

One of the most interesting reading experiences is that of rereading contemporaneous works. What Gadamer in *Truth and Method* calls "temporal distance" shows itself here in a particularly emphatic way. The distance which separates the reader from the time in which a work originated is not experienced as a natural feature of historical consciousness. This prevents a work from unproblematically being considered a classic; one reads the work accompanied by the recollection of the texts contemporaneous with it and is therefore more attentive to the signs of anachronism.

While rereading Adorno's *Aesthetic Theory* these signs intrude rather strongly. Within the context of the aesthetic debate carried on today, Adorno's project can no longer be considered contemporary. The reason for this is that the current debate about aesthetics stresses elements that are fundamentally different from those emphasized by Adorno. To the extent that the structure of aesthetic experience and the possibility that it can be demonstrated by means of argument are topics of discussion, the debate is marked by a decisive movement "Back to Kant." Stimulated by Foucault, the debate is equally occupied with the question of an aesthetic construction of life, of the art of living, and extends, in this way, to ethical problems. Here it is a question of an 'unlimited aesthetics' whose motto reads Back to Nietzsche. The attempt undertaken by Adorno to conceptually determine the work of art according to the prototype and antitype of Hegelian aesthetics has an untimely effect.

However, more important for Adorno's untimeliness is his commitment to an aesthetic canon, the artworks of so-called aesthetic modernism, which has since become historical while not being able to become "classical" in the precise sense of the word. After Beckett and Celan became figures of literary history, which they had not yet become for Adorno, it was finally clear that already in 1970, the year it appeared, Adorno's *Aesthetic Theory* presented itself as a work *post festum*. For the art that Adorno had labored to penetrate conceptually essentially belongs to the second half of the previous century and the first decades of this one: Beckett and Celan are late products of a bygone artistic epoch.

The anachronistic feeling with regard to *Aesthetic Theory*, which, incidentally, was already capable of being expressed a good ten years ago,[1] should by no means give us a sense of superiority. Whoever wants to view themselves as superior to Adorno on the basis of their own historically matured perspective will be asked by him to show some restraint. No subsequent reader can see the historical character of *Aesthetic Theory* more clearly than Adorno himself saw it.

Aesthetic Theory rests upon the doubt "whether art is still possible at all."[2] Adorno considers it "conceivable" and not merely an "abstract possibility" "that great music—a late development—was only possible during a limited period of human existence." And to elucidate this remark he adds the following: "The revolt of art . . . has become a revolt against art; it is futile to prophesy whether art will survive it. The complaints once made by reactionary cultural pessimists cannot be quelled by the cultural criticism that, as Hegel thought 150 years ago, art may have entered an age of decline" (*AT*, 13). It is not particularly difficult to find a great deal of evidence for the validity of this diagnosis, and thereby for the problematic character of an aesthetics which presents itself as a philosophy of art. To this extent, the move from philosophy of art to aesthetics appears fully justified. The "modern" artistic methods such as collage and aesthetic shocks are adapted from trivial media, with the result that they no longer are provocative but at best entertain: advertising spots today live off of surrealistic effects. The revolt of art against art, the putting into question of artistic procedures in art itself, takes place, if at all, in informal, esoteric exhibitions, concerts, and publications. And finally, the playful eclecticism and epigonism of contemporary works, which we have become accustomed to call "postmodern," underscores the emphatic claims with which the art of so-called modernity presented itself. If anywhere, it appears that Paul Feyerabend and Cole Porter got it right in the case of art: anything goes.

Such observations as these, however, do not necessarily coincide with *Aesthetic Theory*'s claim to truth. The text's claim to truth is made with complete awareness of the conceivable—and in the meantime no longer merely conceivable—historicity of so-called modern art. Adorno does not merely count on the end of art, but also ties its authenticity to its temporal character; art is not authentic or true in spite of, but rather in its temporality. Thus we read:

> For a reorientated aesthetics, the knowledge developed by the later Nietzsche against traditional philosophy, that that which has become [*das Gewordene*][3] can also be true, is axiomatic. The traditional perspective, which Nietzsche demolished, is turned on its head. Truth is only as something which has become. What appears to be a work of art's proper lawfulness is a late product of an internal, technical evolution. (*AT*, 12)

Truth is only as something which has become: this does not mean that whatever has become is therefore true, but rather that something is true in its becoming. The "proper lawfulness" of art, its autonomy, is for Adorno the index of truth insofar as it articulates an experience of time, and in a particularly intensive manner. The experience of aesthetic truth with which *Aesthetic Theory* is concerned is the aesthetic experience of time, and this in a double sense: the works of art whose authenticity or truth Adorno wants to work out are themselves centered around a "temporal core" (*AT*, 50). For this reason, their authenticity or truth can be experienced only temporally.

However illuminating these reflections may appear to be, they are perhaps insufficient to dispel the feeling that *Aesthetic Theory* is anachronistic. And if one then attempts to explain the intransigence of this feeling, one could point to the experience of time itself. One could then say that the intensive experience of time in the "internal-technical revolution" of modern art loses its intensity from the perspective of historical consciousness. The time in which the autonomy of art is realized is not coincident with the time in which art is experienced as soon as the latter is an experience of historical consciousness.

However, one ought to avoid considering the dimming of artistic intensity to be a fact beyond question. It could be the case that Adorno merely did not have adequate conceptual means at his disposal for clarifying the "simultaneity" of the works that were decisive for him with the experience of these works under the conditions of historical consciousness. If this suspicion is substantiated, then the feeling that *Aesthetic Theory* is anachronistic will in no way be confirmed. The feeling of anachronism would be found to be without foundation, and must once again be put into question. The conceptual or categorical weaknesses of philosophical theory do not allow themselves to become otiose, particularly if they also provide clues as to how they might possibly be corrected. The weaknesses of a theory also can reveal what is at issue.

In what follows I would like to develop a corrective to *Aesthetic Theory* in this sense. I will attempt to show that the point of departure for this corrective is supplied by Adorno himself when he makes reference to the thought of Walter Benjamin in the context of the problems sketched above. The central weakness of *Aesthetic Theory* will be shown to be that Adorno can only think the aesthetic experience of time temporally, only according to the measure of time. Because this is not the case with Benjamin, one can develop a corrective to *Aesthetic Theory* in connection with him. The result of my reflections will be that it is possible in this way to give a more plausible account of the categories which Adorno, in unparalleled fashion, had attempted to delimit, namely, the categories of aesthetic modernity. The strength of *Aesthetic Theory* is to have represented art's claim to truth with a view to its modernity; its weakness lies in its conception of the aesthetic experience of time and hence of modernity as well. In order to clarify this, I must first consider more precisely the connection between modernity and authentic art as it is represented in *Aesthetic Theory*.

Adorno's reflections begin with a historical determination of art that is reminiscent of Hegel in that it overturns the Hegelian valuation of art and religion. For Adorno art arises by freeing religious symbols from their original context. A work of art is the negation of a religious symbol. That is to say, in itself it is still determined by the fact that it makes reference to something other, to something beyond the existing world. However, what is here designated as "the other" can no longer be interpreted religiously, and, correspondingly, the referring object has lost the character of a symbol. Unlike the religious symbol, the work of art no longer refers to something that is present in the work of art. Art has freed itself, as Adorno puts it, "from an unmitigated claim to the truth of redemption" (AT, 10). The autonomy of art is due to this alone; works of art can on longer be understood within the transcendent context of religion, and hence as positively determinable epiphanies.

The referential character of works of art cannot be understood in this way as a mode of reference to something beyond the existing world without further explanation. To be sure, works of art, like religious symbols, form an open place in this world by expressing a renunciation of the world. This lies in the form of works of art, even if, after the negation of the symbolic, the referential structure alone remains. However, this referential structure, which has now become empty, equally presents itself as something connected to the existing world. The autonomy of art can be realized only if the artistic productive process creates an image that is internally harmonious. In its freedom from a determinate context, the image is freely available and presents itself to be conveyed "to the world in which art is to be found" (AT, 10). This is what Adorno means when he says that "owing to its renunciation of empirical reality" art sanctions "its predominance" (AT, 10).

In this way autonomous art finds itself in a twofold dilemma: it can no longer be a religious symbol, and yet in spite of this it cannot renounce the claim to refer to something beyond the existing world. As a determinate negation of the religious symbol it remains determined by its referential character. It cannot be assimilated into the existing world, and yet precisely because it is distinct from the existing world it cannot prevent being assimilated. Every picture which refers to something seeks to be understood as a picture of something.

This dilemma would not be resolved at all by making art once more into a religious symbol. For the autonomy of art cannot be revoked. The attempt at such a revocation would be tantamount to an unbelievable restoration. Moreover, religious symbols were seen to be problematic precisely because they claimed to be fulfilled. Religious symbols belong to the existing world as well, and for this reason they cannot make good on their claim. Although it may at first appear as if autonomous art is, in its way of being present, connected to the fulfilled past of religion—where art reveals the questionableness of this past—art remains dependent upon itself in its way of being present. By the religious past of art showing itself to be questionable, the possibility of a fulfilled future is also closed off. To be able to awaken hope of redemption, the work of art must be a religious symbol, which it essentially is not. On the basis of this diagnosis Adorno can express his agreement with Rimbaud's "postulate of an art of the most progressive consciousness, in which the most advanced and variegated procedures penetrate the most advanced and variegated modes of experience" (*AT*, 57): *Il faut être absolument moderne.*[4]

Modern, in Adorno's sense, is not the art of a particular, historically determinate epoch. Rather art is modern in general in the radical way in which its autonomy is made present. If one wishes to historically date—modern—art in the context of an epochal scheme, one already must have been orientated to this way of being present. If the experience of a radical way of being present is principally constituted by means of art, one must certainly be orientated to art in order to understand modernity.

This, in fact, is Adorno's belief. In his estimation, philosophy is incapable of achieving a radical way of being present like art. Philosophical reflection, considered by itself, cannot negate the referential character of the religious symbol in the same manner, for where philosophy appears as the negation of the religious, it is incapable of saving the referential character of the religious. Philosophy can, to be sure, turn against the existing world and capture its incapacity for redemption; however, philosophical reflection does not articulate itself in forms which, like artistic ones, refer to something beyond that which exists, even when philosophy is articulated artistically. In this way, the paradigmatic character of art is confirmed once more. An aesthetic experience of a radical way of being present is, therefore, possible only if it is not solely devoted to an affirmation of the existing world. And if this radical way of being present only expresses itself in art, an aesthetic experience of a radical way of being present can only be artistic or bound to works of art.

The plausibility of Adorno's starting point naturally depends upon whether the aesthetic experience of a radical way of being present can convincingly be tied to the structure of works of art. With respect to this, it is not an exaggeration to say that Adorno devoted practically the entire conceptual effort of *Aesthetic Theory* to this task. Accordingly, I can only present his solution in sharply abbreviated form, formulating it with a view to the point which, I believe, Adorno's conception is in need of correction.

To this end, it is apposite to first observe that the radical way of being present, as it is expressed in works of art, is not unhistorical. To be sure, art is prevented from making reference to the past of religion and, in this way, to a fulfilled future as well; it is precisely this that constitutes its radical way of being present. But the radical way in which artistic autonomy is made present does not simply exist, but rather must always be produced anew. In artistic production the empty referential structure of art must be put to work again and again, because only in this way can a restoration of religious symbolism, as well as assimilation into the existing world, be avoided. Put another way, art needs to continually attack its autonomy, in order to be able to confirm it. Art can only protect its referential character by having every work of art interrupt the possibility of making reference to the existing world and hindering the fulfillment of its referential structure. This is only possible in that every work of art bests all other works of art and is, in this way, historical. This is the point of Adorno's double superlative in his talk of the "most advanced and variegated modes of experience."

One can designate what Adorno has in mind here as "form of a second order." Every work of art that does justice to the claim of absolute modernity dissolves the immanent, lawful obedience to form and harmony of its predecessors by having predetermined forms at its disposal. Carried to its logical conclusion, the result is apparently that no formal solutions are left standing which could make a claim to enduring validity and bindingness. Each newly discovered solution is the destructive element par excellence, and in this way construction and destruction, as modes of experience, cannot be separated from one another. This second order form refuses the expectation of complete intelligibility, and therefore offers no interpretative model for the existing world.

In spite of this, the idea of the bindingness of art cannot be rejected. Art which does justice to the claim of absolute modernity only has a form of the second order, but it nevertheless has a form. Just as the destructive element belongs to artistic construction, this destructive element can only be realized constructively. An autonomous work of work is understood, for Adorno, by understanding how, on the basis of this competitive dynamic, something utterly individual can be realized. A work of art is radically present in virtue of the fact that when a work successfully surpasses the formal solutions of other works of art, it asserts its exclusive presence. Historical ordering does not do justice to it because it does not recognize the authority of the successful form. At the same time, however, individuality is formally successful only as it surpasses what has gone before. It does not appear to be content in itself, but originates in a historical moment. The way of being present of a successful work of art is not a fulfilled, timeless presence; there is no eternity which does not belong to the schema of time. Or, as Adorno himself puts it, "every work of art is an instant [*Augenblick*]" (*AT*, 17). It is, completely in the sense of Plato's *Parmenides*, without place between time and timeless presence (156d–157b).

Adorno's radical avant-gardism can only be grasped in light of these ideas. The avant-gardism of art stands in the service of aesthetic instantaneousness [*Augenblicklichkeit*], and in this way alone it distinguishes itself from the power-laden, competitive movement of a dialectic of enlightenment, whose concern is to maintain the position of the victor now and in the future. Aesthetic avant-gardism aims solely at the aesthetic instant of the individual.

However, the aesthetic instant cannot be understood on the basis of aesthetic avant-gardism. The aesthetic instant is not the consequence of well-calculated effects, but is that which is precisely "the Other" to the calculative. In Adorno's words: "The new is, out of necessity, something desired, but as the Other it would not be the desired" (*AT*, 41). The referential character of art for Adorno consists in this, that in a work of art material elements are brought together and given a form capable of being experienced which cannot be constructed as such. A work of art can only have a referential character where its competitive dynamic is transformed into something that is not arbitrary, into what Adorno calls the "nonidentical." The competitive dynamic, to which works of art are indebted, is, taken for itself, the principal of the existing world. Avant-gardism is artistic enlightenment, but in this way avant-gardism merely designates the condition of artistic truth, not this truth itself. The truth of works of art lies in their instantaneousness and not in their historicity. This truth rests upon a temporal boundary.

But then the particular truth of a work of art, which is subordinate to the standard of absolute modernity, cannot become meaningless for those who come later. To this extent Adorno must certainly grant limited place to aesthetic historicism, since the respective form of autonomous works of art can be understood only by considering the correlative state of artistic expressive possibilities. However, if a work of art is more than the result of well-calculated effects, then the work cannot, in this way, be experienced in its aesthetic truth. What, for example, is authentic about Wagner's *Tristan und Isolde* in Adorno's sense does not remain reserved for musicologists who can reconstruct the relevant historical situation. However, it does not have permanent validity in the sense of classical works of art, which can be confirmed again and again.

Hence the experience of modern art is neither tied to contemporaneousness, nor is it ahistorical, resting upon the foundation of a continuity which maintains itself amidst the change of time. A work of art will be experienced in its truth only if it succeeds in recognizing its instantaneousness.

However, when it is a question of saying more precisely how this occurs, Adorno comes up against the boundaries of his conceptual possibilities. He can only think the authentic experience of art according to the model of a competitive dynamic. Even where the experience of a work of art is not governed by the perspective of artistic production, it should be avant-gardist in character. The correspondence between earlier and later works of art also has the character of a critique for Adorno, namely, a critique "in accordance with the present state of things" (*AT*, 67). But this does not really allow the works that have been realized to speak; they also remain connected to a new instantaneousness, even when it is not at all a question of its being realized in a new work of art. Because Adorno's principle remains caught within a competitively dynamic dialectic of enlightenment, he cannot admit the instantaneous presence of noncontemporary works of art, without being able to challenge them.

Within the context of *Aesthetic Theory* this leads to a strange partial solution. Early works of art remain, as Adorno says, "eloquent," but their eloquence is a kind of murmur behind closed doors: "What has once been true in a work of art and was contradicted in the course of history, becomes capable of revealing itself again only when conditions have changed; for their sake this truth must be cashed out. So deeply imbricated are aesthetic truth and history" (*AT*, 67). If truth and history are "so deeply imbricated," *Aesthetic Theory* fails to recognize the fact that modern art, together with its competitive dynamic, is becoming part of the past. Even if one can and should read Hölderlin differently after Celan, Celan's poetry no longer marks "the present state of things." Adorno admits that the "present state of things" cannot always offer a convincing standard when he says that in the "afterlife of works qualitative differences [would be] revealed which in no way coincide with the degree of modernity of their period" (*AT*, 67). This is then followed by an astounding sentence: "In the secret war of all against all which constitutes the history of art, the older modernity, as that which is past, might be victorious over the more recent" (*AT*, 67–68). The older work can be "more modern" than the newer, for, to speak with Adorno once again, "time alone is no criterion" (*AT*, 67).

If time alone is no criterion, then the experience of works of art in their instantaneousness clearly can be bound no longer to the "present state of things." It is not necessary to dispute that the artistic negation of past formal possibilities can lead to instantaneousness. That, however, can only be reconstructed by art historians, viewing works of art with a historical consciousness, while the experience of instantaneousness itself is not necessarily tied to competition. Adorno's conception of the aesthetic remains too firmly tied to artistic production for it to be able to assimilate these thoughts. And it remains fixed upon the idea that art must prove itself to be ceaselessly incommensurable with the existing world. Adorno clearly cannot imagine that artistic form as such already marks a caesura with respect to the world. For this reason his conception is in need of a corrective; it requires a corrective so that its central thought of aesthetic instantaneousness can manifest itself without being distorted. What *Aesthetic Theory* is lacking is a hermeneutic of the instantaneous and hence a hermeneutic of absolute modernity.

It speaks in favor of *Aesthetic Theory* that it points the way out of these difficulties itself. In almost all of its essential determinations, the ideas of Walter Benjamin shine through. That is evident by merely counting them up. When Adorno says that the experience of aesthetic instantaneousness is not possible in the absence of a critique, one cannot help but think of the central role which the concept of critique plays in the opening passages of Benjamin's essay on Goethe's *Elective Affinities*. When Adorno declares the truth of works of art to be an indeterminable harmony, he is able to adopt the concept of the 'constellation' which is central to Benjamin's work (*AT*, 127). And when he comes to speak of the "correspondence" between earlier and later works of art, he reminds one of Benjamin's reflection that there is a "historical index" which belongs to the past, according to which the past does not merely belong to a particular period, but rather can only first be understood in a particular period (*GS* V.1:577). Adorno does not merely take up Benjamin's ideas, however, but reinterprets them. While for Benjamin critique is the separation of the material content of a work which can be reconstructed historically from its atemporal truth content, Adorno ties critique to the "present state of things." While Benjamin understands the concept 'constellation' as the atemporal meaning of connected elements and this meaning as "idea,"[5] the harmony of elements for Adorno has a material character; it consists in a reference to a nonidentical nature which emerges in radical construction. And while for Benjamin the "historical index" of the past indicates how it could later be understood, Adorno sees in it the later possibility of its being surpassed. Taken by themselves, all of these reinterpretations are naturally not illegitimate; considered in themselves they are merely a further example of how philosophical conceptions arise through the interpretation of others. Nevertheless, in order to carry out his own program of an aesthetics of absolutely modern art, Adorno would have done well to have taken up Benjamin's ideas in their original form.

This is particularly clear when we consider the central idea of *Aesthetic Theory*, aesthetic instantaneousness. Here, too, Adorno's use of Benjamin takes the form of a radical reinterpretation which destroys the opportunity to do justice to the experience of the instantaneous. For Adorno, the presence of a work of art only has meaning in that its truth allows time to appear, namely, the time of fleeting illumination and disappearance. The work of art is, as Adorno puts it, "the paradoxical attempt to capture this most fleeting of moments." He continues as follows:

> In works of art that which is momentary is transcended; objectification transforms the work of art into an instant. We must consider Benjamin's formulation of a dialectic at a standstill, which is outlined in the context of his conception of the dialectical image. If works of art are, as images, the continuation of something transitory, they then become concentrated by appearing as something momentary. To experience art means as much as to recognize its immanent processes even as in the instant of its standstill. (*AT*, 130–31)

The time of which Adorno is speaking here should not be understood in a Heraclitean sense as the time of eternal flux in which finally nothing more can be experienced, as Socrates works through this idea in the *Theatetus* (181b–183c). The "most fleeting of all moments" is, for Adorno, altogether a harmonious appearance, "apparitions" of moments which take a form like the configurations of a fireworks pattern which appear (*AT*, 49–50). Works of art are fireworks patterns which persist. To the extent that their truth lies in that which belongs to time, the persistence of a work of art itself is revealed as appearance.

That is, for Adorno, the characteristic form of aesthetic instantaneousness. Standing without place between time and atemporal presence, the instant can be thought only by interpreting it equally in relation to time and atemporal presence while concurrently holding on to its difference from both. This occurs, in Adorno, because the duration of the instantaneous as appearance and its temporality are no longer interpreted from the perspective of historical time, but rather merely as the time of periodic appearing and disappearing. It is not difficult to recognize that within this conception temporal interpretation is given priority: the aesthetic instant is, for Adorno, pure time, a time in which the competitive dynamic is no longer possible, a time without self-assertion, without memory of that which has been overcome and without anticipation of future existence. In a word, it is the time of the non-identical. For Adorno, the nonidentical can be experienced only in the pure time of the instant.

The plausibility of this idea can be doubted if only for the reason that, for Adorno, the nonidentical which works of art bring to appearance are also said to have the character of a constellation, a harmonious assemblage of individual elements. But constellations can be recognized and observed in spite of their fluidity. That they are not mutually exclusive but rather challenge one another was something that Benjamin was able clarify by understanding the fluidity of appearance as its *readability*, and its duration as an *index of this readable meaning*. This occurs in connection with the determination of the "dialectical image," to which Adorno makes reference. The decisive note for our purposes comes from the pages of the *Arcade Project* and reads as follows:

> It is not the case that the past casts light upon the present or that the present casts light upon the past, but rather the image is that within which what has been coalesces in lightening like fashion with the now. In other words, the image is the dialectic in a standstill. For while the relationship of the present to the past is a purely temporal one, the relationship of what has been to the now is dialectical and has an imagistic rather than a temporal character. . . . The interpreted image, that is to say, the image in the now in which it is recognized, bears, to the highest degree, the stamp of critical, dangerous moments, which are the basis of all reading. (*GS* V.1:578)

The standstill of time of which Benjamin is speaking here becomes comprehensible by clarifying why the relationship of what has been and the now cannot be understood by means of a temporal scheme. If this relationship were understood temporally it would be either as tradition, in which the validity of what is earlier is confirmed by the later, or as a historical meditation, in which the earlier appears in a reconstruction from the perspective of the later. In contrast, the earlier is, in a strict sense, *concurrent* with the later, when it reveals itself as something readable; in this context this also means the concept of the constellation. The constellation is not merely the harmonious assemblage of individual elements in such a way that something reveals itself as readable, but rather is the coherence, in a single entity, of readability and the possibility of interpretation. A constellation can be experienced only in a constellatory manner; the concurrence of the readable with its interpreter is just as instantaneous as readability itself.

However, Benjamin's decisive idea, and the idea which is lacking in Adorno, is that the instantaneous is the readable. It does not merely appear fleetingly and resists being grasped in a determinate manner; rather its fleeting appearance means that the truth can elude us, as a thought eludes us when we fail to recognize it.[6] Having a thought does not consist in recognizing it; recognition can and should merely make reference to the thought, just as the interpreted text does. Both in the text and in recognition meaning first emerges.

Just as the interpreted text stands in a relationship to the recognition which occurs in reading so that what can be understood does not elude us, so the work of art is related to interpretation. Interpretation stands in the service of what is experienced in a work of art. However, the work of art is dependent upon interpretation insofar as it appears as something which can be read.

Of course one need not remind Adorno that works of art and interpretation cohere. But the elucidations of the relationship of work and interpretation in *Aesthetic Theory* do not remain focused on the instantaneous cohesion of both, but rather waver between an overemphasis of the work and an overemphasis of interpretation. The following passage is an example of the former: "The better one understands a work of art . . . the less . . . it clarifies what is essentially enigmatic about it" (*AT*, 184). As an example of the latter, Adorno can describe "the need of works for interpretation" as a "sign of their inaccessibility" and add that the "objective" element sought in works of art is never achieved by them (*AT*, 194). This last passage must be understood as saying that interpretation remains behind the work to the extent that it can never be directed toward that which appears instantaneously, but rather only toward the structurally formal aspects of the work. However, the interpretation must say what the work itself cannot say, namely, that the manner in which works of art bring the true, the nonidentical, to appearance is, taken by itself, untrue. What gets lost by overemphasizing the work and interpretation in this way is the readability of the work, the instantaneous appearance of meaning which takes the form of an instantaneous constellation.

Speaking with Benjamin and against Adorno, one must say that aesthetic experience is the instantaneous experience of meaning and not merely the experience of the precarious relationship of inaccessible truth and the appearance of accessibility. When elements coalesce into a constellation in a work, something determinate can be understood, and not merely an appearance on the order of a fireworks display which can only be observed fleetingly. At the same time, the successful articulation of what is understood does not reduce it to the obviousness of the existing world. Where the readable is interpreted, it is not incorporated into an extant and obvious context. Rather, everything that could be obvious is annulled by that which is proper to the readable. The meaning which emerges from the simultaneity of the readable and its interpretation belongs neither to the past nor to the present. It has the character of a simple presence and can be articulated in interpretation without one thereby being able to determine it. It forms the play-space in which what is past and what is present appear in a form in which they can be understood. The meaning which is produced in the instantaneous meeting of past and present is not the temporal meaning of the temporal. It is clearly only experienced in the perspectival abbreviation of the particular instant, and this is precisely what gives the experience the character of modernity. Modernity is the instantaneous experience of the historical and the present in their meaning, a simple presence which is revealed in no other way than in their particular constellations.

Adorno's *Aesthetic Theory* comes close to these ideas without advancing them itself. If one follows the penetrating determinations in which it develops the competitive dynamic of modern art and its transformation into instantaneousness, one can understand why just the works of modernity present themselves, with particular intensity, as readable. The more decisively art moves away from the obvious, the greater the chance that its works will have the character of constellations. In this way they can enter into the constellation of their interpretation. And by articulating the interpretation, the present and the part of the past that is incorporated into the work of art are placed in a new light. Modern art and the experience in which it is articulated together constitute the possibility of an experience of history which is no longer caught in a temporal schema, be it that of an age of decline or one of progress. The dialectical images of modern works of art make clear in an exemplary way that one can just as little understand the past on the basis of the present as the present on the basis of the past. One can understand both only in the moment of absolute modernity, and to this extent the aesthetic experience of time is not something temporal.

Insofar as one is not willing to renounce understanding aesthetic experience as an experience of history in this sense, philosophical aesthetics must remain a form of the philosophy of art. And it would be a mistake to deny the aid which *Aesthetic Theory* can give us in clarifying these questions. The suspicion that this text is anachronistic would then be only a sign that one does not understand oneself within modernity, in that one believes that modernity can be understood as a fundamental feature of a past or passing epoch. But if modernity is in truth not a historical concept, then Rimbaud's demand remains obligatory. If it has become plausible that one cannot do justice to modernity by conceiving of it in terms of a competitive dynamic, then my reflections have achieved their aim.

9

Art as World Representation

"A timeless way of being present is part of art insofar as it, like religion and philosophy, is detached from and independent of all historical and social conditions. Art, too, claims to be absolute by extending beyond all historical temporal differences."[1] These lines from one of the recent essays on the philosophy of art by Hans-Georg Gadamer are easily recognizable as a commentary on Hegel. However, they are not meant to be simply this. Rather, with these sentences Gadamer seeks to articulate an idea which he himself wishes to champion, and they assume thereby the character of a well-planned provocation. In the era of "post-metaphysical thought" talk of the Absolute has an unusual effect. It becomes a protest against the *Zeitgeist*.

This has still greater weight if one considers that Gadamer need not have restricted himself to citing Hegel alone as a source for the idea of the absoluteness of art. Philosophers of art who unmistakably acknowledged the authority of the conditions of modernity did not wish to let the absoluteness of art be viewed as a hypostatization which had, in the interim, come to be regarded as questionable. Walter Benjamin's utterly un-Hegelian philosophy of art would not be what it is without this idea. In a 1923 letter, which is programmatic even for his later works, Benjamin pursues the question of "how works of art relate to historical life," and here Benjamin considers it "as settled that there is not such a thing as the history of art."[2] As an explanation Benjamin adds that the work of art is to be understood differently than human life, essentially not as the "concatenation of temporal events."[3] There is nothing which would link works of art with one another in the sense of an ancestral relationship or generational sequence. For Benjamin the work of art is "in its essence ahistorical."[4] Out of the alterations of historical life and its multifarious temporal relations, the work of art emerges as simply present.

Theodor W. Adorno certainly could not have readily agreed with this; however decisively his *Aesthetic Theory* might also have been influenced by Benjamin. Insofar as Adorno seeks to understand art as the intensive articulation of the rationality that is otherwise also at work in society, he need not merely say that the "social element" is "constitutive of the work of art." He also understood works of art as an "unconscious writing of the history of their epochs." However, as Adorno adds, it is precisely this which makes works of art "incommensurable with historicism, which, instead of pursuing their own historical content, reduces them to external history" (*AT*, 272). It is not difficult to recognize the central thought of Benjamin's programmatic letter in this remark. The work of art is in its essence ahistorical.

However, Adorno and Benjamin are perhaps not such advantageous allies when it is a matter of defending the absoluteness of art. For it is precisely when they attempt to think consequently under the conditions of modernity that there emerges what for many has become problematic about modernity. From a perspective that is skeptical about modernity, Benjamin's and Adorno's thinking appears to be an echo of that romantic metaphysics which furnishes art and the experience of art with a nobility that is considered odd today. A rereading of Adorno's *Aesthetic Theory* in particular can be felt to be instructive on the point that here a past artistic epoch is once again conjured up and celebrated: the so-called classical modernity which grew out of romanticism together with its claims, now regarded by many as rather strange, to the purity of artistic form and the despairing hope that the collapse of tradition could be countered with creative restoration as the acceleration of the technical age could be countered with static poems.

Certainly here one ought not express the suspicion of anachronism too loudly before one has become clear about its presuppositions. And it is then evident that one must be clear about what it is that one contests. Whoever speaks of the past of classical modernity thereby articulates a historical consciousness that just as little exists on the basis of the past as on the basis of one's own present. Every statement about putatively past and now morbid works of art and their historical significance presupposes the possibility that they can be experienced, and this, in turn, is only granted by the way of being present of the works themselves. It is because the works are present that, as Adorno would say, their historical content is accessible at all. The work is not so much in time as time is in the work.

This brings the state of affairs which Adorno had in mind and which Gadamer also has in mind to the fore in a more pregnant manner. Whoever claims that works of art are ahistorical does not contest that they have significance in relation to history. Rather, it appears as if the historical experience could then be articulated rather well if it occurs within a space that is not subordinate to history.

Gadamer once formulated this in relation to Hegel's thesis about the historical character of art and in the process validated, as it were, the cunning of artistic form as opposed to its philosophical interpretation. It is well known that where Hegel speaks of the historical character of art, he wants to indicate that art has lost its religious commitment. Nature has been "emptied of gods,"[5] with the result that the representation of nature no longer communicates the experience of a comprehensive meaning. And no matter how worthily we find "God the Father, Christ and Mary" also represented, "it is no help; we bow our knees no longer" (13:142/ 1:103). But only where the alter image is removed from the context of the sacred does it first become a form of art which is able to be the "present of the past."[6] That is, as Gadamer emphasizes, something completely new—one could also say, something modern. Where works are no longer inscribed in the context of a historical world—and they remain so, where they play a decisive role in allowing this context to become manifest—they come forth in a simultaneous manner. This is what first makes it possible to speak of "the" art. However, as Gadamer says, through this "essential simultaneity of all art something comes to consciousness which represents a final victory over history. In a certain sense this found its first, nascent self-consciousness in Hegel's thesis."[7]

We are now in a better position to understand what it actually meant by Gadamer's thesis of the absoluteness of art cited at the outset. Clearly it does not mean that art is the representation of the Absolute. Rather, art becomes absolute when it ceases to be a representation of the Absolute. This formulation should not lead to a conceptual confusion. There is no equivocation and also no furtive displacement in the meaning of this discourse of the Absolute. In both cases the Absolute means that which is in itself, that which has been removed, and hence the antithesis of the relative. Yet these are different interpretations. Hegel saw the absoluteness of art in the sensuous appearance of the idea. Here free individuality realizes itself in the work of art, and in this way the individual comes to appearance inasmuch as it is not simply an instance of the universal, but that which is actual in and for itself. On the other hand, the talk of art that has itself become absolute signifies the freedom of a work of art in the face of a history to which the figures of religious consciousness meanwhile also belong.

With his formulation of the "essential simultaneity of all art," Gadamer already indicated how this freedom of the work of art is to be experienced. This formulation does not merely suggest that the works of absolute art can, even if they stem from different epochs, exist side by side and in this way constitute the well-known context of a *musée imaginaire*. Above all, the formulation designates the relationship of these works to their readers, listeners, and viewers. It takes off from the accessibility of the works, which is not mediated historically. Where one engages a work of art, one must, as Gadamer says, "not know from what past, from what distance and foreignness one encounters something." Rather, the work has "its presence and will not be considered to be something foreign, but rather draws one into its spell—there might also at first be a great deal that is foreign which must be overcome" (WB, 376). A work of art that addresses us addresses us immediately, and in this way reveals its binding force. By saying more precisely what this binding force consists in, one makes, at the same time, the absoluteness and the unhistorical character of art more comprehensible.

To this end, it is helpful to take up Gadamer's reference to the possible foreignness of the work of art once more. Without this, the experience of art would hardly have the character of a claim.

A work that immediately and directly closes off its own possibilities for understanding never even appears as a work of art. It would be obvious and would, in this way, only allow itself simply to be incorporated into the context of one's life and one's way of understanding the world. Correspondingly, only what is not obvious, only what falls outside of, or is external to, the context of what is familiar can be challenging. The foreign is therefore the initial form of that which makes a claim upon understanding.

However, one can only engage what is challenging in this sense when it is something which addresses us at the same time. The promise of comprehensibility must be bound up with it, that is to say, what appears as something foreign must be able to demonstrate that it is comprehensible in the experience of one's own interpretation, elucidation, and understanding, without it thereby becoming obvious.

With this something essential has been said about the character of what appears as foreign. One will not do justice to what is foreign, in the sense sketched above, if one traces it back to what is proper to oneself or if one is able to integrate it successfully into a context with which one personally has nothing to do and in this way is successful in explaining the foreign. Both deprive the foreign of the possibility of being challenging. Its claim is ignored when one allows it to disappear into the obvious, or if one lets it pass as something that is different from what is proper to oneself.

A usual way in which the latter is enacted is historical ordering. Where one believes one has overcome the foreign by having placed it in a putatively appropriate historical context, one has overplayed and concealed the conditions characteristic of understanding. One conceals the only situation in which the explanation could have offered a way out. The explanation could even be correct; nevertheless, the matter is not advanced, and instead, as Gadamer remarks, "the experience of art is harmed by the self-gratification of historical education" (WB, 377).

The integration of something into the obviousness of the context of one's own life and the fixing of the foreign within the framework of historical knowledge often belong together—and always whenever a matter is so complex that it is not simply obvious or completely, and hence in an indifferent manner, foreign. The foreign that is challenging appears as something comprehensible, and the attempt to make good on its comprehensibility can be enacted in the difference between the comprehensible and foreign elements. Where that occurs under historical premises, historical consciousness first actually becomes manifest. It emerges as historical consciousness is caught in the schema of time. Historical consciousness cannot express itself other than in the distinction between the present and the past, and then the possibility of a nostalgic flight from the present into the alleged authenticity of the past is just as possible as the limited and self-righteous attack of the present on the past. One disrespects oneself in one's own present, or everything that is not obvious and cannot be reconciled with the representations and institutions of the present becomes a victim of the overestimation of the present.

One can see, at the outset, how absolute art stands in relation to this. No work of art is capable of impeding the one-sidedness of historical consciousness. However, works of art do provide a standard which allows this one-sidedness as such actually to be identified, and, what is more important, works of art open up another possibility for the experience of the historical. Its binding force is constituted by both. In art the historical can unfold as something meaningful, so that one is capable of engaging with its meaning by experiencing works of art. Works of art pull us out of what belongs to daily life and is obvious. They open up the possibility to have experiences that are not already prefigured in what is usual and familiar. And no less do they present the foreign, hence also the historical, in such a way that it no longer appears in its previous context. What is encountered in works of art is released from its historical context, just as the spectator must step forth out of his immediate present, in order to adequately relate to the work. The work belongs neither to an earlier time, nor to a present that is distinct from such a time. Seen from the perspective of historical consciousness, it constitutes, as it were, neutral ground. It is the ground upon which one can encounter the past as someone who lives in the present, upon which the past can appear as present. For this reason, the experience of the historical is possible in those works of art that are neither given over to the historical, nor are self-righteously orientated to the present; for this reason works of art offer an experience of one's own present which is open to the historical.

When the present is elevated above itself and the past achieves a presence that addresses the present, it emerges that both cohere without either being an element of a homogeneous or continuous whole. The past need not be reconstructed as the prehistory of the present and the present need not position itself in the tradition of the past in order for the coherence of the two to become apparent. Rather, in its presence the works create constellations of the past and the present; they show how little present experience is exhausted by the obvious, and they indicate the past in such a way that the manner of pointing to what comes later becomes clear. In art that "hidden index" emerges which, as Walter Benjamin said, carries the past with it in order to be referred to redemption.[8] The "secret agreement between past generations and our own" is codified in works of art.[9] (694/254). By means of a characteristic shortening and shading, but also in their peculiar breadth and precision, these works keep open a context which can no longer be understood on the basis of the opposition between the proper and the foreign. It is a context in which the tension between the proper and the foreign can be played out in such a way that the proper, in its confrontation with the foreign, is transformed and reconstituted once more, and the foreign as such only appears in that it addresses and challenges the proper. It is a context that refers the present to the past and gives the past the possibility to lead that which is in the present out of its narrowness. Under the presupposition that one can understand this context of an interpretative existence as a world, one can say of the works of absolute art that they represent a world.

One certainly must elucidate what this means more precisely, even if it has already clearly emerged that we are not here thinking of a copy of an existing world that is otherwise immediately accessible. If, instead, one understands by the representation of a world the explicit presentation of a context of life, it then appears that the distinction between absolute and nonabsolute art has not been considered satisfactorily. For it is precisely nonabsolute art, such as painting that is tied to a particular space; architecture; poetry understood as a form of social play; or music appropriate to the courtyard of a grand house, a church, or a bourgeois home that allows the particular contexts of life to be experienced. Art of this type is itself even the preeminent manner to enact a life within a context and, at the same time, to allow it to become manifest. Absolute art is clearly not world representation in this sense. It no longer constitutes its absoluteness by being bound within the context of aristocratic, religious, or bourgeois life. Nevertheless, the relationship of absolute art and the world can be determined in connection with it.

Where art becomes absolute, an essential possibility of world representation and world experience is clearly lost; this is surely what Hegel meant in his thesis on the end of art. But if one does not wish to grant that this is equivalent to the loss of the world in general or that art has thereby lost its meaning with respect to the world, a new relationship with the world is established by art becoming absolute. One could describe it as world representation which is enacted as the disclosure of the world. It is a world representation that seeks to investigate the world from continually changing points of view and ever-new perspectives, and the details and supplements bound up with them.

It is not difficult to recognize these reflections as variations of Heidegger's view of art as the "setting up of a world."[10] On the one hand, however, Heidegger did not mean this in the sense of an absolute art, and on the other hand, Heidegger grants much more to art and demands much more from it. As the example of the Greek temple which he employs demonstrates, art for Heidegger is world representation in the sense that it makes explicit a context of life in its unity; the work of art "fits together" and "gathers" life in its significance—that is, the "paths and relations" characteristic of a context of life, (GA 5:27–28/42). However, art is only in a position to do this, Heidegger thinks, insofar as its works open up the context of a world. Because this opening up is a happening of the origin, art is not merely able to represent the world anew, rather it essentially sets up a new world. Art is the production of a world.

What is problematic about this thought is its radicalness. In particular, it does not do justice to the manifold and multiplicity of works of art. If the temple actually opens up a world, if Hölderlin's poetry is really in a position to establish a new relationship to the gods who have been and thus to decisively mark the historical situation, then there is no longer a need for other works of art once this has taken place.[11] At the very least, they could not constitute a world in the same way, and then one asks oneself what their character as art actually consists of.

In order to be able to constitute a world, including its religious relations, art would have to be absolute in a sense other than the modern. If it were fixed in an already open world, it could not have the character of an origin that is able to bring something new into existence that Heidegger wants to attribute to it. However, where a new world arises by means of art and is now open as a world, it would have to again lose its absoluteness; henceforth it would have to allow the constituted world explicitly to become manifest. In other words, Heidegger grounds religious experience in art in order to understand art solely on the basis of the religiousness articulated through it.

However, if one grasps the particular achievement of absolute art as the disclosure of a world, this indicates that the world is experienced explicitly with the works of art in an unmistakable, irreplaceable, and unsurpassable manner. But where something merely becomes explicit, it does not then first come into being. Where the world is not produced by means of art in the Heideggerian sense, this process of disclosure precedes the disclosedness of the world. By contrast, that which has always already been disclosed first shows itself to be what it is in its particular disclosure. Absolute art is the confirmation of something which, for all that, one cannot experience in a determinate and articulated manner without it.

In order to answer the question of how this is to be thought more precisely, it is apposite to defer this question for the moment and pursue another question which will prove to be closely related to it, namely, the question of what the status of a work of art actually is. Gadamer has answered this question with a pithy sentence: "Art is in performance [*Die Kunst ist im Vollzug*]" (WB, 391). This means that art does not fulfill itself in a work in such a way that one can understand the work as a manifestation of a type of knowledge that is separate from the productive process and derives its meaning from it. And correspondingly, when one genuinely experiences a work of art, one does not remain at a distance, judging a finished product which one then begins to use. What one designates as the production of a work of art by means of the problematic analogy with productive craftsmanship, with *téchne*, has, in addition, the character of a world disclosive experience for the artist himself. Drawing and painting, writing verse and poetry, and even improvisation and composition are enactments of understanding and interpretation which articulate themselves in production without having their essence lie in mere manufacturing. And correspondingly, the experience of a work consists in engaging in understanding and interpretation, the only means by which the work can actually manifest itself.

Just how little the work of art is something autonomous will perhaps become clearest in understanding and interpretation, which explicitly have the character of representation. To read a work of poetry or perform a piece of music is a relationship to the work in which the work is what it is only in the enactment of performance. One must attend to the work completely if the representation is to succeed. And this holds true also for understanding and interpretation in the sense of reading, listening, and contemplation. Whoever reads a novel ought, while reading, to be able to forget the author. Where this is not possible, it speaks against the novel. If such an absorption in the enactment of the work is also essential to the activity of the artist, one could in fact, like Gadamer, speak of the "hidden sameness of the creation and the absorption" (WB, 391). One could also cite Jorge Luis Borges, who, in the dedication of his first volume of poetry, addresses the reader and declares it to be a meaningless and contingent fact "that you are the reader of these exercises and I the author."[12]

Clearly we have not adequately determined the performative meaning [*Vollzugssinn*] characteristic of art. In order to do justice to the essence of production and experience in their sameness, the enactment of both must be described in such a manner that their directedness to the work is considered to the same degree as the bond between the work and its enactment. In order to grasp the "way of being of the work of art" in this sense, Gadamer introduces the Aristotelian concep of '*enérgia*' and understands it, in turn, against the background of the concept of 'becoming toward being' introduced in Plato's *Philebus*, which needs to be understood differently than that of 'being in becoming' (WB, 385–87). What is meant by this is that what is determinate only emerges in movement, just as movement is always the movement of something determinate. The work first emerges in the movement of creation or performance, and at the same time it is this which first allows the movement to be this particular thing. With every stroke upon the canvas, with every sentence he forms, the artist is bound to something which he first makes accessible through his activity—which he creates. Whoever contemplates a picture or reads a piece of poetry proceeds in the same manner, but with the difference that he engages with an ordered framework in order to provide the work with the movement appropriate to it. In both cases there is an interplay between an effective element and the actual movement, and this is what Gadamer's reference to the idea of *enérgia* seeks to make plausible. Just as the experience of the completed work in its derminateness, the enactment of production is always what it is and constitutes, at the same time, the being of that which it has always been. In this manner the binding force of the work of art can be grasped without making it autonomous in an inappropriate way.

But if one does not wish to defend the reification or objectification of a work of art, one ought not overlook a difficulty with the thesis that the being of art consists in its enactment. When Aristotle elucidates the essence of *enérgia*, it becomes clear that in the case of its effective as well as its actual elements, phases of movement are at issue. One sees and has always seen, one thinks and has clearly always thought (*Metaphysics*, 1048b 30–35). It is difficult to dispute that the effective character of the work cannot be grasped in its essence in this way; accordingly, the coherence of the effective and the actual elements here must also be understood otherwise. In contrast with the enactment which is proper to it, the work of art is unique.

The singularity of the work in contrast with how it is experienced becomes explicit in the experience of the work itself as soon as it is repeated. Then the inexhaustibility of a work of art becomes apparent. It reveals that one can see every picture in a different way, every poem can be read otherwise, every piece of music can be heard or performed differently. No matter how different these experiences also are, they nevertheless remain the experiences of the same work. In its sameness the work, in turn, resists being grasped directly. The work itself cannot be placed next to experiences of it, but rather always only shows itself in experience.

The relationship of work and experience can now be determined by designating the work as the free-space of its possible experiences and by grasping the experiences as representations of this free-space. The ordered framework of the work allows for particular possibilities of representation, and in every representation this framework of possibilities emerges in a particular way. Hence the free-space of the work is only actual in the enactment of its representation. However, the enactment of representation belongs to the free-space of the work.

While the experience of a work of art is bound to the work as its free-space, it is nevertheless distinct from the productive activity of the artist. In the discovery and the production of a particular form of work, the artist might be bound to the outline which he makes of the work form—he might carefully follow the stubborn properties of the material itself—yet one will not be able to say that the artist, in his activity, represents the free-space of a work. He first produces this free-space so that others will be able to represent it. It is, to return once more to Borges, perhaps truly a "contingent fact" that the reader is not the poet. But if he were to become the writer of the text which he is reading, he could no longer be the dedicatee of the work, the reader in the sense of one who is addressed. By playfully taking the reader into his confidence and suggesting that he feels himself to be the author, Borges makes this distinction evident to the reader of the written text, who no longer needs the author.

Nevertheless, it remains true that no work of art is simply the autonomous product of a productive process. It remains true that artistic activity does not exhaust itself in production; it is a form of understanding and interpretation which is enacted in the mode of production, and in this it is in fact again similar to the experience of the work of art. With his productive work, the artist allows possibilities of life to first become present. The form that is expressed in the telling of a story, for example, is concurrently an understanding and interpretation of this story—the understanding and interpretation of a context which could also have been expressed otherwise. By emphasizing particular elements and repressing others, by creating particular continuities and relations, there first emerges what one understands as the story that has been told. But a context emerges that is known to the narrator and to a certain extent is familiar to him, without his being able to express it otherwise than by means of the telling of particular stories. This context first acquires a form by being told. The past, which has determined the present in a manner that is for

the most part opaque and that clearly or less clearly remains preserved in memory and influences thinking and imagination, becomes explicit by being told. At the same time, the disclosure of
something present has established itself as true in the "plastic
power"[13] of formation and construction. From the infinite possibilities for action within the context of one's life, one has now been
determined.

One can also express this by saying that here the world has
taken a definite form and has come to be represented as something definite. The disclosedness of a play-space of possibilities of
understanding oneself and the context of one's own existence coa-
lesces, together with an openness to this context, into a constellation in which both elements become determinate. However, in the
work of art they become manifest as a constellation in order to remain open to further experiences. Where the understanding and
interpretation of the artist manifests itself in the work, it transforms itself and becomes the play-space for further experiences.

One will be referred to the play-spaces opened up by the works
of art all the more vigorously the more complex the possibilities of
a world are and the less fixed the openness to it is. Where a world
no longer can be experienced in its institutions, or at least no
longer directly, where the ties that decisively determine the understanding of being-in-the-world withdraw, where, therefore, to
speak with Nietzsche, the world has "once again become 'infinite'
insofar as we cannot reject the possibility that it contains infinite
interpretations" (*GS*, 374), works of art can be determinative if
only for the reason that they prove themselves to be the play-
spaces of understanding and interpretation. In their determinate
form they draw a boundary for the experience of the world and in
this way disclose the world in a particular horizon. What is disclosed in this world is itself once again quite clearly capable of
many, ultimately infinite, interpretations. However, these interpretations are bound to the form of the work and are tied thereby
to the sameness of its play-space. The play-space of works, in
turn, is the disclosed representation of a world horizon. Only
when works of art become detached from the world in which they
have arisen and by so doing acquire their absoluteness, can they
disclose this world within the boundaries of a form.

Naturally it is a question of whether and how art is able to be
establish itself in its absoluteness. The idle exercises of an old and

sterile avant-gardism can just as little be convincing here as the market- and media-dominated presentations of what is pleasant and sensational. As a standard for what is here demanded and what, in great works, is achieved, we can look to what Gadamer, in a clear reference to Paul Celan, calls a "speech crystal" [*Sprachkristall*]. This word designates how it is "whenever the stream of speech achieves a valid form in poetry." And, Gadamer continues, "as the crystal in its formation and the fixity of its structure begins to emit its fire whenever light falls upon it, so it is also the linguistic achievement of poetry that it approaches the hardness, fixity and the constancy of the crystal and does not captivate by means of a pleasant form, but rather through a flash of light" (WB, 371–72). By understanding a text of the kind that is meant here, one understands more than the text. In this sense Gadamer's reflections can be developed through an image of Ernst Jünger: "The transparent formation is the one which concurrently illuminates depth and surface to our gaze. It can be studied in the crystal, which one could designate as an entity that is capable both of constructing an inner surface and of turning its depths outwards" (*AH* 2, *SW* 9:182).

10

History as Destiny and the Presence of History
Determining Philosophy with and without Hegel

Philosophy is not possible today without considering its history. No matter how diverse the questions and orientations may be, none of them is so obvious and self-contained that they can be represented convincingly without a view to their presuppositions and origins. Anglo-Saxon philosophy has also recently attempted to justify itself historically.[1] In the debates of continental thought the historical perspective is built-in, as it were, and in a manner which can easily be recognized today. Where the possibility of a "postmetaphysical thought" is considered and debated, one thinks within a historical schema, irrespective of whether one's approach is deconstructive, discursive-theoretical, skeptical, a cautious antirealism, a form of transcendental pragmatism or a search for ultimate foundations. One must justify one's own tradition when it is no longer obviously valid, but one must also engage traditions when one wishes to think against them, without them, or otherwise than them. And finally, even if one could avoid becoming engaged in the history of philosophy, it would not be very clever to do so. For as Hans-Georg Gadamer has remarked, it is a weakness of philosophical thought when one does not seek to test oneself against the tradition "and prefers to play the independent fool."[2] What one thinks oneself has usually already been thought elsewhere and often more subtly than one could work it out oneself. Philosophical avant-gardism, which can only comprehend the most modern thing, is foundationless; its tempo is the *furioso* of the ephemeral.

Contemporary philosophy is, therefore, historical, and as historical philosophy it still remains in the shadow or light of Hegel. For Hegel made philosophy historical; he created a situation in which, philosophically, one did not merely look to the history of philosophy secondarily. Since Hegel one experiences what this means in a different manner than Aristotle or Plato. One considers the opinions of one's predecessors not merely to clarify the sphere of one's own questions and then get on with the real work at hand. The confrontation with earlier thought is not merely a means to refute or bolster an unquestionably contemporary position. Rather, one thinks with Plato or Aristotle, with Kant or Nietzsche, with Heidegger or Husserl, with Frege or Wittgenstein, and in the process one acknowledges, more or less explicitly, more or less decisively, the authority of earlier thinkers.

The particular difficulty of historical thought is rather apparent when one considers that everything which is encountered in historical consciousness possesses a particular ambiguity. What is experienced as having a binding power has, at the same, its bindingness threatened here. For this reason there is hardly a question more significant or treacherous for historical philosophy than that of the "contemporary relevance" of a thinker or a theory. With this question one asserts, willingly or unwillingly, that something is historical, and yet not just historical, that something is possibly of some importance to the present, but just possibly, because in itself it belongs to another time. With this question of contemporary relevance, historical thought exposes itself by explicitly recognizing its insecurity. History belongs to those who come later, but it does not simply belong to them.

The question of contemporary relevance has a certain affinity with the question of the aesthetic significance of a work of art. What is aesthetically meaningful demands the attention of a reader, an observer, or a listener because it cannot immediately be assimilated into the context of her life. The aesthetic does not belong in a world which is certain, in a rather obvious way, of its taste and its judgment; for this reason it can also remain part of an art collection or an archival record. Aesthetic consciousness belongs together with the institution of a museum, through which one can stroll almost indifferently. In the same way, historical thought proceeds with a concern for the tradition in which one always has to confront the nonbindingness of what is handed down.

Since philosophy has become historical it has not suffered from a lack of attempts to overcome the difficulties sketched above. For nothing less is at stake than the persuasive power of philosophy after its historicization. It contradicts the essence of philosophy to be subject to the criterion of contemporary relevance. Philosophical efforts which can be historically relativized in their entirety lose their meaning. After its historicization, philosophy is dependent upon its ability to successfully elucidate historical consciousness in a manner compatible with the essence of philosophy. It cannot withdraw into the history of philosophy and thereby become ignorant with respect to the issue at hand, namely, philosophical thought that is oriented to genuine philosophical issues. And it cannot reduce itself, in the manner of the hit parade, to being concerned with only that which pleases the public, without suffering the loss of every possibility of being understood. Any philosopher who wants to be trendy has already lost.

With respect to an elucidation of historical consciousness compatible with the essence of philosophy, Hegel undertook such a project when he allowed philosophy to become historical and to come forth in its historicity. Hegel conceived of a philosophical history of philosophy by means of which he wanted to oppose the danger of assimilating philosophy into history by giving a philosophical interpretation of history. One always does well to begin with Hegel if one wants to grasp the relationship of philosophy and history. For even if one disputes Hegel's solution or remains skeptical in the face of it, Hegel's account elucidates the structure of historical consciousness so clearly that one is given the possibility in connection with Hegel of understanding the inception and justification for later attempts to solve this problem. With Hegel modern philosophy begins, a philosophy which has an essential relation to history. And with Hegel philosophy begins to assert its modernity. Hegel saw the difficulties of such a philosophical self-assertion so clearly that he also prepared the ground for a critique of his own solution. One can better think without Hegel by first thinking with him.

In the introduction to his "Lectures on the History of Philosophy," Hegel clearly formulated the decisive problem of his undertaking:

> The thought which may first occur to us in the history of philosophy, is that the subject itself contains *an inner contradiction*. For philosophy aims at understanding what is unchangeable, eternal, in and for itself: its end is *truth*. But history tells us of that which has at one time existed, at another time has vanished, having been expelled by something else. Truth is eternal; it does not fall within the sphere of the transient, and has no history. But if it has a history, and as this history is only the representation of a succession of past forms of knowledge, the truth is not to be found in it, for the truth cannot be what has passed away.[3]

In his outline of a philosophical history of philosophy, Hegel attempts to reconcile the "inner contradiction" of truth and history. Upon closer inspection it becomes quite clear that Hegel merely succeeds in underscoring this inner contradiction in all its sharpness. Without wanting to do so, he demonstrates the inner contradiction between truth and history as their truth.

However, in order to see this truth is it necessary to first engage Hegel's conception. Hegel's conception rests upon the conviction that the history of philosophy is to be understood as a *development* and contemporary philosophy as its *product*. As a result of the historical process, contemporary philosophy is "the latest, most recent, most modern philosophy [*die neueste Philosophie*]," as Hegel describes it, but at the same time the "most developed, the richest and the most profound" (61/41). And even if hardly anyone else would make the same assertion, it would be false to take this formulation as evidence of Hegel's inflated sense of self-importance. That the most modern philosophy is the "richest and most profound" is explained by the state of its development, and with regard to this there is in fact no philosophy which developed upon a richer historical foundation. However, that does not mean that the most modern philosophy would necessarily also do justice to the state of its development, for it also can lag behind what it actually is.

What Hegel says to elucidate the concept of 'development' is also true of the most modern philosophy: "That which is in itself must become an object for human beings, must arrive at consciousness; in this way it comes to exist for human beings" (40/21). What it is in itself will first come to exist *for* the most modern philosophy by its retrospectively assuring its own development. Its richness must be weighed, its profundity measured—only then is the most modern philosophy truly itself. The fact that it is also the most developed signifies to the most modern philosophy not an accomplishment, but a task. For this reason Hegel weighs his words carefully when he speaks of the most modern philosophy in the form of an imperative: "In it everything which at first appears to be past must be preserved and retained; it must itself be a mirror of the whole of history" (61/41).

The question, whether the most modern philosophy is not overwhelmed by the demand that it be a mirror of the whole of history, thus renewing the suspicion of inflated self-importance, should be taken up first. This question has an obvious answer if we first clarify more precisely how Hegel conceives of the preservation of the past in contemporary thought [*gegenwärtiges Denken*]. To this end one ought, in turn, pay attention to the meaning of the splendid metaphor of the mirror that Hegel introduces here. A mirror and what is reflected in it are essentially *distinct*, and if the past is reflected in the present, then the past remains the Other with respect to the present. It appears that the highest and ultimate goal of Spirit, as Hegel says, that Spirit "unites with itself" (41–42/23) is not reached with the reflection of the past in the present.

This view is, from the beginning, contradicted by Hegel's ideas. It only appears that the process of mirroring is not a unity if one does not think the unity of Spirit as Hegel wants to understand it. For Hegel does not at all have in mind a simple sameness in which all difference disappears. Rather, the unity of present and past consists in the fact that the past, as the present, appears in its Otherness or, as Hegel himself puts it, "that for which the Other is, is the same as the Other" (41/23). Present and past are the same, but the past is the same as the past insofar as it is in the present in a different manner.

In the metaphor of the mirror one can see the following thoughts: what is mirrored is in fact identified with its mirror image. It is the same, but merely appears elsewhere and then upside down. However, the autonomy of the image and its inversion do not justify us in understanding that which appears as an Other in the sense of something foreign. One only experiences it this way if one does not know what a mirror is and does not recognize one's own image as such. But in thought, Hegel says, "all foreignness [is] transparent, absent; Spirit is absolutely free here" (42/23). The Other is no longer something foreign, but rather a part of oneself. Spirit is not bound to anything which would be other than itself. It is independent and thereby "absolutely free."

Hegel's thought of a reflection which achieves unity of self-consciousness is so well known that it now appears superfluous to have insisted on the difference of present and past in connection with the metaphor of the mirror. And it would have been superfluous if the idea of knowledge of oneself in Otherness could simply be reconciled with his determination of the relationship between present and past. That, however, is not the case.

When Hegel says that the present must be a mirror of the whole of history, then history is that which is reflected while the mirror image appears in the present. If one connects this with the thought of self-knowledge in Otherness, then one must also understand the philosophical history of philosophy, as Hegel wants to write it, as a form of self-knowledge of history, and not of the present. It would be more precise to say that contemporary philosophy, the most modern philosophy, recognizes itself in history. Contemporary thought recognizes itself, then, by looking into the mirror of history.

But Hegel does not say this, and for good reason. If the most modern philosophy is the product of a historical development and its richness and profundity lie in nothing more than in this development, then the most modern philosophy is actually nothing which could be reflected. It itself has no content which could be compared with the content of past philosophies; it does not have a proper face which could appear to it as an image in the mirror of the past. Considered from the perspective of content, the most modern philosophy is nothing that could be grasped for itself. Where one is not fully aware of this, one engages in prophetic attempts to determine the "present situation" or the "present state of things." One wants to determine historically that which resists historical concretization. The self-historicization of the present is no less absurd than the attempt to view one's own back by quickly turning around.

What distinguishes the contemporary, most modern philosophy from the philosophy of the past is, for Hegel, not its content but rather its form. This form even represents "an enormous difference" (40/21). This difference consists in the fact that the philosophy of the past has, in the most modern philosophy, ceased being part of the past. The most modern philosophy should, as we have noted, preserve and embody "what at first *appears* as past of the past." Everything that has been preserved is contemporary, and it only appears to be part of the past if for some reason it no longer fits into the present, like a tool one no longer has any use for today or a piece of clothing that has gone out of fashion.

However, the "scientific products of reason" are not of this kind: they "are not things that belong to the past" (57/39). The products of reason can have their place only in thought, in the enactment of thought, which can be nothing but contemporary. For to critically engage an idea means to take it seriously in the present, and in this sense to experience it in the present. This is not equivalent to the interpretation of texts that have been handed down, even if the interpretation of texts is, at the same time, a necessary presupposition of historical philosophical thought. It is something different, because for thought the thought itself is what counts. It is true that one becomes acquainted with it in connection with the text, but the thought is then taken up on its own. One can, for example, speak about Plato's doctrine of ideas from the perspective of the historian, but one cannot understand Plato's texts from this perspective. When one understands his texts, one critically engages with their ideas in a manner that is not quite positive. This occurs in thought alone.

Hegel gives expression to this idea when he describes the products of reason as "effects and works which are neither negated nor destroyed by subsequent ones." He continues as follows: "They have neither canvas nor marble, neither paper, representation, nor memory as media in which they can be preserved. These media are themselves transient, or are the ground for what is transient. Rather, they have thought (the concept), the permanent essence of Spirit, which neither moths nor thieves can penetrate" (58/39). That which initially appears to be part of the past has its presence, therefore, in thought's way of being present. It is a presence, which, if one follows Hegel, cannot be understood temporally. Thought is "the permanent essence," because everything that is thought, that is thought philosophically, can only be illuminating or implausible, enlightening or unimportant, but not old or bygone. Contemporary thought is the mirror of the past, which allows the traces of time to disappear without becoming beautiful or flattering. The mirror image of the past is its only authentic image.

At the same time, however, this image is also the sole content of contemporary thought. "The conquests of thought, when constituted into thought, make up," as Hegel says, "the being of Spirit itself" (58/39). Contemporary thought is also comparable to a mirror in that from the perspective of its content it is only what appears in it. Using another metaphor which is perhaps more helpful in making the idea comprehensible, one could speak of contemporary thought as a *space of appearance*. In its way of being present, thought is a space for the appearance of a past, which has lost its pastness by becoming the content of contemporary thought. And contemporary thought becomes greater and richer in content the less it excludes it, by distinguishing between its content, as something which belongs to the past, and itself. The more contemporary thought allows itself to be a mirror or a space of appearance, the less it will remain dependent upon that which it does not wish to be and which appears opaquely foreign to it. That is, contemporary thought has its freedom as a mirror or a space of appearance. As a mirror or a space of appearance it is, corresponding to Hegel's expression, "absolutely" free, hence not merely free through the negation of another.

The metaphor of the mirror or space of appearance could be misleading in a decisive respect. One should not allow this metaphor to entice one to be of the opinion that the essence of contemporary thought is openness and receptivity. Thought is neither a wax block nor a dovecote,[4] but rather "conceptual thought [*begreifendes Denken*]" (46/27). Of course, the openness to the past is not produced in the present. However, the mirror which thought is, is transformed again and again, as it were, in the enactment of thought, while the space of appearance which it is, is again and again reshaped in the enactment. This occurs to the extent that thought engages what already has been thought in a particular way and does away with the foreign element in a particular way; it occurs in the conceptual articulation of what has been thought, by means of which contemporary thought gains its own voice.

What contemporary thought certainly does not—and cannot—gain by articulating what has been thought are its articulative possibilities. The articulative possibilities of contemporary thought must presuppose the articulation of what has been thought previously, for otherwise it would acquire these possibilities at the same time as what was previously thought; and then one could again only conceive of contemporary thought according to the model of the wax block or the dovecote. Therefore, only two alternatives remain: the articulative possibilities of contemporary thought simply must be particular to it, insofar as it is a type of thought, and then these possibilities would be immutable and the same for every contemporary thought, for each particular philosophy which was the most modern; or the articulative possibilities of contemporary thought are formed as it develops. This corresponds to Hegel's thesis, according to which the most modern philosophy is the product of a development, and of the two alternatives named above, it is quite clearly the more plausible. After Hegel one cannot think in the same way as before him, the same is true after Nietzsche and after Heidegger; this will also be the case after every thinker of comparable rank yet to come.

Hegel knew this, and he expresses this thought when he says: "Every philosophy is the philosophy of its time, a link in the whole chain of spiritual development; it can, therefore, only satisfy those interests which are appropriate to its time" (65/45). The consequences of this are very great. If one accepts the temporal limitation of contemporary thought, that which has been handed down is not understood once and for all in the present, but rather the way it is understood corresponds to the particular state of "intellectual development." This state of development is, as it were, the material, the substance, of which the mirror of thought in its changing particularity consists.

With this the point is reached at which the "inner contradiction" Hegel spoke of in reference to the history of philosophy comes to the fore. It is evident in the fact that contemporary philosophy brings the past to presence, and yet is itself not atemporal. In the mirror of contemporary thought what is thought loses its temporal character, and yet the mirror itself is temporally determined. In this way the temporal proves itself to be the ground of timeless presence; timeless presence is temporally conditioned.

To be sure, this is a conflict for Hegel only so long as one does not see how time and presence here cohere. Hegel's attempt to demonstrate this coherence is tantamount to his attempt to resolve the conflict. For him it is a matter of showing "that the entire history of philosophy is an inherently necessary and consistent progression" (55/35). If the history of philosophy as a whole leads to the most modern philosophy, the richest and the most profound, then it leads to the philosophical possibilities of articulation in which the history of philosophy as a whole is articulated. And thus Hegel also believes that he could make plausible the understanding of history as self-consciousness in the form of contemporary thought. In the mirror of contemporary thought the development of the mirror itself is reflected, and it is ensured that the history of philosophy which has been understood is understanding itself in its Otherness. Thus the inner conflict of the unity of self-consciousness is resolved.

It is a sign of Hegel's integrity that he himself formulated the first steps of the decisive objection against his attempted resolution. That is to say, Hegel's resolution of the inner contradiction of time and presence, of history and contemporary thought, does not represent the end of philosophy, to say nothing of the end of historical periods—Hegel had nothing to do with fantastic ideas of any sort. At the end of his *Lectures on the History of Philosophy*, Hegel characterizes the "standpoint of the present time" and says that "with it the series of spiritual forms is concluded for now" (20:461/3:552). Note that Hegel says merely "for now." Corresponding to this is the remark from the introduction, made with methodical caution, that the continuation of philosophical development has "an absolute goal, *too*" (54/35; my italics). In addition, Hegel says with all the clarity one might ask for that conceptual thought does not stand outside the development of Spirit: "Philosophy," Hegel says, "is . . . for itself the apprehension of this development and, as conceptual thought, is this development in thought" (46/27).

Conceptual thought is itself development. But this also means that by extending the history of thought into the present, conceptual thought takes it one step beyond that which was understood hitherto. Just as no one can obtain essential insights into her own life without having this knowledge change her life, so, too, an understanding of philosophical development cannot be without consequences for the articulative possibilities of philosophy. But the substance of the mirror does not itself then appear in the mirror. By articulating itself, contemporary understanding has already exceeded the development hitherto. The particular enactment of understanding cannot be comprehended on the basis of what it has understood.

There is yet another rather different reason for the fact that contemporary thought cannot understand itself as a product of what is understood within it. Hegel's thesis that contemporary thought can be experienced as the product of a development is not merely contradicted by the development of thought in time, but also by its way of being present. Hegel's thesis implies that every subsequent philosophy that does not undercut the position of an earlier one, has preserved the earlier philosophy within itself. Aristotle's philosophy is then the truth of Plato's philosophy. But we know that Plato's philosophy can also be the truth of Aristotle's philosophy. A philosophy can have the effect of allowing us to read the earlier philosophy itself in a new way and to see it in particular respects as equal, if not superior to, the later. This shows that the schema of development is suited, in a quite limited way, to understanding the relationship of philosophical conceptions to one another. Philosophies whose rank is comparable at all do not, at the very least, stand in a merely effective relationship to one another, but rather they can and must be read and interpreted as supplements of previous philosophies; alternatives are also supplements in this sense. This is even one of the consequences of Hegel's idea that past thought ceases to appear as something past in the mirror of the present. Great ideas are contemporaneous with one another. This is what allows us, for example, fruitfully to consider Aristotle and Kant jointly from a systematic perspective. Every systematic interpretation which presents philosophical reflections from diverse times annuls the historical ordering. Rather, philosophical conceptions belong in the simple presence, as is their lot in the light of the present.

If this is the case, then contemporary thought can interpret the philosophical conceptions of the past only at the cost of narrowly fitting them into a strictly linear development, which leads up to contemporary thought itself. Instead, contemporary thought sees itself faced with the task of considering its evaluations always as possible ones and to seeing the contemporary past as a field in which to articulate itself as contemporary thought. The past does not let itself be forced into the domesticated mold of a previous history; it cannot be exhausted in any one particular articulation. This is due to the mirror of the present, in which fundamentally everything past must appear, even if its present might only be capable of being articulated in a particular respect. Contemporary thought is always richer than its particular determinateness. By being the realm of appearance in which the past appears, it is at the same time the *play-space* of its particular articulation. It is, to employ a concept of Heidegger, not merely interpretation, but also disclosedness.

For this reason, contemporary thought can never take a closed form. For as the ideas are articulated by means of a particular present, they assume rough edges. Every particular image which is projected by a contemporary thought is characterized by the particular inclination of the mirror; therefore, to see it more sharply is to see it as something else. Foreground and background are arranged differently in every present. Rediscoveries or renaissances are possible only because certain forms of thought at various times retreat into the background without actually becoming lost.

Thus the play-space of thought impresses itself in every present in a highly particular way, and yet the play-space of contemporary thought itself is not the only thing which plays a role in explicit understanding. To be sure, one only observes the play-space in a perspectival, detailed form, just as one experiences a city perspectively as one moves through its streets. However, in a city essentially every street can be reached. As different as are the paths one takes, every path belongs to the whole of the city that is disclosed. Whoever chooses a particular path knows that the path belongs to a net of paths and streets. In this way every thought belongs to the whole of what has and can be thought. Everything that has been thought can be thought anew; nothing thinkable can be so new that it would not belong within the framework of what has been thought. However unmistakable and singular the philosophy of a particular period might always be, it is only because it is a perspectival representation of philosophy in general that it can be discovered again in other perspectives. If it were otherwise, one would be forced to say that with each perspective philosophy forms itself completely anew. Every material coherence of different conceptions would then be illusory. This assumption would be the end of philosophical interpretation.

How thought expresses itself in the play-space of the present depends upon how, in each particular case, contemporary thought is the product of the past. That it is a product of the past can hardly be doubted. At the very least, every thought expresses itself in concepts not of its own making, and where thought has coined its concepts, it has received what it has then transformed. No thought begins first with itself, and it is part of being in the present to know this. In every act of understanding one experiences how concepts themselves are transformed, enriched, and made more subtle by the process of understanding. One experiences that the past has an effect when one turns to it. In no present does philosophy itself produce the questions which it elucidates, the problems which is seeks to solve. The past would be incomprehensible if the existing possibilities of understanding did not belong to it. Every contemporary thought is the product of the past.

But it nevertheless remains equally true that no contemporary thought can understand itself as this product. Every act of understanding is a constellation of concepts and what can be understood. Every act of understanding demonstrates the coherence of concepts and what can be understood. It is just for this reason that the concepts themselves cannot be understood on the basis of, or from, what has been understood. The past affects contemporary thought, but how it operates remains, because of its effect and in its effect, hidden. Conceptual thought is representative, and as it represents it is not present as something particular. Concepts which genuinely disclose the past are not *present* as something which can themselves be grasped, but rather they *make present* in light of the present, in the play-space of present possibilities.

To the extent that contemporary thought is the product of the past, it is in a substantial sense historical—historical in what it is. Understood in this way, its historicity has the character of a destiny; it is, to speak with Goethe, the law according to which the present appears. However, when one turns to the past in the present, one does not encounter the genuine, substantial historicity, rather history appears in the present. History is presented as the disclosed domain which one experiences and articulates as the play-space of thought. Its historical substance remains, as it were, behind thought, while it can be in the simple presence which history achieves in the present. This presence is the freedom of thought, and such freedom can exist because destiny hides itself in its operation. Destiny and freedom are, to return to Hegel's metaphor once more, the two sides of the mirror. Only both sides together produce an image.

We are this mirror itself, and if, for this reason, we also do not know what is going on behind our backs, as it were, we nevertheless experience how the past achieves its particular presence in the space of appearance of the mirror. We experience history in the oscillation of this particular presence. Destiny contributes the particularity of this presence, so that the presence itself is represented in history.

However, we do not understand history without the simple presence of contemporary thought. Where we articulate history by understanding the forms of thought according to the order of time, we remain within a simple way of being present. What is encountered in the schema of time and history has, for conceptual thought, already entered presence. Within the schema of history, thought itself is, therefore, a representation of this presence; history represents itself in this presence.

Again and again we experience this divide between time and presence and with it all the uncertainties and imponderability of historical thought. We experience that the historical can be grasped only in present freedom, while it conceals itself in its historical substantiality. We experience that the play-space of freedom gives presence to everything that appears within it, and that we, in its openness, can only exist and pass through it temporally—just as we gradually wander through a city which is present to us as a whole, taking different paths. Time and presence stand in an irreconcilable conflict; only on this account do they play off one another and allow us to be as we are.

The conflict between time and presence, between becoming, passing away, and being, has animated philosophy since its Greek beginning. This has certainly also been the reason why philosophy has remained the same over the centuries. The apologists of being share a common identity just like the apologists of becoming and passing away; they belong in conflict with one another just as the figures of Aristotle and Plato in Raphael's "School of Athens," the one pointing to the earth, the other gesturing to the heavens. Here the conflict becomes visible as a conflict between two thinkers. However, this is only an image. Every great philosophy plays out this conflict, more or less explicitly, within itself.

Hegel wanted to reconcile the two sides of the mirror for the sake of the bindingness of historical thought. He wanted to show that the tain of the mirror could appear in the mirror at the same time. The subject ought to be able to become clear about its own substantiality, so that the subjectivity of contemporary thought, could, in the end, also prove itself to be the actuality of the historical substance.

As we have seen, however, Hegel's intention to reconcile these two elements has confirmed the truth of the conflict. The category of development cannot mediate between the present and history, and thought, therefore, cannot find its historical substance. No thought is capable of ordaining its destiny; no thought begins with what it understands. Because of this inability, every thought, in order to be able to express itself, must be guided by the history that is made present to it. Its freedom, the play-space of the historical thought that has been made present, is the only thing that is open to it. However, it can be guided by history without having to sacrifice its own relativity and independence; every philosophical path belongs to the present play-space of thought. What philosophy is comes to light on every path. The freedom of thought, its play-space, is, at the same time, its bindingness.

11

Last Gods
Hermeneutic Theology in
Nietzsche and Heidegger

— 1. —

A human being cannot say what a god is. For this reason, the persuasive power of the stories about the divine, about God or the gods—myths, therefore—is transitory. As soon as we become conscious of the stories as such, they are subject to doubt and critical questioning. Yet conceptual thought has always attempted to counteract this doubt and to transform this critical questioning into a more or less emphatic recognition. This is the reason why, for as long as there has been philosophy, there have also been different forms of philosophical theology. In order to defend the meaning of the divine stories, it must be possible for their meaning to be articulated conceptually. One must be able to say what a god is in the concepts of philosophy.

Where this claim is made, the strife between conceptual thought and divine stories, between *logos* and *mythos* is naturally renewed. Now thought no longer doubts the meaning of these stories, but rather claims, more or less explicitly, to be able to articulate this meaning better than the stories themselves. By so doing, thought threatens to undermine the meaning of the stories once again, for the stories do not seek to say what the divine is, but merely to

155

give an intimation of it. This is what gives them their persuasive power; however, it also gives rise to doubt and to critical questioning.

The weakness of these stories is that they are equally bad at defending themselves against the critical claims of conceptual thought as against its claims to have more to offer than these stories; but the weakness of conceptual thought is that it can be so faultlessly robust with respect to myths. When a genre such as the divine stories is so quickly crushed in the grip of thought, the damage that is produced ultimately redounds upon the culpable party. It was not able to do justice to the genre to which it turned its attention. The problem lies not in the fragility of the genre, but rather in its destruction.

Because the possibility of enabling different experiences belongs to its essence, conceptual thought does not of course necessarily remain caught within this failed orientation to the nonconceptual articulation of the divine. The failed orientation of conceptual thought can be designated in the very form of this thought. We become aware of it in this way, and in this way it appears as a problem.

Clearly this does not solve the problem. And it is also not solved where conceptual thought simply leaves the stories which it otherwise attempts to decode or exceed to themselves. Even if this occurs as a gesture of recognition, it remains a dressed-up form of indifference, an evasion in which conceptual thought exaggerates its own defeat.

But if not only the grasp of conceptual thought which seeks to unmask or exceed but also its putative reserve are not adequate to myths, if nothing of the sort can shed light upon them, the possibility remains open that conceptual thought will give up any attempt to adapt intentionally to myth and that its failure will lead to a self-transformation. Conceptual thought must transform itself into a thinking that intimates. Such a thinking is adequate to myth because it speaks as myth does.

Correctly understood, this does not mean that thought has become a kind of narrative speech, that *logos* has become *mythos*. Even if such a transformation were possible at all, it would be insincere, because once conceptual thought has constituted itself, it can return to its previous form only by denying itself. A thinking that aspires to intimate like myth should not challenge the abyss which separates it from *mythos*. It can speak *like mythos* only by not attempting to speak *as mythos*.

We can call such a thinking "hermeneutic," at least if we understand the word as Heidegger elucidated it in his "Dialogue on Language."[1] Hermeneutic is then a thinking which expresses that which, at the same time, conceals its occasion from it. It is a thinking that can speak only by silently preserving the relationship to its subject.

That might sound more obscure than it actually is. For although the talk of what is hermeneutic here no longer refers to the problem of a "theory and methodology for every kind of interpretation (*GA* 12:92/11), it is still thought completely from the circumstances of an interpretation. What is at issue in the interpretation of a text is to express the understood meaning of the text. And yet as every experienced interpreter knows, this cannot succeed without there being some gaps and remainders which are not captured by the interpretation, because in the course of interpretation one stays within the context of the text. In this situation, one cannot articulate the context of an interpretation, because the interpretation belongs in its context and is first made possible by it. Texts that require interpretation are always richer than an interpretation. Hence the process of interpretation is always an articulation from a horizon of understanding directed toward a possible understanding.

The structure sketched above takes a more radical form if the interpretation or exegesis is no longer that of a text, but rather is a matter of expressing oneself in one's own way of being. In such a "hermeneutic of facticity," as Heidegger puts it in a lecture course from the summer of 1923, there arises a "possibility for Dasein to be and become for itself in a mode of *understanding*."[2] However, because Dasein is not an object, Heidegger adds that the "evidence character" of an interpretation of one's own being remains "fundamentally labile" (*GA* 63:16). The reason for this lability is not simply the fact that one can never completely objectify oneself, and thus gain an undistorted experience of oneself. It arises no less from language, which is clearly not simply a medium for the articulation of Dasein, but rather allows us to first actually be how we are. Because it is not possible to say what language is completely in language, silence remains an irreducible element of every act of speech. Thinking, however, exists in language and can succeed only if does not resist its linguistic character.

Where thinking becomes hermeneutic, it expresses itself, therefore, by intimation. This suggests, at least initially, that ultimately no other manner of articulation than this one is possible for us. The formation of concepts, too, actually belongs within the realm of hermeneutics; no concept sovereignly grasps its own foundation, but rather remains tied to that about which it must remain silent. The grasping and determinative objectification of the conceptual would not be so effective if its assumptions could be grasped more easily. Yet the context within which one moves is usually the most obvious.

However much they might differ from one another, not only does conceptual thought, considered by itself, remain separated from *mythos* by an abyss, but so does hermeneutic thought. The fact that hermeneutic thought has been through the experience of a purely conceptual thought means that it is marked by the playing out of the strife between *mythos* and *logos*. For this reason, the attempt to speak hermeneutically of the divine will certainly also fail if it is guided by the deceptive hope that it can recapture the immediacy of *mythos*.

If, nevertheless, a hermeneutic thinking does not wish merely to remain silent about the divine and hence fall back into the seemingly sympathetic but actually evasive posture of conceptual thought, it must articulate the experience which it has been through. On the other hand, hermeneutic thinking cannot speak of the experience characteristic of it as one thematizes historical events. For hermeneutic thinking has not finished with *logos*, but rather has it within itself, and it has revoked its actual or possible—always possible—objectification for the sole purpose of being able to express itself as *mythos*. However, *mythos* explicitly continues to be an independent form of speech, distinct from hermeneutic thought, which immediately would fall back into the role of a merely conceptual thought if it were to attempt to relate to *mythos* and the divine of which it speaks from outside. To hermeneutic thought there remains no other choice than for it to speak of the divine in its own manner: in a manner, therefore, which speaks only as *mythos* speaks of the divine and is therefore protected from relating to *mythos* in a way which would do away with or exceed itself, in a manner which does not deny the logical character of thought and yet does not lead to the objectification of understanding.

2.

Heidegger concerned himself with such a highly unusual discourse of the divine, at the very latest since the lecture course on Hölderlin given in the winter of 1934 and 1935.[3] This attempt reached its most concentrated form in the last section of the *Contributions to Philosophy*.[4] What Heidegger here wishes to articulate is neither a new mythology, nor is it in a speculative sense theological. Rather, here the loss of the gods should be endured, and such an experience of the divine should be left open. The godless age in which not merely *mythos*, but also a speculative-theological thinking which exceeds *mythos*, has lost its authority, is itself the possible space for the experience of the "last God," who must be called "the last" if only because he cannot be experienced without the loss of the gods.

For Heidegger, however, our age is not godless because antagonism and indifference with respect to religion are dominant. These are merely symptoms for the inability of conceptual thought, taken by itself, to comply with the divine. The loss of the gods can be endured in thought only if thought engages with this inability. It must confront the impossibility of speculative theology in order to be able to enter the domain of the hermeneutic. Thought can intimate the divine and in this way become hermeneutic only by enacting the rejection of speculative theology within itself.

For this reason, the confrontation with Nietzsche's proclamation of the death of God and what it means is, for Heidegger, of central importance. Heidegger's confrontation with Nietzsche is not an episode in a scholarly history of philosophy. It is also not a distancing from a thinker by means of a different position, but rather a necessary, perhaps even the most important, step within the transformation of thought itself, which it must undergo and enact again and again. With Nietzsche, Heidegger avers, the objectified form of conceptual thought, which he gives the name of *metaphysics*, has entered a stage "that is probably its final stage, for inasmuch as through Nietzsche metaphysics has in a certain sense divested itself of its own essential possibility, other possibilities of metaphysics can no longer appear."[5] The grasping and determinative thought which is concerned with nothing more than grounding and consolidating—the determination of the real— finds, with Nietzsche, a form which cannot be exceeded. For Nietzsche made exceeding into a principle of the real itself and thereby took a final, consequent step within the determinative thought of "metaphysics." At the same time, Nietzsche dragged the position of determinative thought into a dynamic which provided that every attempt to ground the real would be only temporarily credible and thus ultimately groundless. With metaphysics, Nietzsche undermined speculative theology, which for Heidegger means the talk of the death of God.

The interpretation of metaphysics sketched above, and particularly Heidegger's Nietzsche interpretation, have not been accepted without question. That is completely in keeping with Heidegger's intention. Did he not, in the "Dialogue on Language," characterize his "originary appropriation" of the history of thought hitherto as something the "success [of which] can and should be disputed?" (GA 12:104/20). In this sense, one can ask whether what Heidegger calls "metaphysics" is really a self-enclosed system of thought, as it not seldom appears to be in his texts. Correspondingly, one can question whether the popular discourse of a "post-metaphysical" thinking which has arisen in connection with Heidegger is really meaningful. When Heidegger says that his concern has been to bring out "the essence of metaphysics, and only thus [to bring] metaphysics back within its own limits" (GA 12:103–04/20), this suggests, at the same time, an attempt to shake a kind of thought from its objectification without rejecting the subject of this thought. A thought, which in Heidegger's sense would not be metaphysical, must be ultimately richer, not poorer, than "metaphysics," while the positions of a "post-metaphysical" thinking reminds one rather of a philosophical clearance sale.

Because it is Heidegger's concern to shake the objectification of conceptual thought, one could ask him whether this attempt has not been undertaken, at times to great effect, again and again within the tradition characterized as "metaphysical." This could be debated, and it would be a debate which would be carried out in the spirit of Heidegger's thought. But then it would be futile to debate, whether Heidegger and not Nietzsche was the first to overcome "metaphysics," while Heidegger remained within its spell.[6] It would be futile, because the idea of a hermeneutic transformation of thought is no less enlightening, if someone did it before him, and Heidegger himself only incompletely carried out this task. If one plays Nietzsche against Heidegger, then either one remains in the tracks laid down by Heidegger, or one implicitly alters the meaning of the concept of 'metaphysics' and speaks about something that no longer has anything to do with Heidegger or his interpretation of Nietzsche.

While it may be unproductive to regard Heidegger and Nietzsche as competitors to overcome metaphysics, it will nevertheless be acknowledged that the issue is fundamentally the same for them both. The question then is to illuminate how close Heidegger and Nietzsche are to one another on the subject of a hermeneutic transformation of thought. That, of course, could contribute to an understanding of this transformation itself. It could show how this transformation could occur in utterly diverse ways, and could, at the same time, reveal the fundamentals of a hermeneutic thinking. The question of a hermeneutic discourse of the divine offers a particularly fortuitous point of connection for the question of Heidegger's proximity to Nietzsche, and, thereby, for Nietzsche's to Heidegger. For like Heidegger, Nietzsche, too, undertook the task of speaking of a god neither in a mythic, nor in a speculative-theological manner. This god is also a god after all gods. For this reason, the talk of him perhaps also comes "too late and not at the right hour," because "today [one] uneasily . . . believes in God and gods" (*BGE*, 238). The god, which Nietzsche gives the name *Dionysus*, is also a god after the death of God, a last god, about which one can speak neither mythically nor theologically.

However, because Dionysus is a last God, he cannot be spoken of without raising the aporia of speculative-theological thought. A hermeneutic transformation of thought makes this possible, in turn, only if it does not take place for the benefit of an antitheological, and in this sense anthropological, alternative. For the anthropological alternative also draws its meaning and eventually its power of persuasion alone from the theological thought which it finds objectionable. Anthropology reacts against theology by positing human beings as the measure of all things, whether as a sign of protest or resignation. If no god is the measure of all things, it must be human beings—whoever thinks this way has failed to understand that he is repeating the cognitive structures which he allegedly opposes. Whoever thinks this way has failed to understand the logic of countermovements: "Counter-movements," Heidegger says at one point in the *Contributions*, "remain caught in their own victory; that is to say, they trap themselves within the confines of the defeated party" (*GA* 65:186).

Nietzsche recognized the problematic character of an anthropological countermovement to theology and drew the obvious consequence that neither a god nor a human being could be the measure of all things. The question of a standard for the correctness of thinking and acting brings to the fore the aporia of theological, as well as anthropological, thought. Where a god functions as the standard of correctness, one fixes that which cannot be fixed; where human beings presume to consider themselves the standard of correctness, the idea of a standard loses its essential binding force. Where one frees oneself from the question of a determinable standard, one arrives at *Beyond Good and Evil*. One is free for experiences which can be considered neither theological nor anthropological. And so it is no coincidence, but rather by design, that Nietzsche prepares the epiphany of his last god under the title *Beyond Good and Evil*.

But even if in the domain beyond good and evil no god and no human being is the measure of all things, it remains undecided whether this domain has a hermeneutic character. It can open up the possibility of there being no measure at all, and thereby be absolutely unhermeneutic, a domain which radically excludes being bound once more to a context of understanding which is not at one's disposal. Heidegger interpreted Nietzsche's word of the death of a normative and thereby "moral" god[7] in this way: with the death of God, dominion is not transferred from God to human beings, but rather "a place can unfold that is identical neither with the essential realm belonging to God nor with that of man, but with which man comes once more into a distinctive relationship" (*GA* 5:255/100). The essence of this domain is expressed by Heidegger with Nietzsche's formula "will to power." *Will to power* is the name for the dynamic of life, posited as a principle, which holds only for what serves to augment it. The will to power is a will which does not fulfill itself in any goal, but only in itself, that is to say, in the possibility of exceeding its current state. Where human beings understand themselves on the basis of the principle of this will, they do not wish to be the measure of all things, but rather to let themselves be carried away by a movement which holds sway over all beings as it then becomes evident in the "landscape of workshops" of the scientific, technical age, as Ernst Jünger would say.

One cannot seriously dispute that Nietzsche's characterizations of the will to power often enough allow themselves to be read in this fashion. And yet at decisive points, they are inconsonant with such an interpretation. In addition to the dynamic side of the will to power, Nietzsche also emphasized the necessary limitation of its actual effects, and, in order to make this comprehensible, interpreted the actualization of the will in terms of the model of textual interpretation. Like textual interpretation, the will to power belongs within a domain which it can never exhaust. It is essential that it belongs within such a domain, and for this reason the will to power also clearly can not be recognized without its limitations being seen to be essential to it.

Specifically, this means that every willing is, as it were, the discriminating and abbreviating interpretation of an immeasurable multiplicity, which, when read in this way, becomes a particular appearance. And the will expresses itself by acquiring a form by means of this appearance. We are the way in which we interpret the world, which we understand as a boundless multiplicity. The will to power, therefore, is the enactment of a unifying representation which can just as little assume a final form as the interpretation of a classical text. The dynamic of the will to power has its foundation then in the essentially openended character of every interpretation. Every interpretation is open to the possibility of being continued, namely, continued in an augmented form. The subsequent interpretation of a text should allow it to be realized in a more precise and more complete manner.

But then the essential boundedness of the enactment of the will to the world, understood as a boundless multiplicity, also belongs to the dynamic of the will to power. The will can be enacted only in the world, and therefore the world, which is never really available to the will, must be affirmed if the will itself is to be affirmed. In order for a will to be able to will its power, which is to say, its own possibility, it must affirm the limitations of its own reality. The will to power is the hermeneutic principle of life.

This thought becomes clearer if one considers that Nietzsche does not understand the world in its boundless multiplicity simply as a synthesizable manifold, but rather as a complex process.[8] The will, which interprets and unifies the multiplicity, is not excepted from this process. Every construction of unity is itself the appearance of a process, which can be experienced only as it appears. Willing is, as Nietzsche says at one point, "something complicated" (BGE, 19), a web of affects, feelings, thoughts, and drives, which, in turn, when experienced, are themselves appearances, "symptoms" (KSA 12:1 [59]). Accordingly, Nietzsche can note that the will is "a false hypostatization" (KSA 12:1 [62]). The will is not a principle; rather the discussion of the will merely indicates the agonistic coherence of occurring multiplicity and the construction of unity.

Consequently, this also holds for the talk of "the will to power" itself. If Nietzsche says that the world is "just 'will to power' and nothing else" (BGE, 36), that is an interpretation in which philosophy does what it has always done; once again it creates "the world in its own image" (BGE, 9). However, by prescribing how the world should appear in this way, one says, at the same time, something about this apparently sovereign act. Interpretation is also part of the world, and correspondingly Nietzsche can add that philosophy is "this tyrannical drive itself, the most spiritual will to power" (BGE, 9). While the dominating character of interpretation is once again firmly underscored, interpretation is just as clearly brought back into the world. What appears as a divine act of creation is not otherwise fundamentally different from the world process. This most "spiritual," most transparent will to power weakens itself by projecting itself into the overpowering world process.

Nietzsche uses the expression "circus vitiosus deus" (BGE, 56) to describe this quality of the will to let itself be overpowered in its own projection. It initially describes the sketched movement of an interpretation which is, as it were, caught within itself in that it must take itself to be its first presupposition. This circle of interpretation is God, deus, insofar as the sovereignty of interpretation is transformed into the affirmation of the overpowering process within which interpretation can exist at all and to which it is, therefore, indebted. The process will be affirmed, in turn, in the perspective of the interpretation, and in this way the interpretation regains its sovereignty in a certain manner. It can affirm the process on whose basis it exists only by affirming itself. But the interpretation cannot protect its sovereignty, because in affirming itself, it also affirms the process which overpowers it. The interpretation affirms the process for its own sake, which it can do only by projecting an image of the process. It makes the process necessary as what it is, and it needs the process to be what it is. And in this way the process is part of a self-transparent interpretation of beings as a whole, which, as Nietzsche puts its, says yes "to him, who needs precisely this spectacle—and makes it necessary, because again and again he needs himself, and makes himself necessary" (*BGE*, 56). The process is not the god, and certainly not the presumed "subject" behind the interpretation, who can only approximate the place of the dead, "moral" god, according to which one had to orientate oneself, and even this only in an interpretation. Rather *deus* is the circle of interpretation in the unifiable motility of its transformation. The name *Dionysus*, then, also stands as a name for this.[9]

3.

Heidegger placed great value on the fact that Nietzsche did not apodectically determine the circular motility of the interpreting process, the occurring interpretation, as *circulus vitiosis deus*, but rather gives this expression the form of a question. Thus the god is not taken to be a computable, absolute certainty. This gives Heidegger occasion to question fundamentally "whether the god possesses more divinity in the question concerning him or in the situation where we are sure of him and are able, as it were, to brush him aside or fetch him forward, as our needs dictate."[10] What Heidegger says here is just as relevant with regard to Nietzsche as it is illuminating with respect to his own motives. When considering the divine, neither Nietzsche nor Heidegger is concerned with certainty. This separates them from speculative theology and demonstrates the hermeneutic character of their thought. Nevertheless, the questionableness of the god expresses itself quite differently, whether it is designated by Nietzsche with the name of the masked god or clothed in the anonymity of the "last god" by Heidegger.

The reason for this lies in the relationship each has to myth. In the penultimate section of *Beyond Good and Evil*, Nietzsche is still playing with myth and alludes to the "art deity" of his first literary effort.[11] The name *Dionysus* is itself a mask, an interpretation. In spite of this, Nietzsche uses this mask to summon up myth, and ultimately this may be related to the shattering of the linguistic and cognitive tension in the late work. The final formula of *Ecce Homo*, "Dionysus against the crucified,"[12] offers an example of this. It intimates nothing more—while understanding also could be criticized for being overbearing—but rather plays desperate positions against one another. Dionysus thus ceases to be a last god. He becomes one god among many and loses himself in a mythology that no longer has any hold over us.

Before the last part of his *Contributions to Philosophy*, Heidegger places a motto which seems to suggest a comparable danger. For the description of the last god as a god "completely other than those who have been, especially the Christian God" (*GA* 65:403), appears dogmatically to assert a counterposition, just as in *Ecce Homo*. However, the formulation "completely other" can also be read as an attempt to exclude every possible comparison. Analogously, Heidegger does not fall back into the rejected monotheistic dogma with his discussion of the most "singular singularity" of the last god (*GA* 65:411); rather the attempt to describe the last god remains what it should be with respect to the matter at hand: hermeneutic.

The danger that Heidegger's attempt to think the last god is transformed into a dogma is avoided, if only for the reason that it is not concerned with the autonomy of a form, whatever name one might choose to give to it. Rather, his concretion employs the discourse of the last god alone in a meditation upon those gods, which Heidegger designates as the "gods who have been presencing [*die Gewesende*]." Of the last god, he says that it *"presences* [*Wesung*] . . . in the sign, the accession and deferment of the arrival and flight of the gods who are presencing and their hidden transformation" (*GA* 65:409).

In order to understand this, one must attempt to hear it in Heidegger's language. But one should know at least one thing, that

Heidegger also is able employ the word *sign*, the word here used to designate the presencing, the occurring tarrying of the last god, as a translation of the Greek *semainein* (*GA* 39:127). A sign is an indication.

The "gods who have been presencing," the gods who are present by having been displaced into the distance, are givers of signs. The word for "have been presencing," *gewesend*, is the perfect of "to presence," *wesen*, in the sense of "tarry," *verweilen*, here formed as a participle. It indicates something that no longer tarries and precisely in so doing remains near. Heidegger characterizes the present by means of a particular crossing of terms: accession and deferment of the arrival as well as the flight. One can translate this as the coming-to-pass and not coming-to-pass of arrival and flight. However, this does not designate a bland undecidability, but rather the intensity of the open: the gods who are presencing do not simply retreat; rather they are present precisely in their withdrawal; they arrive in their flight, and their arrival is at the same time a tarrying.

It is easy to see that this intensity of the open has a temporal quality. Arrival is the present, but in such a manner that it is determined by the not-yet of the future. Flight is the present, but in such a way that it already contains the no-longer of the past. Here a present is thought which is open through the future and the past and owes its intensity to the tension between future and past. Both flight and arrival are continually transformed into one another; they occur and likewise also do not occur. Arrival occurs, but as the nearness of those who are fleeing, and flight occurs, in that what flees has the proximity of what is arriving. Flight and arrival occur by not becoming static conditions. In this way, time remains open. Nothing actually enters into the present, and nothing actually distances itself from it. The openness whose intensity lies in the coming-to-pass and not coming-to-pass of flight and arrival is a past which does not close itself off in forgetting, and a future which cannot be calculated. It is the openness of time, and hence can be designated by Heidegger as the "time-space" [*Zeitraum*] (*GA* 65:412).

The presencing of the last god is indicated with the coming-to-pass and not coming-to-pass of the flight and arrival of the gods. This coming-to-pass and not coming-to-pass at the same time constitutes the openness of the time-space. If one takes them together, then the presencing of the last god can be understood as the coming-to-pass of the time-space, which cannot be experienced apart from the flight and arrival of the gods who have been presencing. What Heidegger designates as the "passage" of the last god is then an agon which occurs by means of the openness of the time-space. And the time-space can only be agonistic insofar as it is experienced as the intensity of the transformation of flight and arrival. What attracts our attention here, by eluding any plan and calculation, is the coherence of presence and absence, the experience of a way of being present which withdraws equally into the past and the future.

This coherence of presence and absence is experienced in the gods who have been presencing. However, the gods who have been presencing are experienced on the basis of the cohesion of presence and absence. The agonistic coherence of presence and absence is the essence of time, the coming-to-pass of time. This coming-to-pass allows the gods who have been presencing to be as they are. It indicates them, just as the charged intensity of their flight and arrival indicates the coming-to-pass of time. The coming-to-pass of time, then, allows the gods who have been presencing first to be experienced in their divinity; it is that which is genuinely overpowering. And, conversely, the coming-to-pass of time cannot be overpowering without the gods who have been presencing. In this bond with the gods who have been presencing, one can understand the coming-to-pass of time, which Heidegger himself designates with the word *event* [*Ereignis*] as the last god.

The connection of the event with the gods who have been presencing is also a *circulus vitiosis deus*. Both bestow, as it were, divinity upon the other: the gods are other than mythical representations that have become lifeless and vapid only in virtue of the event, while the event first acquires a divine quality through the gods who had their time.

One sees quite clearly now how this consideration of the divine coheres with Nietzsche's word of the death of God. Only the death of the "moral God" opens up the domain of a completely other experience of the divine. This is in keeping with the meaning of Nietzsche's note from 1882, according to which what appears to be "God's self-destruction" is "merely the shedding of his skin." "He sheds his moral skin! And you will soon see him once again, beyond good and evil" (*KSA* 10:3 [1]). But what Heidegger undertakes to think, though close to Nietzsche, is also separated from him by an immense distance. One does not live through the death of God in order to see the new God or to see the old God in a new light, as if nothing at all had happened. Precisely this, that something has happened, becomes the point of departure for Heidegger's hermeneutic of the last god. And for this reason one has, in turn, to relate the most extreme linguistic formulations of the *Contributions* to Hölderlin's poetry, which speaks of the very past that is at play in connection with God; in this way, they can be experienced in the play-space of poetry.[13]

Heidegger and Nietzsche differ from one another in that the one orients himself to the expanding agonistic play of augmentation and overpowering, while the other thoughtfully traces the circle of historical experience and the coming-to-pass of time. Their points of departure cohere upon the common ground of a hermeneutic theology. That, in turn, can be understood more specifically, and in attempting this, the true nature of hermeneutic theology becomes evident. It lies in the fact that hermeneutic theology seeks a theological discourse which is not religious. There is philosophical piety, but no philosophical religion.

Heidegger himself most clearly expressed what is at issue here when he rejected the "commonly accepted, but for this reason not any less questionable grouping together of Nietzsche with Kierkegaard." While for Heidegger, Nietzsche belongs to the philosophical tradition, which Heidegger terms "metaphysics," Kierkegaard stands eccentrically opposed to this tradition. For, Heidegger continues, "Kierkegaard is not a thinker but a religious writer, and indeed not just one among others, but the only one in accord with the destining belonging to his age. Therein lies his greatness, if to speak in this way is not already a misunderstanding" (*GA* 5: 249/94).

The religious writer is distinguished from the philosopher essentially in the fact that for him revelation is an indisputable fact, a fact which sets his thinking and writing into motion, keeps it on track, and transforms all philosophical ideas which he takes up. All these ideas cease to be philosophical and are transformed into elements of a religious discourse. To the question of the divine, the religious writer has the answer of faith and confession, instead of pointing to the worldly coming-to-pass of world interpretation and existence in a historical world. The religious writer can name the divine, the revelation of the God which one believes in, directly. His discourse rests upon the completely involuntary decision in favor of what is particular about this revelation.

But the religious writer can, in fact must, also always keep silent about his answer. For he does not speak in the context of religion for the faithful, but rather seeks, as Kierkegaard said, to draw attention to religion without a church office. He seeks to indicate the religious: no matter how radically he may be separated from the philosophers and their theological hermeneutics, he, too, must speak hermeneutically.

12

The Absolute Particular
Individuality and Religion
after Kierkegaard

What is it like to be a bat? Thomas Nagel's essay of this title has received a great deal of attention and has been discussed widely within academic philosophy, not primarily because it solved a problem in an exemplary manner, but rather because it formulated a problem in a particularly vivid way.[1] The question—What is it like to be a bat?—is interesting because while we clearly know a few things about the perception and navigational abilities of bats, we are not able to conceive *how it is* to securely move about in dark caves as if sleepwalking using a perceptual organ guided by sound. We do not possess this knowledge, because, being human beings, we do not have such an organ. While we may be able to say a great deal scientifically about bats, their mode of existence is absolutely foreign to us.

Søren Kierkegaard was not interested in bats. In spite of this, Nagel is working completely within the scope of Kierkegaardian thought. For Nagel is interested in bats only because he is interested in human beings, in how it is to consciously enact one's life.

This was exactly Kierkegaard's question: What is it like to be a human being? And because no one can simply take themselves as an example of the species, Kiekegaard's question is still more radical. It is the question of how it is to be this human being, this unmistakable individual, this person. It is the question of how it is for each person to be himself. In his own quite particular way, Kierkegaard is a discoverer and investigator of individuality, and he himself was exceptionally clear about the peculiar difficulties of such an investigation.

The problems are not inconsiderable. To begin, if we consider more precisely how radical the question of individuality is, we quickly realize that the question produces a paradoxical situation. The discoverer and investigator of individuality relates to the individual as the zoologist relates to bats. Whatever one says about individuality, it remains something general which, in the best case, will apply to all individuals but can never truly represent how it is to be an individual, this individual. Only each individual ever knows this. One knows it, because one is this individual.

This leads to the next problem, for does one really know it? It certainly might be the case that every life has its own particular coloring, that every life is bound within its own particular feeling for life. It certainly might be the case that from time to time one senses the inevitability of one's own inimitable way of being: you must be this way, you cannot run away from yourself. But what comes into view when one performs such an investigation and attempts to isolate it by telling the story of one's own life is no more than an *image* of one's own life. And the more clearly one conceives this image, the more clearly one draws it, the more one forgets its dark, and necessarily dark, side, namely, that one is attempting to construct an image of oneself. One forgets that one always remains the other with respect to one's own image. He who makes the portrait is not the one depicted in it.

Hence the question of each particular life, of the individual, cannot, at least not at first, be concerned with *what* one knows of oneself, but rather only ever with *how* one knows of oneself. And this 'how' is nothing conscious, but rather the *enactment of knowledge*. In principle, one can consciously reflect upon this enactment, one can attempt to make it an object of knowledge, and one does that, for example, when one asks oneself what it was like to construct this image of oneself, to tell oneself the story of one's life in this situation, at that time or a short time before. However, it is also fundamentally true that the question regarding this situation remains unanswered. It eludes the present of the individual, the present that is particular to each person. One eludes oneself in one's own present and, in this way, fails to become master of oneself.

Nothing comes from this difficulty. But just for this reason it was meaningful to illustrate it, for it has revealed what is individual in one's own life. What is individual in one's own life has shown itself by disappearing. It has shown itself as the genuinely ungraspable enactment of one's own life.

It is a short step from here to the surprising result that it is not each individual's knowledge of himself which leads to the secret of individuality, but rather the distance—the dispassionate, abstract determination. The particular person, the individual, who is never realized in any life story, nevertheless can be indicated by an abstract reference to the enactment of life. Moreover, if this still rather vague information is unsatisfying and needs to be explained and developed, it nevertheless serves to confirm that something general can be said about individuality which eludes the individual who seeks to know himself.

One can now therefore understand why it is ultimately not so improper to undertake a conceptual investigation of individuality, and why the investigator of individuality knows even more about individuality than the individual himself if these general concepts are unavailable to him. One can understand how the investigator of individuality is able to communicate to individuals what their individuality is and how it is experienced. The investigator of individuality can even make the individuals aware of their individuality in order to show them how they could actually be in their individuality, namely, by making them aware of the disappearance of their lives as a whole in its enactment and to make allowances for this disappearance.

This was Kierkegaard's program, and he followed it through most consistently in *The Sickness unto Death*. Certainly the book does not immediately appear to be an investigation of individuality. Kierkegaard assigned it the same intention as the rest of his work. Without the authority of a church office it too should "draw attention to religion."[2] *The Sickness unto Death* is also a work of a "religious writer." The subtitle announces its goal: *For Edification and Awakening*.[3]

Nevertheless, the individuality of the individual is what is at stake, for the text *The Sickness unto Death* is about the chronic sickness of individuals. Kierkegaard calls it "despair" [*Verzweiflung*]. And the text is to make it clear to the reader that this despair can be overcome and the individual can become actual and healthy by religious means alone, even in Christian faith alone. By investigating the individual enactment of life in the condition of sickness, Kierkegaard seeks to indicate what Christian faith is. Christian faith is the nondetrimental, unclouded actuality of individuality.

This could easily be misunderstood. Kierkegaard does not mean that only in faith can one be an individual and actualize one's life as one's own. The point here lies in the distinction between the individual and the genuinely individual life. One is also an individual if one is not genuinely an individual; this is also true, if one has not, or not yet, found faith. But then the individuality will not be free, but only reveals itself as it fails to fulfill itself in sickness. And by failing to fulfill itself, individuality reveals how it is a problem for the individual to have to be an individual.

For Kierkegaard, this problematic experience of individuality is the only possible one. More precisely, it is the only experience in which one's own individuality as such appears. However, where one is genuinely an individual and where the problem of individuality no longer exists, that is, in Christian faith, one's own individuality is no longer evident, just as one is not explicitly aware of one's body when one is healthy. One only experiences the actuality of individual life where one neither seeks it nor avoids it oneself.

It also follows from this that Kierkegaard can only investigate and represent the problematic relationship of the individual to his individuality.[4] In addition, individuals can be reached only by the pronouncements of the investigator where individuality is problematic for them—and only then *is it essential* that they also be reached by these pronouncements. The investigator of individuality speaks to individuals like the doctor at a sickbed. His goal is therapy, and everything that he says is subordinate to this goal. The genuinely individual life, that genuine and healthy life of the individual, remains untouched by what the investigator of individuality has to say.

Kierkegaard's undertaking has now been outlined in all its complexity. To be sure, the conceptual analysis of individual life is orientated to the genuinely individual life, but this is not its theme. The genuine and healthy individual life only comes into view conceptually when it fails to fulfill itself, just as the doctor is interested in health only in view of the sick. Health does not interest the doctor, and yet he is concerned with nothing more than health.

But just as the doctor must possess a concept of the human being which allows health and sickness to be thought in like manner, so Kierkegaard must have a conceptual definition of individual life at his disposal which holds despair and faith together and is adequate to both. He needs a conceptual determination of individual life which is equally adequate to the healthy actuality of this life as its failure, a determination which relates failure to actuality and is able to account for the fact that nothing positive can be said about this actuality.

Kierkegaard develops such a determination at the very beginning of *The Sickness unto Death* by designating the human being as "spirit," spirit as "the self," and in connection with this, saying how he understands the concept of 'self.' The concept of the 'self' is the kernel of Kierkegaard's therapeutic anthropology.

"The self," he writes, "is a relation which relates itself to its own self, or it is that in the relation that the relation relates itself to its own self" (*SD*, 146). That sounds more complicated than it is. The human being, which is what Kierkegaard is aiming at, is a relation between two elements which can be grasped in distinct and opposed determinations. The human being is a relation, a "synthesis," namely, a synthesis of finitude and infinity, of possibility and necessity, of the temporal and the eternal. But in addition, the human being is characterized by the fact that she is herself in the synthesis which she is and toward which she *comports* herself. Seen in this manner, this comportment in human being toward human being is the self.

In order to understand more precisely what all this means, one must first clarify how Kierkegaard precisely elucidates the elements of the synthesis distinguished by him and, in this way, human being. Finitude, for Kierkegaard, is the particular determinateness and narrowness of life, what, therefore, one *is* as someone with particular characteristics, a particular ancestry or membership in a particular generation, particular talents and limitations. By contrast, infinite is what one is not, and this is clearly an unlimited quantity.

However, under particular circumstances one can be what one is not, and in that case it is no longer simply infinite, but *possible*. The relation in possibility consists in *wanting to be* something that one is not. One discovers the infinite here, as it were, by realizing it by means of a plan or a desire.

In the case of such discoveries one naturally comes up against boundaries from time to time, for one cannot be everything that one wishes to be. When one realizes this, one acts in the determination of *necessity*; one is then determined by what is and how it is, and that can go so far that one no longer takes pleasure in plans and desires—just as, in the converse case, one can lose the security of one's own boundaries in plans and desires.

This now brings an important aspect of Kierkegaard's determination of human being to the fore, and it reveals, at the same time, from precisely which observations it arises. The life of human beings is not fixed by its determinations, but rather it can—and must—be enacted between them. But in this way life is always characterized by a *lack*. Whoever only holds on to what he is has a lack of infinity and, because he does not wish to be anything other that what he is, a lack of possibility. Whoever does not see his definiteness and narrowness has a lack of finitude, and to the extent that he always wants to be other than he is, also a lack of necessity. From these conceptual characterizations, the first steps toward a pathology of despair, one can easily imagine the corresponding character types. The romantic or the fecklessly active dreamer, the self-satisfied member of the bourgeoisie or the person full of resignation and despair. Kierkegaard sketches them in strokes that are as brief as they are precise.

All of the elucidations of Kierkegaard's determinations essayed to this point have been related only to the comportment of human beings *in* the synthesis of their opposed determinations. That is to say, it was explained how life is enacted in the synthesis, but not *how it is* to live in a synthesis of the kind elucidated above. For the lack of finitude and necessity and the lack of infinity and possibility need not become explicit to the person who has them, just as little as one senses a bodily lack in all circumstances. To put it another way, one can have a lack and not *suffer* from it. But then one does not become cognizant of how one is. The synthesis, together with the opposed determinations of human being, do not enter consciousness.

Where this occurs, the situation becomes more complicated, but for the investigator of human beings and its pathology, also more interesting. For now one will no longer be able to do justice to the neglected determination with the simple diagnosis of a "lack." To the extent that one becomes conscious of the neglect, it has consequences for this comportment that the determination which is set against it is neglected. Whoever consciously always wishes to be otherwise than she is comes up against and is disturbed by the necessity to which she ought to submit. Whoever still persists in her determinateness and narrowness with such a low degree of explicitness is confronted by the disconcerting, vertigo-inducing ability to be otherwise.

This brings the last, and hitherto ignored, two determinations into play: the temporal and the eternal. Everything that has a beginning and an end is "temporal." "Eternal" is the simple presence that is not divided into a past, present, and future. Presence, in this sense, is the structure of human being, namely, that one is a synthesis and has to comport oneself in it—one does not leave this behind oneself in life, and it does not stand before one in life.

But this unquestionably places all comportment, be it planning and desiring in possibility or adherence to necessity, in a framework to which there is no longer any alternative. It is constitutive of the play-space of life that one can play or desire or be persistent. But that every plan and desire is, as every act of persistence, bound up with its opposite, that every form of life is framed by the basic form of the synthesis, this is the fact of this play-space itself.

Now the fact of this play-space of life is certainly not of the kind that one could simply take note of it or consider it of no consequence. On the contrary. As soon as the pain from the lack in one's particular comportment first appears, as soon as one has become conscious of the synthesis as such, one has already begun to comport oneself in relation to the synthesis, to the fact of the play-space of life. And the more intensive this experience becomes, the more intensive the tension between the possible and the necessary that one is comes to the fore, the clearer it becomes that this tension cannot be avoided or just as little resolved. But as a result of the fact that no resolution of the tension within life can be effected within this comportment, the comportment itself comes to the fore. The more conscious the failure of life becomes in despair, the more insistent the comportment also becomes. And what obtrudes in this way is the enactment of one's own life, namely, that one has to run one's own life.

We have now fully brought together the two sides of the sickness through which human being, for Kierkegaard, is marked. Where we become conscious of the fact of the play-space of life and the comportment in it, it becomes clear that one can only fail in one of two ways. One can seek to come to terms with the deficiencies of one's own life, and in so doing one merely confirms that one is unable to exhaust the synthesis' play-space of life. Or one can attempt to exhaust the synthesis by betting everything on the effort to construct one's life oneself. Here the same thing is confirmed, because this project, undertaken in spite of life, cannot be completed successfully. One must conduct one's own life, and one can just as little conduct it sovereignly as one can successfully refuse to manage it.

In both cases, one despairs, and despairs intensely. One does not desire one's own life, and yet one desires it. As Kierkegaard himself puts it, one wants to be oneself in despair by not wanting to be oneself, and one does not want to be oneself in despair by wanting to be oneself. This means that one wants to accept the synthesis but not enact it, because one cannot accept it in the process of enacting one's life. Or one wishes to enact one's life oneself, and then one does want it as just that life that it is; one does not want it as that life which does not arise in the enactment.

Although the flaw of human life lies in despair and is revealed by it, despair is far from being merely a disadvantage. It is, as Kierkegaard says, what distinguishes the human being from the beast (*SD*, 148). It is therefore that which first makes the human being human at all. Despair is the essence of the human being.

Furthermore, despair is the essence of the human being in such a way that one experiences this essence individually, and one experiences oneself, therefore, in despair as an individual. Each is his own despair, and if it were then possible to narrate one's life story in such a manner that one did not obscure or twist what is told through the process of the telling, if it were not the case that in every life story the history of the story is necessarily lacking, if every presentation of a life sickness told by the one who is sick were not always also a symptom, every life story would have to be the presentation of a particular case of despair. It could not be anything other than this. However, if this were the case, autobiographies would only show how, despairing, one has attempted to come to terms with one's life and has not mastered it as a whole. If one were able to measure one's despair oneself, one would not despair. But the attempt to do this is itself an act of despair.

Where one attempts to make oneself understandable to oneself, the enactment of this very attempt becomes elusive.

Against despair neither the brooding, resigned attempt to accept it nor the resistant effort to overcome it is helpful. Both are merely symptoms of despair, and in both cases the despairing one merely digs himself deeper into his despair. For this reason, the only thing that can help is "moving away from oneself infinitely" and therein "returning to oneself infinitely" (*SD*, 162–63). One can only help oneself by no longer worrying about oneself, for every act of worry, no matter what kind, is despair. However, it is clearly not helpful if the renunciation of worry is a form of flight from the flaws of one's own life. For this reason, freeing oneself from oneself must be a return to oneself. One must accept the unavailability of the play-space of life and the comportment within it. That, in turn, must not have the character of a resigned acceptance, which would be despair once again. It must distinguish itself from this acceptance by the fact that both the enactment of life and the play-space of life—life in the totality of both its opposed determinations—are affirmed. One must wish to be as one is. And that cannot ultimately mean that one wishes to bring about the accord of the opposed determinations oneself, for that, too, would be despair once more. One must wish to be as one is without attempting to do so by overcoming the play-space of life.

To accept life without resignation, to want life without violence, for Kierkegaard, are characteristics of faith. In faith one accepts the play-space of life but in such a way that the releasement [*Gelassenheit*] becomes concentrated in the strength of one's will. One wants to be oneself in the play-space of life, but in such a way that this willing gradually ceases in the releasement of acceptance.

This characterization is quite clearly oriented to the conflict of one who is despairing. Without giving priority to possibility, one can just as little think willing as one can think acceptance with giving priority to necessity. To comport oneself within the "synthesis" of the self always means to be subordinate to one of the two elements of the synthesis. The conflict of the elements of the synthesis is the motility of life.

The foregoing confirms that in describing the "self" one can only follow despair. One can name the health and actuality of the "self" only in reference to the synthesis and the comportment which exists in the tension between the two elements of the synthesis. In characterizing faith, one must also focus upon the tension between willing and releasement. For this reason, too, every conceptual determination of faith remains abstract and inadequate. The circumstances of health can be grasped and represented only on the basis of the elements of despair. Thus it would appear that one has silently traced faith, together with religion, back to the structure of the self. What can be said equally well or better conceptually would seem then to have been expressed religiously in mythical form. However, that is impossible, because the self is always a comportment in human being to human being, and this comportment necessarily fails to fulfill human being. One cannot, on the basis of the self, make a reconciled life comprehensible to oneself.

To be sure, Kierkegaard did not shy away from conceptual elucidations where it was a question of the health of the self. In *The Sickness unto Death* he even offers a concept of God when he says that God is "that all things are possible" (*SD*, 173). However, all of these elucidations have a provisional and indicative character. They do not seek to replace the religious with the conceptual, but rather to indicate the religious. That everything is possible in this sense means that which is unthinkable according to human standards. It means that which eludes the conceptual, the simple, that is to say, the absolute particular—the particular that is comparable to nothing, that is distinct from nothing, and thus does not belong within any context.

The religious, however, is not like this, because then the experience of the religious would be individual, and only each person would know how it is to have such an experience. Rather, the religious is absolutely particular because it has at its center an absolutely unique event. One does not experience oneself religiously, but rather the binding force of the absolutely contingent. The absolutely contingent cannot be understood as an exception to a rule, and just as little can it be understood as a side effect of something meaningful. It cannot be understood at all, but rather is, as Kierkegaard—once again only suggestively—says in his *Training in Christianity*, the "absolute paradox."[5] It is the particular which opens up a domain of ungraspable bindingness, and thus releases one from the immanence of the play-space of one's own life. The particular in this sense does not correspond to an aspect of life, but rather to the individual himself. In the fact of the absolute particular lies freedom *from* the facticity of life, freedom from one's having to resolve one's life within the play-space itself.[6] However, in the absolutely particular also lies freedom *to* the facticity of one's own life, freedom to accept the play-space and the comportment in it, because one is no longer caught within the spell of its immanence. By having a relation to the absolute particular, which is not oneself, one is released from oneself and achieves something that cannot be achieved in the immanent enactment of life. The enactment of life contains an actuality which is no longer subordinate to the tension of the play-space of life and for this reason is able exist as an actuality. Where one is not mindful of one's own actuality but turns to the absolute particularity of the religious, the enactment of life is unhampered and one can tranquilly exist in the play-space of one's own life.

For the Christian, man becoming God is absolutely paradoxical, and for this reason, binding. It is not an event that one can take to be true or question. Like every revelation, man becoming God is only comprehensible in faith, and for this reason it is a misunderstanding of religious tolerance to attempt to uncover a common kernel in the different religions in order to reconcile them with one another. There is no religion without the absolute particularity of the revelations that are originary for them. The more clearly this is seen, the more people will be inclined to have respect for other religions.

The absolute particular of a religion cannot be integrated into a life plan, rather one can only subordinate one's life to it through the immediate decision of faith. If one were to see faith as one possibility or necessity among others, then one would have misunderstood the decision character of faith. One would have reduced the religious to something comparable to other things, and in so doing one would also have forsaken the freedom to be free from oneself. To enter into a religion is to accept that one's own life has a predetermined meaning, which, strictly speaking, is not at one's disposal in this life. The absolute particular of the religious believer is meaningful because it grants a meaning to freedom without allowing itself to become fixed as a moral standard. The path leading from it does disclose a duty which one has to satisfy, and which one could also therefore fail to live up to; without the movement of life, religious meaning cannot be grasped. It is a meaning which simply must be actualized in the movement of faith. The meaning of faith is a pure performative meaning because it is free.

If one considers the religious to be a possible alternative, it has already lost the power that is characteristic of it. In its exclusiveness, the religious is therefore also particularly impotent against the doubt which it encounters from outside. As soon as this is successfully articulated, the religious withers away leaving its forms and institutions empty behind it. The freedom that it is has then closed itself off.

There is, to be sure, also some doubt, an uncertainty in the religious person, which belongs within the context of a religious life. For Kierkegaard this uncertainty is even of decisive importance, because without it faith degenerates into an insipid truism. The meaning given to life as a whole that is opened up by revelation must be accepted again and again. However, this means that faith presupposes despair from the beginning. Not merely a concept of faith, but also the experience of faith is only possible on the basis of despair, and in faith one must then also be able to accept despair, the ever-present possibility of despair. Without the possibility of the struggle between resignation and self-assertion, releasement and willing are not able to reach an equilibrium. The freedom of the religious exists only because it cannot be guaranteed. And for this reason, it also only exists where it remains open. Without the uncertainty of possible doubt, it does not remain open. However, the doubt must be adequate to faith and may not fix it in place if it is to allow the leap into faith. Despair must remain a present possibility so that the freedom of faith does not close itself off.

The releasement of faith arises, therefore, because in the play-space of one's own life one no longer has a relationship to it but is engaged with the absolute particular of a specific religious revelation. Where this revelation determines one's life, the experience of the enactment of one's own individual life has receded. The recovery of the individual is therefore equivalent with the loss of individuality insofar as this is disclosed in the tension of the elements of life, or ultimately in the tension of the play-space of life and its comportment. In this tension, the basic possibilities of an unsuccessful life are not merely laid out but are actually given. The individual is its illness. It can be healed only by renouncing itself, by no longer wishing to be realized by means of the comportment in the play-space of life.

Nevertheless, this is no mere loss of self, no demise of the individual as occurs during intoxication, under anesthesia, or in fanatical devotion, It is the experience of oneself as the other in the absolute particular, so that one cannot secure oneself in it. But precisely in this way faith leads back to despair. One can only say that one experiences oneself as reconciled from a position in which one is not reconciled. The sickness of individuality and its healing ultimately belong together. And so Kierkegaard did not merely describe the strife in the individual's enactment of life, but in addition the necessary strife of intransigence and reconciliation, of despair and faith. He showed how the nonreligious belongs to the essence of religion. It also belongs to the essence of religion that this cannot be reversed.

13

Trusting the *Logos*
On Plato's Rhetoric of Philosophy

For Michael Theunissen

Rhetoric, one reads in the *Gorgias*, is the producer of belief (453a). It is, according to the *Phaedrus*, a guidance of the soul by speech (261a). Whoever has mastered the art of rhetoric can make others believe what he wishes, and whoever believes a rhetorician has acquired beliefs without knowing whether they are true or not. Rhetoric is, on this account, an art of flattery (*Gorgias*, 463b) that is comparable with cosmetics. Just as cosmetics produce the appearance of beauty, so rhetoric produces the appearance of knowledge.

The counterpart to rhetoric, if one follows the *Gorgias*, is a type of knowledge that is capable of proof because it manifests itself in a work—knowledge in the sense of craftsmanship [*téchne*]. In the *Phaedrus* one can read something similar. Here rhetoric is called an "artless pursuit" (260e),[1] and is contrasted with dialectic, that ability to experience what phenomena are in the interplay of the one and the many. Only he who is in a position to practice dialectic, he who has mastered *dihairesis* and *synagoge*,[2] is capable of a kind of speech that is coupled with insight (266b). Rhetoric, therefore, is neither craftsmanship nor philosophy.

This much is generally familiar even to the superficial reader of Plato. The way in which philosophy and the philosopher are here contrasted with their counterparts, rhetoric and its sophistic defender, became such a fundamentally widespread belief that the assertion that philosophy is itself rhetorical was able to assume the character of an unmasking, a deconstruction of philosophical claims and stylizations. Because the philosophical claim against rhetoric is intended as a claim to knowledge, the originator and virtuoso of this game of unmasking, Friedrich Nietzsche, drew the logical consequences of this claim and doubted "that a 'drive to knowledge' is the father of philosophy." Nietzsche assumed "that another drive has here, as elsewhere, employed knowledge (and misunderstanding) as a mere instrument" (BGE, 5). This is a drive that, preserving and intensifying itself, seeks to master and therefore to dominate beliefs—a rhetorical drive that aims to dominate by means of the strongest interpretation and, perhaps for this very reason, expresses itself with the claim to truth in a particularly subtle and effective manner. Now Nietzsche intended this to be an enlightening thought. Unmasking the claim to knowledge, he makes the claim to know what philosophy in truth is. One could regard this gesture of enlightenment itself as a problematic echo of the Platonic tradition, and correspondingly, it does not pay to expose it, for this would be merely a continuation of an inconsequential game, but simply to dismiss it. A recognition of the rhetorical character of enlightenment represents the last flash of philosophical insight before philosophy finally dissolves into rhetoric or literature. Paul de Man wanted to hold onto this moment of dissolution as he established the impossibility of a deconstruction of philosophy.[3]

However, Nietzsche can just as little founder as a deconstructor of philosophy as Plato, as the originator or at least the most influential representative of the claim to philosophy, can be deconstructed. With regard to Nietzsche, the idea of a rhetoric which would be a medium of truth is for him quite conceivable. A speech can aim to produce belief and nevertheless uncover something, raise something out of concealment, by representing it. Every speech is appearance, but appearance for Nietzsche is "reality once more, as selection, intensification, correction" (KSA 13:14 [168]). That and that alone constitutes the rhetorical character of speech: rhetorical is the interpretative representation of a "reality"—which can be represented only through simplification and abbreviation—by means of which one's own interpretation seeks to demonstrate its persuasiveness. Rhetoric is the tribute, happily paid by most, to the perspectival character of all reality.

Nietzsche's critique of knowledge is not, therefore, as radical as it sometimes appears. Correspondingly, Plato does not defend such an unmitigated claim to knowledge as his deconstructors assume. To be sure, it cannot be denied that the Platonic Socrates contradicts the self-understanding of the rhetorician in the *Gorgias*. Rhetoric is not a *téchne*, but just as little is it philosophy. The "political art," of which rhetoric is taken to be an imitation (*Gorgias*, 463d) is, as philosophy, not a form of knowledge which can be learned and mastered, but rather that relationship to the greatest and most important things which Socrates, in the *Apology*, says cannot be reached by means of a *téchne*. Socrates allows the rhetorician's claim to possess a skill or craft to fall short by showing that a craft is a form of knowledge. However, it does not follow from this that philosophy is a form of knowledge in the sense of a craft.

The situation is similar with the conception of dialectic discussed in the *Phaedrus*. Only superficially could it be regarded as a knowledge of determinations and definitions that is unproblematically at one's disposal. For whoever engages with the many in order to see it related to a single unity engages with the boundlessly many and multiple. The many is always subject to further differentiations, and that it coheres in a single unity in one way and not another is therefore never certain. This also holds for the converse path from the one to its multiplicity of aspects and forms of appearance. For one is once more concerned with what is contingent, and it is therefore not unambiguously fixed how far one should carry the process of differentiation. Because the dialectician attempts to ascertain the form of an object, he cannot orient himself to this form; dialectic is therefore also marked by the manner of approach taken by those investigating the phenomena. There are dialectical detours and dead ends, as is shown by the first attempts of the sophist to arrive at a definition in the *Sophist*.

Where there are no compelling paths of interpretation, where simple and certain evidence does not reveal that something is such and such and and not something else, there remains a play-space for the introduction of rhetorical means—especially if the aim of dialectical research is to instruct someone with less experience.

For dialectic reveals itself to be exactly that guidance of the soul by speech which characterizes rhetoric. Or, at the very least, dialectic has rhetorical characteristics and, accordingly, the discussions of the relationship between rhetoric and dialectic in the *Phaedrus* do not aim to discredit rhetoric, but rather to preserve it within dialectic. Where one is intimately familiar with a field of knowledge, the possibilities of rhetoric have been domesticated and no longer threaten to produce a confusion of mere persuasion and insight. The ironically detailed statements on behalf of a putative artistic doctrine of persuasive speech in the *Phaedrus* amount to a brief for a kind of speech that does not merely naively offer something resembling the true, but rather one that comprehends that which resembles the true and therefore knows how to handle it (*Phaedrus*, 273d). The distinction between truth and appearance serves to allow one to discover the truth in appearance.

However, philosophy does not always remain in a domain that is ultimately secure. It cannot always count on the fact that it will be concerned with representations of the true or that representations of the true even exist. And it cannot, for this reason, always accept the relative contingency of representations or even use them to guide the soul. Philosophy is challenged in another, completely different manner when it itself is at issue. Where it is doubtful whether the decisive questions can be answered philosophically, the orientation to knowledge and the knowable must itself be justified. The domain of knowledge does not then constitute the obvious horizon of a speech which elucidates by means of dialectic and, correspondingly, the rhetorical is also not dialectically domesticated.

This holds true for the *Phaedo*. And because it holds true for it alone among all the Platonic dialogues, it is the most radical of all Plato's texts. Nowhere else is the claim, indeed the possibility of philosophy, so unreservedly hazarded as here. For while the young Socrates might, in the dialogue *Parmenides*, be thoroughly frustrated by the objections of the Eleatic, Parmenides does not put philosophy as such into question, but rather even explicitly holds that one must not allow oneself to become confused by dialectic in the face of all specific difficulties that arise (*Parmenides*, 135b–c). While the sophistically educated Callicles might, in the *Gorgias*, condescendingly doubt the worth of philosophy, Socrates need not allow himself to be deceived by this and can demonstrate the groundlessness of the position which Callicles defends. In the *Phaedo* something more and quite different is at issue, namely, whether philosophy can endure in the face of things that, quite simply, cannot be understood or imagined. What is at issue is whether one who is imminently facing death can trust the philosophical *logos*. Because the extreme situation only brings to light what generally is the case, the question concerns the trustworthiness of the philosophical *logos* in general. This question clearly cannot be answered within the framework of the essential possibilities for the *logos*. However, should the question be answered and not simply decided, this would have to occur in a manner that is primarily rhetorical, and it will have to be established thereby what a trust in the philosophical *logos* would look like. Correspondingly, the speeches in the dialogue are marked by a rhetorical vocabulary in a quite striking manner. What is required is for the soul to be guided to the *logos*, at which point, however, the limits of demonstration and argumentation, the limits of the *logos*, are open to view.

The beginning of the actual dialogue which follows the introductory conversation makes it clear that these limits have, for Socrates, already been crossed. In the time that remains of his life Socrates has turned to poetry, to myth, and taken leave of the *logos*. This can be traced back, as Socrates says, to an injunction in a dream, which he wishes to explore like the oracle of Apollo, as he set about to test whether none of the Athenians was wiser than he. Socrates had this dream, as he says, often in his life and understood it in the same sense as the oracle—as an exhortation to philosophy (60e–61a). If he does not now practice the greatest of the arts, but rather popular music, he will fulfill the dream completely and free himself from every merely possible sin of omission (61a).

However, that is not the real reason why Socrates now expresses himself in myth. One discovers this when Socrates reflects upon the relationship of pleasure and pain. Both never occur concurrently, and yet they cohere, so that whoever seeks to attain the one is compelled also to take the other upon himself. However, the coherence of the opposed elements is adequately expressed in myth. Things which exclude one another in the *logos* can be represented as connected in a story (60b–c). This also concerns life and death. Immediately before death one should, as

Socrates says, talk about the journey there in stories [*mythologein*], and say what one believes it to be (60e–61a).

Cebes, one of the two Pythagoreans no longer bound by tradition with whom Socrates carries on the conversation, does not want to accept this. He doubts that it is suitable for the philosopher to see death as a desirable goal of his life, and implicitly he thereby also puts into question the mythical speech with which Socrates arrives at a conception of the transition from life to death. Cebes always seeks, as Socrates says, something that he can present as an objection [*lógous tinàs*] and refuses to immediately believe what is said to him (63a). Certainly that is not meant merely as a reproach. And yet it must surprise us that here Socrates evidently expects that Cebes should believe him, that he should allow himself to be convinced. For that is, following the sophist and rhetorician Gorgias, the goal of the art of rhetoric.

That what is at issue here is actually a rhetorical situation and not a philosophical conversation in the usual sense becomes clearer when Socrates interprets the questioning of his mythical images of death as an exhortation to a defense. Cebes and Simmias expect a defense, and one "as before a court" (63b), whose goal it should be to convince them both (63d). When Gorgias explains that the goal of rhetoric is to persuade the audience, he refers to the example of a speech in court first of all (*Gorgias*, 452b). Evidently is it the speech that aims to convince par excellence.

The *Phaedo* stages an utterly different kind of defense. After Socrates had to justify himself before the Athenians in the *Apology* and before the laws of the city in the *Crito*, he must now supply the arguments that are demanded of him. His defense is enacted before the court of philosophical thought, which Cebes and Simmias—certainly not perfectly but with youthful vigor—defend. Socrates is asked to translate into the *logos* what he himself now believes to be able to articulate mythically: his philosophical life and the readiness for death which has been granted him.

If Socrates, with his turn to myth, truly accords with the situation immediately before death, he cannot possibly fulfill Cebes' demand, at least not as it was raised. But he may also not refuse it, for what he articulates in myth is to be the result and sum of a life that was essentially determined by an obligatory commitment to demonstrative and argumentative speech, to *logos*. There remains only a single way out. Socrates must attempt to make the coherence of *mythos* and *logos* itself believable and to accord a role to *logos* which actually befits *mythos*. He must, then, demonstrate that the *logos* can convincingly play this role, and because this attempt is, in turn, confronted by the demand for a justification in terms of the *logos*, the success of this endeavor remains precarious. Yet the attempt also remains clear. The rhetoric of the Socratic defense is aimed at the *logos*, and for this reason alone it cannot lead to an opaque belief; it remains confronted by a doubt which appeals to the *logos*. However, Socrates must have no less but rather more than the *logos* to offer. The Socratic defense must itself speak in the manner of the *logos*, without it being the case that what is at issue can actually be grasped by the *logos*.

Because it is worthwhile to speak on behalf of a position which its defenders regard as the originary philosophical position, Socrates first seeks to acquaint his interlocutors with the philosophical element of his outlook. He represents the coherence of philosophy and the readiness for death more precisely by describing death as the separation of the soul from the body, and philosophy as an anticipatory form of death that can be enacted in life. To live philosophically means not to make oneself a slave to desire and, what is bound up with this, to desire to attain that purer and more precise knowledge that is above the uncertainty and unclarity of experience marked by the senses. Of decisive importance here is that Socrates must, as a consequence of his analogy of dying and philosophy, understand the state following death exactly as the fulfillment of life, just as he understands the relationship to the thinkable that is no longer obscured by the senses as the fulfillment of the philosophical striving. Philosophy, the more or less known, therefore should provide insight into the unknown of the beyond.

Socrates hopes that he will have been convincing with this, more convincing [*pithanóteros*] than in his defense before the Athenian judges (69e). Yet considered more closely, what he says does not go beyond the mythic speech with which Cebes and Simmias were so dissatisfied. The existence of a beyond can only be articulated mythically, and accordingly the analogy between philosophy and death breaks down at its most important point. Cebes immediately objects that among human beings there is "great disbelief" [*pollèn apistían*] (70a) about whether the soul still exists after death and whether knowledge that is not oriented to the physical world and not entangled in it is possible. Correspondingly, it requires "no little persuasion and faith" [*ouk olíges parmythías deitai kaì písteos*] (70b).

The first attempt at persuasion fails—it had to fail because the thinking which expresses itself in the *logos* cannot simply follow myth. It can be persuaded, if at all, only by finding once more in myth that which can also be grasped through argument—if it succeeds, that is, in translating into myth that which can be grasped by argument. This is the goal of the next attempt, and it appears not to have encountered the difficulties of the first. At least Socrates maintains with great vigor that Cebes and the others have not been tricked into agreement [*ouk exapatómenoi homologoumen*] (72d).

Socrates illustrates the mythical discussions of rebirth and becoming in general by demonstrating that everything arises out of its opposite (70e). If that is the case, one also could find it understandable that living beings originate out of the dead. Thus the faith in a life beyond, which Socrates claims is the essence of philosophy, also appears to be justified philosophically. That first appears to be the case after the idea of the circle of becoming is supplemented by the idea that all learning is a recollection; one only understands something by understanding it on the basis of something that one previously understood (74c–d; 75e–76a). And if that it is the case, one can experience in thought how little that which is present is what it is for itself alone. Together with the circle of becoming, this makes it plausible that the soul of every human being existed before its birth. The text shows how decisively Socrates portrays his subject (77c–d).

However, it is not only Cebes, the most stubborn skeptic among men (77a), who will not follow the argument, but the much more obliging Simmias also doubts whether the preexistence of the soul equally guarantees its continued existence after death (77b). In the context of the previous reflections, this doubt is actually not justified. If the idea of the circle of becoming is genuinely illuminating, one must not fear that the soul is dispersed as dust after the death of a human being, and that this also signifies the end of its being (77b). In the circle of becoming, nothing can be lost.

That may be, and yet the two skeptics are not wrong. They have certainly understood something from the interpretations sketched by Socrates, yet they have not understood what they wanted to understand. Hence as the idea of recollection is introduced and considered, it is used only to indicate an experience which originates prior to the present and not one which crosses over it into the future. The fact that this is not captured by means of the idea of the circle of becoming brings into sharp focus how little ultimately is achieved with the translation of *mythos* into the realm of the comprehensible if no experience corresponds to that which can be grasped in thought. The *logos* remains abstract and for this reason unavoidably acquires the character of a merely persuasive device when the most concrete phenomena are at issue.

Cebes openly admits that this is the case and even appears to want to be satisfied with this. He speaks, at any rate, of the child in us that wants to be persuaded and convinced so that he no longer fears death like a ghost (77e). What is usually referred to as the second proof of immortality is a further attempt at persuasion of this kind, an attempt to persuade by means of the *logos*. By demonstrating the permanence of the thinkable, the ideas, Socrates seeks, at the same time, to make the permanence of the thinking soul believable.

In principle this is a modified repetition of the previously introduced coherence of the representation of the beyond and the philosophical liberation from the entanglement in sensuous perception. It is modified by the fact that Socrates now no longer relies solely on the myths of the beyond, but rather returns to the thinkable and the atemporality characteristic of it. The atemporality of that which thinks certainly cannot be deduced from the atemporality of the thinkable. The thinking soul is certainly "most like" the thinkable in its atemporality, but at most what this says is that the soul is "almost" indissoluble (80b). For a proof of immortality that is rather insufficient. It is so obviously insufficient that the attempt at persuasion almost annuls itself. Where the *logos* wishes to persuade, its limitations come into sharp focus.

Whoever comes to know the limitations of the *logos* and will not accept them succumbs to misology, a hatred of a speech that raises expectations without fulfilling them. As Socrates says, the hatred of the *logoi* arises, exactly like the hatred of human beings, out of an all too great and disappointed trust. It arises where one "has trusted without craftsmanship" [*pisteusai àneu téchnes*] (89d), and one goes from the extreme of an untainted, positive view of the explanatory possibilities of the *logos* to the other extreme of bitter rejection.

One understands immediately that blind trust is naive and unreflective. Why it should be "without craftsmanship" first becomes clear when one thinks not of the opposed concept of an applied craft, but rather of the ability to make distinctions and judgments. Craftsmanship, as Socrates speaks of it here, is not a normal *téchne*. It demonstrates its reliability above all by knowing its limitations. Whoever is proficient in it understands the distribution of knowledge and ignorance, of truth and falsity. In the *Apology* it was named "human wisdom" [*anthropíne sophía*] (20d). In virtue of this human wisdom Socrates is able to test a person's claim to knowledge and to decide what someone understands and what they do not.

Human wisdom, therefore, is not merely the art of critique, but more essentially the art of recognition. Whoever is experienced with it demands too much neither from human beings nor from speeches. It is for this reason the only means against the hatred which arises out of the disappointment of a naive trust. At the same time, however, the art of recognition is thereby directed against the claim to sovereign mastery. That is less evident, but it nevertheless first makes it understandable why Socrates here speaks of art in the sense of craftsmanship at all. Whoever believes to be able to manage human beings and speeches from a superior height and therefore considers himself to be the most wise, soon has the experience that no one and nothing is trustworthy anymore. The more radically and thoughtlessly one claims to possess the craft of mastery, the less it can be employed. For this reason, thoughtless reflectivity is ultimately more dangerous than naivete. It destroys the domain within which it is effective by seeking to master it. Only where one recognizes a domain of action can one accomplish something. The most essential element in an art lies not in success, but in the fact that one understands the limitations of the craft, and in this way first liberates the craft. The art of recognition is the secret essence of every art. It manifests itself in philosophy.

When Socrates here refers to those who, arguing, occupy themselves with controversial speeches [*hoi perì toùs antilogikoùs lo-*

goùs diatrípsantes] (90c) and ultimately believe that they are the most able, clearly the sophists and the rhetoricians are meant. They claim to possess an applied craft and are not in a position to employ it because they are not clear about the elements of an art which are necessarily not at one's disposal. Yet in the *Phaedo* Socrates has nothing to do with the rhetoricians and sophists— his warning about misology is directed at Cebes and Simmias. By demanding that Socrates defend himself before the court of philosophy with compelling arguments and proofs, they are threatened, therefore, with the groundlessness of sophistic thinking and speech. As a result of their skeptical questions and their demand for justification, the danger arises "that the *logos* will die and that we will not be able to bring it back to life" (89b). Cebes and Simmias speak in the interest of philosophy and yet come close to betraying philosophy. The problem of the dialogue is thereby put in the most extreme terms possible: philosophy itself is at stake in a radical way.

When Socrates attempts to acquaint his interlocutors with a trust, bound to art, that is contrary to the hatred of the *logoi*, he seeks, correspondingly, to save philosophy. One must trust the *logos* and adapt oneself to its limitations in order for philosophy to be possible. Having come to know its limitations, the trust is not blind but is equal to the trust operative in an art. One should explicitly recognize what cannot be grounded and yet first makes it possible for one to do one's duty, because only in this way can one avoid the groundlessness of the sophists. One certainly does not avoid it by finding more secure ground. What one recognizes also can be put into question and have its validity questioned.

In order that the philosophical conversation with Cebes and Simmias does not die, Socrates must attempt to imbue them with a trust in the *logos* that is transparent to itself. He must, as he himself expresses it, overcome and subdue their doubt by defeating the doubting, self-destructive *logos* (89c). The metaphors are unambiguous: Socrates must persuade his interlocutors and thereby be rhetorical. However, because he wants to persuade them to a kind of trust, he is prohibited from making use of Cebes' and Simmias' thinking. He must be rhetorical in a manner that is unrhetorical and ultimately antirhetorical. The *logos* needs rhetoric so that it does not destroy itself. But rhetoric must turn against itself. It needs a rhetorically enacted reversal of rhetoric.

Socrates enacts this reversal first by openly admitting the rhetorical nature of his speech. He does not comport himself philosophically [*philosóphos*] but argumentatively, with an eye to victory [*philoníkos*]. Where that is stated openly, one has renounced the most effective means of achieving victory; conversely, one best persuades others by asserting that one is speaking truthfully. And Socrates adds immediately that he is not at issue (91a). However, only in this way can Socrates reach his goal, for he does not wish to persuade Cebes and Simmias to adopt a particular opinion, but to bestow trust upon the *logos*.

That is not possible without Socrates himself trusting the *logos* and articulating his trust in such a manner that the others are able to receive it. The less the others are at issue, the greater the chance that they will ultimately let themselves be persuaded. Correspondingly, Socrates says that it does not worry him whether those present consider what he says to be true or at most to be something incidental [*ei mè eìe párergon*], but that to him it preeminently appears to be so (91a–b). To persuade others can, in truth, always only be something incidental. It occurs most quickly when one represents his or her own convictions and in this way indirectly communicates what one wishes to say. This must be done persuasively, but at the same time without strategic intentions. Then one ultimately, albeit indirectly, effects what one is prohibited from primarily aiming to achieve. That which is incidental becomes the major work. Rhetoric realizes itself in this reversal.

What it means to trust the *logos* cannot be communicated to a radical skeptic. This is certainly also true of someone who believes that what is most important can be immediately revealed by the medium of demonstrative speech. The seriousness of a philosophical life is not demonstrated alone, or even primarily, in the conclusive discussion of material questions. For this reason it would not help at all in the context of the *Phaedo* if the to and fro of suppositions and deliberations would finally come to an end and that which for a very long time was not spoken about in an almost insistent manner was expressed. The entire deliberation over the immortality of the soul remains unresolved not lastly because it is not said what the soul actually is. Yet what one might expect as a Socratic initiative only comes from Simmias and Cebes, both of whom have an idea of what the soul is. And Socrates would have had a relatively easy time of turning the problematic elements of their attempts at clarification into the starting point of an attempt with better prospects for success. That, however, does not occur. Rather, Socrates picks up on Cebes' reflections only to move away from a thematic interpretation of the soul. It will be shown that this putative wrong turn is the only correct path.

Instead of an elucidation of the soul, Socrates engages in a far-reaching narrative of his introduction to philosophy, in which it is revealed why it belongs to the essence of the *logos* in general not to be able to arrive at any final certainty. The orientation to the *logos* is the second best solution, which is only necessary because the world does not prove to be immediately comprehensible. The question of the cause, the origin and foundation of the world as a whole cannot be answered, and thereby the question of how the many beings in the world cohere and are meaningfully bound together. Whoever asks from whence and by what means the many beings in the world meaningfully cohere will not receive a direct answer. But it is also revealed thereby how little the soul is, as Cebes had asserted, a beginning and a ground. As beginning and ground it must be comprehensible to itself. Instead, the soul is connected to a *logos*, which does not grasp but merely represents the beginning and foundation of the whole.

For such a representation it is essential that it assumes a position between arbitrariness and necessity. A simple, merely arbitrary speech cannot be representative; it reveals nothing that would be distinct from it, and speaking would be an empty and futile game. Just as futile would clearly be a speech in which one could be completely certain that it hits upon its intended subject matter. In order to ascertain that, the matter that is represented would have to be immediately accessible, and when that is possible, one has no need of representations. To trust the *logos*—that means, therefore, to consider it as representative.

Socrates does not merely carry out what this means; above all he demonstrates it. When he comes to speak about what is for himself the most powerful *logos*, he is not concerned with explaining his original philosophical decision and making the doctrine of ideas plausible to the two young Pythagoreans. That would be futile after all three had previously spoken of the ideas as if they were completely obvious. The most powerful *logos* for Socrates—that *logos* which became hackneyed by being discussed again and again—according to which one assumes that there is a Beauty that is itself in accord with itself,[4] and a Good and a Magnitude and everything else (100b). This *logos* is here brought into play so that something can be represented in it. Hence the doctrine of ideas is not the final stage of philosophical wisdom, but rather a manner of thinking and a *façon de parler*, which indicates that which cannot be understood directly.

In keeping with the theme of the dialogue, what cannot be understood directly is, naturally and above all, immortality. Using the doctrine of ideas, Socrates seeks to identify and demonstrate the cause for the immortality of the soul [*tén aitían epideíxein kaì aneurésein hos athánaton he psyché*] (100b). In keeping with the conversation hitherto, the strength of the Socratic *logos* naturally can only prove itself in this way. Yet it cannot prove anything more than its strength; it cannot confirm its truth, but rather only that one may trust the *logos* of the doctrine of ideas if one does not demand too much of it.

The question, whether it is possible to demonstrate the immortality of the soul dialectically by means of the ideas, can be answered easily from the perspective of logical consistency. Socrates shows that something can be warm only if it participates in warmth and, correspondingly, something can be alive only if life is within it. Warmth and life show themselves, in turn, only in particular forms, as fire and as soul, respectively. The soul cannot exist without life, and because life and death are mutually exclusive, it cannot die. It does not accept death and is therefore immortal, without death, to put it precisely (106a–b). Yet that could still mean that the soul simply disappears when death approaches, that it is dispersed as dust, as Cebes had feared. With regard to this, Socrates can still add that if anything at all is permanent, it is the idea of life itself. Insofar as the idea of life necessarily inhabits the soul, the same holds true of it (106d).

With this Socrates has achieved what he wanted to achieve. He has identified the cause of the immortality and permanence of the soul: the idea of life. And Socrates has, at the same time, thereby justified the decision not to ask about the soul itself and to give the question of the cause a different direction in answering Cebes. Animation, which is immediately experienced as the soul, cannot be shown to have an immortal element. For this one must turn to life, which necessarily inhabits the soul as the idea of life.

Yet because this idea is, as we have seen, not identical with the soul, it cannot be positively determined on the basis of the soul. The idea of life withdraws, like the god with which, for Socrates, it coheres. The god at any rate and the idea of life are, as he says, permanent (106d). In contrast with the god, one can at least ask about the idea of life in the context of demonstrative and argumentative speech. The idea of life is capable of being interrogated philosophically and is, in every walk of life, the effective form of the god. If this is the case, it is identical with the idea of the Good articulated in the *Republic*.

This idea is capable of being interrogated philosophically by interpreting beings in their context—in accordance with the second best solution, which is, at the same time, that of the most powerful *logos*. When Socrates introduces it, he compares the second best solution with the attempt to consider the sun in water or in something else (99d–e). The philosophical examination of phenomena on the basis of the ideas, that is, dialectic, is an investigation into causes in the representative medium of the *logos*, which is able to comprehend the coherent order of beings only in terms of their harmony. One can ask how everything that exists meaningfully coheres in virtue of a cause, yet this cannot be quickly or completely understood. And what ultimately can be interrogated in this way, the idea of connection and meaningful coherence is, in turn, only that barely visible image of the god in the *logos*. It indicates the god, who, according to the *Apology*, is responsible for Socratic philosophy and so, too, for the persuasive power of Socrates.

Philosophy, as it emerges with Socrates, is the attempt to consider and represent that which exceeds every thought and representation. Philosophy has no ultimate ground to which it could, by means of a self-justification, return. It proves itself to be abysmal when one seeks ultimate foundations, and for this reason it must, in its own way, be rhetorical if it is not to degenerate into a form of conceptual technology. For the sake of its truly philosophical character, its *logos* must be defended as the most powerful. This occurs best with the persuasive power of a philosophical life by showing how one trusts the *logos*, knowing that there is no more here than trust, because the most important things are not found in the *logos*.

Because philosophy is rhetorical in its representations and self-representations, one ought not to expect it to produce definitive explanations. The effect of the Socratic power of persuasion ultimately remains significantly divided. Cebes is convinced, but the originally much less skeptical Simmias admits that he still holds some doubt [*apistía*], as he says, because of the enormity of the subject of the discussion and because he does not have a great deal of confidence in human weakness (107a–b). Socrates agrees with Simmias: one must investigate the first foundations of philosophical thought still more exactly, even if they are worthy of trust [*pistaí*] (107b). Philosophy can become persuasive, and hence a mark of a serious life, only through much practice. Simmias understood this better than Cebes, and to this extent philosophical rhetoric ultimately had a greater effect upon him. He at least senses that philosophical discourse seeks to indicate that which it does not itself have dominion over. The *logos* is trusted only by those who understand its hermeneutical limits and only then its hermeneutical possibilities.

Notes

1. TN. This is a literal translation of the German *Spielraum*. This term, which figures prominently in Figal's text, designates the space of possibility or openness within which something can occur.

2. TN. Figal's reference is to fragment 53 of the standard edition of the fragments of Heraclitus, canonized in the Diels-Kranz edition of the writings of the pre-Socratics, *Die Fragmente der Vorsokratiker*, ed. H. Diels, 6th edition revised by W. Kranz (Berlin, 1951). Fragment 53 begins with the assertion that "war is the father of all things." The word translated as war is the Greek *polemos*, which, as Figal notes, can mean both war in a literal sense and strife or conflict more generally. It is this latter meaning which Figal means to capture with the German *Streit*, which I have consistently rendered as strife throughout the text. See Charles Kahn, *The Art and Thought of Heraclitus* (Cambridge: Cambridge University Press, 1979), 67.

3. For a positive interpretation of the concept of 'strife,' see Michael Theunissen, "Hesiods theogonische Eris," in *Eros und Eris*, ed. P. J. M. van Tongeren (Dordrecht: Kluver, 1992).

4. Plato, *Timaeus*, trans. Benjamin Jowett, *The Collected Dialogues of Plato*, ed. Edith Hamilton and Huntington Cairns (Princeton: Princeton University Press, 1963), 1161. TN. In most but not all cases the translations cited have been followed with-

201

out modification. Substantial departures from the published texts have been noted, while more minor emendations have not. All other translations are my own.

CHAPTER 1.

ON THE SILENCE OF TEXTS: TOWARD A HERMENEUTIC CONCEPT OF INTERPRETATION

1. Cited from Plato, *Works*, ed. John Burnet, vol. 4 (Oxford: Oxford University Press, 1900ff.). The English translation cited is that of W. C. Helmbold and W. G. Rabinowitz (New York: Macmillan, 1985).

2. This is chiefly the thesis of Jacques Derrida, variations of which can be found in numerous essays and books. Programmatically speaking, the clearest of these texts remains "Structure, Sign, and Play in the Discourse of the Human Sciences," in *Writing and Difference*, trans. Alan Bass (Chicago: The University of Chicago Press, 1978). Derrida's reading of the *Phaedrus* and the Platonic conception of the *phármakon* is elucidated in "Plato's Pharmacy," in *Dissemination*, trans. Barbara Johnson (Chicago: The University of Chicago Press, 1981). On the debate over deconstruction and hermeneutics see *Text und Interpretation: Deutsch-französische Debatte mit Beiträgen von Jacques Derrida u.a.*, ed. Philippe Forget (Munich: Wilhelm Fink Verlag, 1984); *Dialogue and Deconstruction*, ed. Diane P. Michelfelder and Richard E. Palmer (New York: State University of New York Press, 1989); *Transforming the Hermeneutic Context: From Nietzsche to Nancy*, ed. with an introduction by Gayle L. Ormiston and Alan D. Schrift (New York: State University of New York Press 1990); Manfred Frank, *What is Neostructuralism?* trans. Sabine Wilke and Richard Gray (Minneapolis: University of Minnesota Press, 1989).

3. Hans-Georg Gadamer, "Text und Interpretation," in *Gesammelte Werke* (Tübingen: Mohr, 1986–1995) 2:340; "Text and Interpretation," trans. Dennis J. Schmidt and Richard E. Palmer, in *Dialogue and Deconstruction*, 30. Hereafter cited as TI with references to the German edition, followed by the English.

4. TN. The word translated as "constraint" is the German *Verbindlichkeit*, which has no direct English equivalent. The root of this substantive is the verb *verbinden*, which is close in meaning to the English infinitive *to bind*. Literally speaking, *Verbindlichkeit* is the quality of being bound or tied to something. Gadamer uses the term to express the idea that interpretation is bound to the work of art, and it is in this sense that the word constraint should be understood.

5. Hans-Georg Gadamer, *Wahrheit und Methode, Gesammelte Werke*, 1:124f; *Truth and Method*, ed. G. Barden and J. Cumming (New York: Crossroad, 1989) 106f.

6. See *Wahrheit und Methode*, 119f.; *Truth and Method*, 102f.

7. The structure of anamnesis is articulated in a particularly pregnant manner in the *Phaedo*. The first such passage reads as follows: "So long as the sight of one thing suggests another to you, it must be a cause of recollection, whether the two things are alike or not" (74c–d), trans. Hugh Tredennick, in *Plato: Collected Dialogues*. That which is remembered in this way allows, in turn, the perceived object to first be understood. This is what is said of those things that are perceived to be equal: "So it must be through the senses that we have obtained the notion that all sensible equals are striving after absolute equality but falling short of it" (75a). Nothing of what we perceive is simply that which it is understood to be.

CHAPTER 2.
AN ESSAY ON FREEDOM:
ONTOLOGICAL CONSIDERATIONS
FROM A PRACTICAL POINT OF VIEW

1. TN. The word translated as "essay" is the German *Versuch*, which means "attempt," "trial," and "experiment." The word *essay* can have these meanings in English as well, and they should be heard in the title along with the more conventional meaning.

2. Peter Strawson's subtle and instructive reflections are motivated by this mistrust against attempts to ground human freedom metaphysically. For this reason Strawson also can be counted as a particularly interesting advocate of a practical concept of freedom. To be sure, Strawson's determination of the practical concept of freedom is quite close to an ontological grounding. To this extent, the idea which I develop in what follows can be considered as an attempt to draw consequences that Strawson himself did not draw but which his arguments support. See Peter Strawson, *Freedom and Resentment and Other Essays* (New York: Methuen, 1976).

3. The recent literature on the critical confrontation with liberalism has grown rather voluminous of late. For a preliminary orientation, see Axel Honneth, "Grenzen des Liberalismus. Zur politisch-ethischen Diskussion um den Kommunitarismus," *Philosophische Rundschau* 38 (1991). An overview of the most important positions within the debate between liberalism and communitarianism can be found in Honneth, ed.,

Kommunitarismus: Eine Debatte über die moralischen Grundlagen moderner Gesellschaften (Frankfurt: Campus-Verlag, 1993).

4. I pursue this project in *Martin Heidegger: Phänomenologie der Freiheit* (Frankfurt: Hain, 1991).

5. TN. The expressions which Figal highlights in this passage are taken from colloquial German. I have translated them literally, albeit awkwardly, in order to preserve Figal's point, which is that our use of the word *freedom* and its cognates is not strictly limited to describing persons and their characteristics.

6. Ludwig Wittgenstein formulated this epistemological indeterminacy most pregnantly: "The freedom of the will consists in the impossibility of knowing actions that still lie in the future." See *Tractatus Logico-Philosophicus*, trans. D. F. Pears and B. F. McGuiness (London: Routledge & Kegan Paul, 1961), 5:1362.

7. TN. The distinction Figal pursues here can be made much more easily in German than in English. Until this point, the term translated as "representation" is the German *Darstellung*, which can also mean "presentation," "depiction," "portrayal," or "description." In this sentence Figal contrasts *Darstellung*, an implicit mode of representation, with *Repräsentation*, a form of representation that is explicitly recognized as a representation in a political sense. This distinction parallels that between depiction and representation; the former makes no reference to political forms of representation, whereas the latter has specifically political connotations. Since there is no English correlate for this distinction, I have adopted the convention of italicizing representation when it is used to translate *Repräsentation*, while retaining the translation of *Darstellung* as representation in plain text.

8. Hannah Arendt, *The Human Condition* (Chicago: University of Chicago Press, 1958).

--------- CHAPTER 3. ---------

THE INTENSITY OF THE POLITICAL: CARL SCHMITT'S PHENOMENOLOGY OF ENMITY AND THE END OF THE IDEOLOGICAL WORLD CIVIL WAR

1. Carl Schmitt, *Der Begriff des Politischen* (Berlin: Duncker & Humbolt, 1963), 54; *The Concept of the Political*, trans. George Schwab (New Brunswick: Rutgers University Press, 1976), 53. Page references will be given parenthetically in the text to the German edition first, followed by the English.

2. TN. Emphasis and quotation marks in original, but omitted in the English translation.

3. See Walter Benjamin, *Urpsrung des deutschen Trauerspiels*, "Erkenntniskritische Vorrede," in *Gesammelte Schriften*, ed. R. Tiedemann and H. Schweppenhäuser (Frankfurt: Suhrkamp, 1974–1989), vol. 1; *The Origin of German Tragic Drama*, "Epistemo-Critical Prologue," trans. John Osborne (London: New Left Books, 1977). Hereafter cited in the text as *GS* with volume and page number.

4. This is the interpretation offered by Heinrich Meier, *Carl Schmitt, Leo Strauss und 'Der Begriff des Politischen': Zu einem Dialog unter Abwesenden* (Stuttgart: Metzler, 1988), 34.

5. This is title of the fourth part of *Leviathan* (1651), whose full title is *Leviathan, or The Matter, Forme & Power of a Common-Wealth Ecclesiasticall and Civill.*

6. Leo Strauss, "Comments on Carl Schmitt's *The Concept of the Political*," in Schmitt, *The Concept of the Political*, 103. This essay first appeared in the *Archiv für Sozialwissenschaft und Sozialpolitik* (1932).

7. TN. Although Schmitt published this address together with "The Concept of the Political," it is not included in the English translation. References to the "Address on the Age of Neutralization" are to the edition of *Der Begriff des Politischen* cited in note 1 and are given parenthetically in the text as AN.

8. Leo Strauss, "Comments," 103.

9. Friedrich Nietzsche, *The Gay Science*, trans. Walter Kaufmann (New York: Vintage, 1974), section 374. TN. Following common practice, Nietzsche's writings will be cited by section, not by page number. For this reason, references will be given to the German text only in the case of Nietzsche's posthumous notes, for which there is, as yet, no English edition.

—————————— CHAPTER 4. ——————————
PUBLIC FREEDOM—
THE STRIFE OF POWER AND VIOLENCE:
ON HANNAH ARENDT'S CONCEPT OF THE POLITICAL

1. Hannah Arendt, *The Human Condition* (Chicago: The University of Chicago Press, 1958). A German edition of the book, overseen by Arendt, was published under the title *Vita Active oder Vom tätigen Leben*, 2nd edition (Munich: Piper, 1981). The German edition can, therefore, be

regarded as a second first edition. Page references will be given in the text to the German edition first, followed by the English. TN. Because Arendt made some minor changes to her text for the German edition, it has been necessary, in order to preserve the coherence of Figal's argument, to modify the English text where it differs from the German.

2. TN. The expression *space of appearance* is Arendt's own translation of the German *Erscheinungsraum*. While this translation has the advantage of literality, it will not seem entirely idiomatic to speakers of English. Nevertheless, in this context it seemed best to employ Arendt's translation rather than attempt to find a less awkward English equivalent.

3. This is essentially already the point of Kant's reflection on the "public use of reason." See Immanuel Kant, "Beantwortung der Frage: Was ist Aufklärung?" A 45; "An Answer to the Question 'What Is Enlightenment?'" in *Foundations of the Metaphysics of Morals*, trans. Lewis White Beck (Indianapolis: Bobbs-Merrill, 1959), 87. For a detailed account of the history of this concept, see Lucain Hölscher's entry under "Öffentlichkeit" in the *Historisches Wörterbuch der Philosophie* (Basel, 1984), 6:1134–40.

4. The concept of "freedom" sketched above can be traced back to Martin Heidegger. See my *Martin Heidegger: Phänomenologie der Freiheit*, as well as chapter 2 below. Hannah Arendt's implicit references to Heidegger in T*he Human Condition* would be worth investigating independently. The idea of openness to the action and speech of others is the starting point for a sociophilosophical theory of recognition. See Axel Honneth, *Kampf um Anerkennung: Zur moralischen Grammatik sozialer Konflikte* (Frankfurt: Suhrkamp, 1992). If one understands the political as the authentic freedom of the space of appearance, then such a theory would itself be a contribution to the phenomenology of freedom.

5. Hannah Arendt later attempted to clarify what constitutes the particular character of political action by relating it back to the Kantian concept of 'reflective judgment.' See her *Lectures on Kant's Political Philosophy* (Chicago: The University of Chicago Press, 1982). This attempt remained unfinished. For a reconstruction, see Ernst Vollrath, *Die Rekonstruction der politischen Urteilskraft* (Stuttgart: Klett, 1977), as well as Hannah Arendt "Kritik der politischen Urteilskraft," in *Die Zukunft des Politischen: Ausblicke auf Hannah Arendt*, ed. Peter Kemper (Frankfurt: Fischer, 1993). In connection with the concept of 'authentic freedom,' one can interpret reflective judgment as an attempt to relate particular situations of action and particular goals of action to something common to them both—which one cannot actually ascertain—and

thereby to represent this common element. Whether this can be played off against the Aristotelian conception of practical wisdom (*phronesis*) by designating the common element of judgment as something which does not exist (Vollrath, in *Die Zukunft des Politischen*, 49), is certainly questionable. The upshot of this is that the common element would become a fiction. For an attempt to reconcile *phronesis* with the faculty of judgment, see Otfried Höffe, "Universalistische Ethik und Urteilskraft: ein aristotelischer Blick auf Kant," *Zeitschrift für philosophische Forschung* 44 (1990).

6. Jürgen Habermas, "Hannah Arendts Begriff der Macht," in *Philosophisch-politische Profile*, 3rd and expanded edition (Frankfurt: Suhrkamp, 1981), 232; "Hannah Arendt: On the Concept of Power," *Philosophical-Political Profiles*, trans. Frederick G. Lawrence (Cambridge: The MIT Press, 1983), 175.

7. Thucydides, *The Peloponnesian War*, ed. John H. Finley, Jr. (New York: Modern Library, 1954), II, 41. TN. I have modified the translation in accordance with those of Figal and Arendt.

8. TN. This passage was added to the German edition and therefore has no correlate in the English text.

9. The concept of 'intensity as a determination of the political' was introduced by Carl Schmitt. See *The Concept of the Political*, 38. If Hannah Arendt's concept of power also can be understood in the sense of an intensity, then both will have taken account of the dynamic of the political in rather different ways. Anticipating subsequent reflections, the relationship of the two conceptions can be determined by saying that Carl Schmitt obtained his concept of the political by concentrating on the phenomenon of violence, while Hannah Arendt principally focuses on power. Clearly it is hardly informative or helpful, therefore, to designate Schmitt's concept of the political as "rudimentary," in what has become a widespread ritual (Oskar Negt, "Zum Verständnis des Politischen bei Hannah Arendt," in *Die Zukunft des Politischen*, 62). Rather, this concept determines one of the two aspects of the phenomenon with rare precision. In addition, if one believes, with Negt, that the coherence of politics and enmity cannot be grounded "in any genuine tradition of the West" (ibid.), one should reread Plato's *Republic*, 373d–3, as well as the first book of *The Laws*.

10. Aristotle, *The Nicomachean Ethics*, 1141b 23–29.

11. Habermas, *Philosophisch-politische Profile*, 235; *Philosophical-Political Profiles*, 176.

12. I have borrowed the distinction between lawmaking and law-preserving violence from Walter Benjamin, "Zur Kritik der Gewalt," *GS*

II.1; "On the Critique of Violence," in *Reflections*, trans. Edmund Jeph-cott (New York: Harcourt Brace Jovanovich, 1978).

13. Hannah Arendt, *The Origins of Totalitarianism*, 2nd expanded edition (New York: Meridian Books, 1958). A German edition of the book, overseen by Arendt, was published under the title *Elemente und Ursprünge totaler Herrschaft* (Munich: Piper, 1986). TN. The two passages cited by Figal were added by Arendt to the revised, German edition of her book. Page references will, therefore, be given to this edition alone.

14. TN. This passage was added to the German edition of *The Human Condition* and therefore has no correlate in the English text. The context of this remark is to be found in the discussion of Pericles on page 205 of the English text.

CHAPTER 5.
THE INTERMEDIATE TIME OF MODERNITY:
HISTORY AND NIHILISM, EUROPE AND
FATHERLANDS, IN NIETZSCHE'S PERSPECTIVE

1. Friedrich Nietzsche, *Beyond Good and Evil*, in *The Basic Writings of Nietzsche*, trans. Walter Kaufmann (New York: Modern Library, 1968), section 245. Henceforth cited as *BGE*.

2. TN. This sentence incorporates an untranslatable play on words. The German word *Ausklang* can mean both "last chord" and "epilogue." In this sentence, Figal uses *Ausklang* in both senses.

3. Friedrich Nietzsche, "On the Uses and Disadvantages of History for Life," in *Untimely Meditations*, trans. R. J. Hollingdale (Cambridge: Cambridge University Press, 1983), section 10. Henceforth cited as *HL*.

4. Friedrich Nietzsche, *Sämtliche Werke, Kritische Studienausgabe*, ed. Giorgi Colli and Mazzino Montinari (Berlin: de Gruyter, 1980), 13:11 [119]. Henceforth cited as *KSA* with volume and fragment number.

5. Ernst Jünger, *Eumeswil, Sämtliche Werke* (Stuttgart: Klett-Cotta, 1978–1983) 17:371; *Eumeswil*, trans. Joachim Neugroschel (New York: Marsilio Publishers, 1993), 375.

6. The term *attunement* should be understood in the sense of Heraclitus' conception of *harmonie*. See Charles Kahn, *The Art and Thought of Heraclitus*, 65, and Diels-Kranz, *Die Fragmente der Vorsokratiker*, fragment 51.

CHAPTER 6.
TYPE AND NUANCE: UNLIMITED
AND LIMITED AESTHETICS WITH NIETZSCHE

1. The distinction between *reconciliation* and *disjunction* has been discussed in a manner that has stimulated the more recent debates concerning aesthetics. See Martin Seel, *Die Kunst der Entzweiung: Zum Begriff der ästhetischen Rationalität* (Frankfurt: Suhrkamp, 1985).

2. I have borrowed this expression from Walter Ch. Zimmerli, "Alles ist Schein—Bemerkungen zur Rehabilitierung einer 'Ästhetik' post Nietzsche und Derrida," in *Ästhetischer Schein*, vol. 2 of the series *Kolloquium Kunst und Philosophie*, ed. W. Oelmüller (Paderborn: Schöningh, 1982).

3. Rüdiger Bubner, "Mutmaßliche Umstellung im Verhältnis von Leben und Kunst," in *Ästhetische Erfahrung* (Frankfurt: Suhrkamp, 1989), 130. In addition, see "Ästhetisierung der Lebenswelt" in the same volume.

4. TN. In this sentence and the previous one, the words *ability* and *force* are used to translate the German word *Kraft*. This word appears in the note "Physiology of Art" cited by Figal above. Its primary meaning is force or power, but it can also denote an ability or power to perform a particular act. Here Figal is drawing on both of these meanings.

5. TN. The term *attunement* is a translation of Heraclitus' concept of *'harmonie.'* See chapter 5, note 6.

6. Martin Heidegger translates the Heraclitean concept of *'polemos'* with "confrontation." See *Einführung in die Metaphysik, Gesamtausgabe* (henceforth: *GA*), vol. 40, ed. von Petra Jaeger (Frankfurt: Klostermannn, 1983), 66f. and 121f.; *An Introduction to Metaphysics*, trans. Ralph Manheim (New Haven: Yale University Press, 1959), 61f. and 113f.. TN. The term Heidegger uses to translate *polemos* is the German *Auseinandersetzung*. On page 113 of the English translation Heidegger writes that *polemos* "is struggle, setting-apart [*Auseinandersetzung*], i.e., not mere quarreling and wrangling but the conflict of the conflicting."

7. TN. The parallel passage from *Twilight of the Idols* can be found in section 6 of the chapter entitled "'Reason' in Philosophy."

8. See *The Republic*, 507c–517b.

9. Friedrich Nietzsche, *Ecce Homo*, in *Basic Writings of Nietzsche*, "Why I Am So Clever," section 5.

10. Charles Baudelaire, "Le peintre de la vie moderne," in *Oeuvres complétes*, ed. C. Pichois (Paris: Pléiade, 1976), 2:695.

11. Charles Baudelaire, "Le peintre de la vie moderne," 695.

CHAPTER 7.
STEREOSCOPIC EXPERIENCE: ERNST JÜNGER'S POETICS OF *THE ADVENTUROUS HEART*

1. TN. Ernst Jünger celebrated his one hundredth birthday on March 29, 1995.

2. The opinion that Jünger's work is a possible key to understanding this century is shared by Peter Koslowsi, *Der Mythos der Moderne: Die dichterische Philosophie Ernst Jüngers* (Munich: Fink, 1991), and Martin Meyer in his less pointed, but for this reason more encyclopedic and instructive book, *Ernst Jünger* (Munich: Hanser, 1990). To be sure, both Koslowski and Meyer pay less attention to the aesthetic character of Jünger's epochal representation. Karl Heinz Bohrer's *Ästhetik des Schreckens: Die Pessimistische Romantik und Ernst Jüngers Frühwerk* (Munich: Hanser, 1978) was a pioneering contribution to understanding the aesthetic aspects of Jünger's work.

3. See the short piece "Historia in nuce: Der Verlorene Posten," in Ernst Jünger, *Das Abenteuerliche Herz*, zweite Fassung [*The Adventurous Heart*, second version], *Sämtliche Werke*, 9:262. *The Adventurous Heart* will, like other texts by Jünger, be cited with reference to this edition of the collected works. The two versions of this text are indicated by the abbreviations *AH* 1 and *AH* 2, followed by the initials *SW* and the respective volume and page numbers.

4. This phrase is the subtitle of the first version.

5. On the theme of Descartes as the father of modernity, see Hans-Peter Schütt, "Descartes und die Moderne Philosophie: Notizen zu einer epochalen Vaterschaft," in *Selbstverständnisse der Moderne: Formationen der Philosophie, Politik, Theologie und Ökonomie*, ed. Günter Figal and Rolf-Peter Sieferle (Stuttgart: Metzler, 1991).

6. Friedrich Nietzsche, *The Birth of Tragedy*, in *Basic Writings of Nietzsche*, section 1.

7. The text of the second version was subject to stylistic revisions and is somewhat more austere. See *SW* 9:228–29.

8. This passage is very similar in the first version. See *SW* 9:197.

9. On the images of nature in *The Adventurous Heart*, see Christoph Quarch, "Die Natur als inneres Erlebnis: Ernst Jüngers Perspektivwechsel in der zweiten Fassung von *Das Abenteuerliche Herz*," *Scheidewege* 23, (1993/94).

─────────── CHAPTER 8. ───────────
AESTHETIC EXPERIENCE OF TIME: ADORNO'S
AVANT-GARDISM AND BENJAMIN'S CORRECTION

1. See Burkhart Lindner, "'Il faut être absolument moderne': Adornos Ästhetik: Ihr Konstruktionsprinzip und ihre Historizität," in *Materialen zur Ästhetischen Theorie: Theodor W. Adornos Konstruktion der Moderne*, ed. Burkhart Lindner and W. Martin Lüdke (Frankfurt: Suhrkamp, 1970).

2. Theodor W. Adorno, *Ästhetische Theorie*, ed. Gretel Adorno and Rolf Tiedemann (Frankfurt: Suhrkamp, 1970), 10. Hereafter cited as *AT*. TN. In light of the fact that the English translation of Adorno's text is notoriously unreliable, I have taken the liberty of translating all citations anew. The page numbers given parenthetically in the body of the chapter are to the German text.

3. TN. The substantive *das Gewordene* is based on the past participle of the verb *werden*, "to become," which, together with its nominal form *das Werden*, "becoming," is a prominent term in Nietzsche's philosophical vocabulary. While a less literal translation would be "the historical," the connection with becoming and Nietzsche would thereby be lost.

4. One must be absolutely modern. This sentence appears in "Adieu," the final part of Rimbaud's prose poem *Une Saison en Enfer*. See Arthur Rimbaud, *Oeuvres complètes*, ed. Antoine Adam (Paris: Pléiade, 1972), 116.

5. See Walter Benjamin, *GS* I.1:214–15.

6. See the fifth of Benjamin's theses "Über den Begriff der Geschichte," *GS* I.2:693; "Theses on the Philosophy of History," in *Illuminations*, trans. Harry Zohn (New York: Schocken Books, 1969), 255. I have elucidated the hermeneutic of history which Benjamin's text suggests in more detail in "Die Konstellation der Modernität: Walter Benjamins Hermenuetik der Geschichte," *Internationale Zeitschrift für Philosophie* 1 (1993).

─────────────── CHAPTER 9. ───────────────
ART AS WORLD
REPRESENTATION

1. Hans-Georg Gadamer, "Wort und Bild—'so wahr, so seiend,'" *Gesammelte Werke*, 8:375. Henceforth cited as WB.

2. Walter Benjamin, letter to Florens Christian Rang, 9 December 1923, in *Briefe*, ed. Theodor W. Adorno and Gershom Scholem (Frankfurt: Suhrkamp, 1966), 322.

3. Ibid.

4. Ibid.

5. G. W. F. Hegel, *Vorlesungen über die Ästhetik*, in *Werke*, ed. Eva Moldenhauer and Karl Markus Michel (Frankfurt: Suhrkamp, 1969–71), 14:137; *Aesthetics: Lectures on Fine Art*, trans. T. M. Knox (Oxford: Clarendon Press, 1975), 1:524.

6. Hans-Georg Gadamer, "Ende der Kunst? Von Hegels Lehre vom Vergangenheitscharakter der Kunst bis zur Antikunst von heute," in *Das Erbe Europas* (Frankfurt, 1989), 67.

7. Ibid., 68.

8. Walter Benjamin, "Über den Begriff der Geschichte" (thesis II), *GS*, 1.2:693; "Theses on the Philosophy of History," in *Illuminations*, trans. Harry Zohn (New York: Schocken Books, 1969), 254.

9. Benjamin, "Über den Begriff der Geschichte" (thesis II) *GS*, 1.2:694; "Theses on the Philosophy of History," 254.

10. Martin Heidegger, "Der Ursprung des Kunstwerkes," in *Holzwege, GA* 5, ed. F. W. von Herrmann (Frankfurt: Klostermann, 1977), 31; "The Origin of the Work of Art," trans. Albert Hofstadter, in *Poetry, Language, Thought* (New York: Harper & Row, 1975), 45.

11. On Heidegger's interpretation of Hölderlin, see my *Martin Heidegger—zur Einführung* (Hamburg: Beck, 1992), 141–158. For the theological context of this interpretation, see chapter 11 of the present volume.

12. Jorge Luis Borges, Preface, *Fervor de Buenos Aires* (Buenos Aires: Alberto Casares, 1993).

13. Nietzsche uses this expression in the second of his *Untimely Meditations*, "On the Uses and Disadvantages of History for Life," section 1.

—————————— CHAPTER 10. ——————————
HISTORY AS DESTINY AND THE
PRESENCE OF HISTORY: DETERMINING
PHILOSOPHY WITH AND WITHOUT HEGEL

1. See Michael Dummet, *Origins of Analytical Philosophy* (Cambridge: Harvard University Press, 1994). A significant sign of the historicization of analytical philosophy is the very title of the volume *Post-Analytical Philosophy*, ed. John Rajchman and Cornel West (New York: Columbia University Press, 1985). The volume is particularly interesting because of the number of contributors who are prominent representatives of analytical or postanalytical philosophy. See also L. Jonathan Cohen, *The Dialogue of Reason: An Analysis of Analytic Philosophy* (Oxford: Oxford University Press, 1986).

2. Gadamer, *Wahrheit und Methode*, 2; *Truth and Method*, xii.

3. G. W. F. Hegel, *Vorlesungen über die Geschichte der Philosophie*, 3 vols., ed. E. Moldenhauer and K. M. Michel (Frankfurt: Suhrkamp, 1969–1971), 18:24; *Lectures on the History of Philosophy*, 3. vols., trans. E. S. Haldane and Frances H. Simson (Atlantic Highlands: Humanities Press, 1983), 1:7–8; the first italicization is mine. Page references will be given parenthetically in the text to the German edition first, followed by the English. Unless otherwise noted, all references are to the first volume of Hegel's lectures.

4. See Plato's *Theaetetus*, lines 191c and 197d, respectively. TN. I have followed Seth Bernadette's translation of the *Theaetetus* (Chicago: The University of Chicago Press, 1986).

—————————— CHAPTER 11. ——————————
LAST GODS: HERMENEUTIC
THEOLOGY IN NIETZSCHE AND HEIDEGGER

1. Martin Heidegger, "Aus einem Gespräch von der Sprache" (1953/54), *Unterwegs zur Sprache, GA* 12, ed. Friedrich-Wilhelm von Hermann (Frankfurt: Klostermann, 1985); translated as "A Dialogue on Language," in *On the Way to Language*, trans. Peter D. Hertz (New York: Harper & Row, 1971).

2. Martin Heidegger, *Ontologie (Hermenuetik der Faktizität)*. Frühe Freiburger Vorlesung, Sommer Semester 1923, *GA* 63; ed. Käte Bröcker-Oltmanns, 15.

3. See Martin Heidegger, *Hölderlins Hymnen 'Germanien' und 'Der Rhein,'* Freiburger Vorlesung Winter Semester 1934/35, *GA* 39, ed. Suzanne Ziegler (Frankfurt: Klostermann, 1980). For an interpretation of this lecture course, see my *Heidegger zur Einführung* (Hamburg: Junius, 1992), 141–158.

4. Martin Heidegger, *Beiträge zur Philosophie (vom Ereignis), GA* 65, ed. Friedrich-Wilhelm von Hermann (Frankfurt: Klostermann, 1989).

5. Martin Heidegger, "Nietzsches Wort 'Gott ist tot,'" in *Holzwege, GA* 5, ed. Friedrich-Wilhelm von Hermann (Frankfurt: Klostermann, 1977), 209; "The Word of Nietzsche 'God Is Dead,'" in *The Question Concerning Technology and Other Essays,* trans. William Lovitt (New York: Garland, 1977), 53.

6. See Jacques Derrida, *Of Grammatology,* trans. Gayatri Spivak (Baltimore: Johns Hopkins University Press, 1976).

7. On Nietzsche's references to the moral God, see *KSA* 10:3 [1], *KSA* 11:39 [13], and *KSA* 12:5 [71].

8. TN. The word that is translated as "process" is the German *Geschehen,* which also can mean "event," "happening," or "occurrence." In the paragraphs that follow it will be rendered as "process" or, in the case of the compound noun *Weltgeschen,* as "world process." In section 3, which is largely devoted to a reading of the figure of the "last god" in Heidegger's *Contributions to Philosophy, Geschehen* has sometimes been rendered as "coming-to-pass," which is in keeping with Heidegger's explicitly temporal interpretation of the event named by the last god, and other times simply as "event."

9. On Nietzsche's Dionysus theology, see the still-suggestive essay by Karl Reinhardt, "Nietzsches Klage der Ariadne," in *Vermächtnis der Antike: Gesammelte Essays zur Philosophie und Geschichtsschreibung,* ed. Carl Becker (Göttingen: Vandenhoeck & Ruprecht, 1966), 2nd edition. On the same theme and equally illuminating, see Leo Strauss, "Note on the Plan of Nietzsche's *Beyond Good and Evil,*" in *Studies in Platonic Political Philosophy* (Chicago: University of Chicago Press, 1983).

10. Martin Heidegger, *Nietzsches metaphysische Grundstellung im abendländischen Denken: Die ewige Widerkehr des Gleichen,* Freiburger Vorlesung Sommersemester 1937, *GA* 44, ed. Marion Heinz (Frankfurt: Klostermann, 1986), 71; *Nietzsche,* vol. 2, trans. David Farell Krell (New York: Harper & Row, 1984), 68.

11. Friedrich Nietzsche, *The Birth of Tragedy,* in *The Basic Writings of Nietzsche,* section 1.

12. Nietzsche, *Ecce Homo*, in *The Basic Writings of Nietzsche*, "Why I Am a Destiny," section 9.

13. On this point, see Heidegger's lecture course on Hölderlin's hymns "Germanien" and "Der Rhein" mentioned in note 3.

CHAPTER 12.
THE ABSOLUTE PARTICULAR: INDIVIDUALITY AND RELIGION AFTER KIERKEGAARD

1. Thomas Nagel, "What Is It Like to Be a Bat?" in *Mortal Questions* (Cambridge: Cambridge University Press, 1979).

2. Søren Kierkegaard, "My Activity as a Writer," in *The Point of View for My Work as An Author*, trans. Walter Lowrie (New York: Harper & Row, 1962), 151.

3. Søren Kierkegaard, *The Sickness unto Death*, in *Fear and Trembling and The Sickness Unto Death*, trans. Walter Lowrie (New York: Doubleday, 1954). Further references will be given in the text with the abbreviation *SD* and the page number.

4. This was first worked out by Michael Theunissen. See his *Das Selbst auf dem Grund der Verzweiflung: Kierkegaards negativistische Methode* (Frankfurt: Suhrkamp, 1991) and *Der Begriff Verzweiflung: Korrekturen an Kierkegaard* (Frankfurt: Suhrkamp, 1993).

5. See Søren Kierkegaard, *Training in Christianity*, trans. Walter Lowrie (Princeton: Princeton University Press, 1944).

6. Emmanuel Levinas has made this thought the center of his philosophy. It is most pregnantly developed in his major work *Totalité et infini* (The Hague: Martinus Nijhoff, 1961); *Totality and Infinity*, trans. Alphonso Lingis (Pittsburgh: Duquesne University Press, 1969).

CHAPTER 13.
TRUSTING THE *LOGOS*:
ON PLATO'S RHETORIC OF PHILOSOPHY

1. TN. For the sake of consistency I have translated citations from the *Phaedo* and the other dialogues cited by Figal directly from his own

German translation, while, at the same time, checking them against existing English translations. The translation of the *Phaedo* consulted is that of Hugh Tredennick (London: Penguin, 1969).

2. TN. Dividing and uniting.

3. Paul de Man, "Rhetoric of Persuasion," in *Allegories of Reading* (New Haven: Yale University Press, 1979).

4. TN. I am here following Figal's literal translation of the Greek, which reads *ti kalòn autò kath'autò*.

Index

Action: appearance of, 44; courses of, 16; determinateness of, 18; diversity of, 27; explicit, 46; freedom of, 16, 17, 18, 43; historical, 105; human, 44; individual, 21, 22, 23; of institutions, 33; meaningful context for, 49; openness to, 46, 206n4; permission for, 46; political, 27, 32, 34–35, 35, 41, 45, 46, 47, 48, 51, 52, 53, 206n5; possibilities of, 17, 20, 21, 25; public, 45; representation of, 22; responsibility for, 13, 19; stages of, 33; symbolic, 25–26; teleological conceptions of, 82

"Address on the Age of Neutralization" (Schmitt), 38

Adorno, Theodor W., 109–124, 126, 127

Adventurous Heart, The (Jünger), 93, 97, 101, 102, 103, 105, 106, 107

Aesthetics, x; agonistic nature of, 78, 85; authentic, 85; coherence in, 80; concept of, 85; contemporary, 78; contingency in, 76, 77, 79, 80, 85; current debate on, 109; disjunctive, 76; interplay in, 76, 80, 81; and knowledge, 78; limited/unlimited, 75–90; multiplicity in, 76, 77, 80, 81, 85; perspectives of, 103, 104, 105; philosophical, 78; reconciliation, 76; tension in experience of, 77; theories of, 75–76; type and nuance in, 75–90; unity in, 76, 77, 80; universalization of, 90; unlimited, 78, 85, 109, 110

Aesthetic Theory (Adorno), 109, 110, 111, 112, 115, 118, 119, 126

Anthropology, 161, 162

Appearance: of accessibility, 123; of action, 44; coming-into, 45; condition for, 46; explicit, 46; forms of, 73; harmonious, 120; instantaneous as, 120; meaning of, 83; of new values, 66; openness to, 46; permission for, 46; political space of, 47, 48; as reality, 83; space of, 46,

217

31; soul of, 51; space of appearance of, 44, 46; strife in, 34; transcending the limits of, 35
Politicization, 30
Poverty: of accessible possibilities, 97; of experience, 94, 95, 97, 103; nihilistic, 64; of self-understanding, 64; of values, 64
Power, 207n9; of adaptation, 69; of the city, 49; community, 27, 53; contempt for, 54; *epos* and *ergon* in, 49; freedom of, 54; and historical freedom, 50; lack of, 64; loss of, 49, 53, 56, 81; plastic, 137; political, 27, 49, 54, 55, 56; relation to state, 50; religious, 182; and space of appearance, 50; state, 27; strife of, 43–57; of synthesizing knowledge, 40; and tyranny, 54; and violence, 54, 55; will to, 82, 162, 163, 164
Provocation, 44

Rationality, 43
Reality: appearance as, 83; elucidation of, 106; empirical, 113; expressions of, 97; fabricated, 83; institutional, 54, 56; knowledge of, 83; perception of, 83; perspectival character of, 187; of the political, 55; renunciation of, 113; valuation of, 83; and violence, 54
Reason: products of, 145; public use of, 206n3
Reflection, 104; aesthetic, 105; philosophical, 114
Relationships: actual/possible, 22; agonistic, 67; commonality/individuality, 22, 23; contingency/necessity, ix; economic, 31; freedom/strife, vii; friend/enemy, 30, 32, 34, 40, 41, 42; of individuals to individuality, 174; moral, 31; past/present, 121; philosophy/history, 141; pleasure/pain, 189; political, 30, 49, 54; power/

violence, 54; precarious, 34; religious, 31; rhetoric/dialectic, 188; with self, 61; unity/multiplicity, 76; work/experience, 135; works/interpretation, 8
Religion: and art, 113; Christian faith, 174; and decisions of faith, 181; experience of, 133; fulfilled past of, 114; indifference to, 159; and individuality, 171–183; negation of, 114; referential character of, 114; symbols of, 114, 115; transcendent context of, 113
Representation, 8; of Absolute, 128; of actions, 22; and autonomy of art, 134; communal, 27; of constancy, 9; of contexts, 24; distinctness in, 22; and freedom, 25; historical, 11; identity in, 22; interpretation as, 9, 26; methods of, 93; modes of, 204n7; multiple, 84; of nature, 127; objectifying meditation on life as, 105; and perspectivism, 84; play-space of, 10, 135–136; political, 27, 204n7; of possibilities, 22, 23, 24, 136; primary, 26; as strife, ix; structure of, 28; transparency of, 85; of the truth, 188; world, 23–24, 25–28, 125–138
Republic (Plato), 85
Responsibility: for action, 13, 19; of citizens, 33; to states, 33; for violence, 99
Revolution, 50, 55
Rhetoric: counterpart to, 185; and dialectic, 185; goals of, 190; integration with philosophy, ix; of philosophy, 185–200
Rights: civil, 50; of others, 19
Romanticism, 60, 126

Schiller, Friedrich von, 60
Schmitt, Carl, 29–41, 207n9
Schopenhauer, Arthur, 71